Designing Socially Just Learning Communities

"There is a great deal that is inspiring about this book. Produced by committed literacy practitioners working for social justice, it is ideal for teacher-researcher communities and study groups."

Barbara Comber, University of South Australia,
Hawke Research Institute for Sustainable Societies

"In a climate where neoliberal policies saturate public and private spheres of life, it is absolutely imperative that educators work as engaged intellectuals in solidarity to challenge and change oppressive practices. This book offers compelling stories about teachers engaging in such social change. Readers also gain insight into the processes through which teachers became people/teachers/researchers/activists who care deeply about social justice."

Stephanie Jones, University of Georgia

"This book is such a gift to educators learning together in study groups, school communities, university classes, and community-based organizations. It helps educators develop hopeful images of what education for social justice might look like, images of teacher learning communities that develop sustained conversations across years, and images of schools and teachers working within the assets and energies of local communities."

Randy Bomer, The University of Texas at Austin

"What comes through most clearly in this book is the power of collective reflection and action. Together and individually the authors show how teaching practice can dramatically improve when educators take the time and construct the organizational means to learn from one another. Reflection, activism, and teaching about difficult issues are addressed in this useful book."

Bob Peterson, Editor, *Rethinking Schools* and
Fifth Grade Teacher at Fratney Elementary School

Rebecca Rogers is Associate Professor of Literacy at the University of Missouri-St. Louis. Her research focuses on language, identity, and power in and out of school contexts.

Melissa Mosley is Assistant Professor of Language and Literacy at the University of Texas at Austin. Her research focuses on critical literacy learning across the lifespan, particularly how teachers and students together use literacy practices toward social action in and out of the classroom.

Mary Ann Kramer is Coordinator for Adult Education and Literacy in the St. Louis Public Schools.

The Literacy for Social Justice Teacher Research Group is a grassroots, teacher-led professional development group dedicated to exploring and acting on the relationships between literacy and social justice.

Designing Socially Just Learning Communities

Critical Literacy Education Across the Lifespan

Rebecca Rogers, Melissa Mosley, Mary Ann Kramer,

and

the Literacy for Social Justice Teacher Research Group

 Routledge
Taylor & Francis Group

NEW YORK AND LONDON

First published 2009
by Routledge
270 Madison Ave, New York, NY 10016

Simultaneously published in the UK
by Routledge
2 Park Square, Milton Park, Abingdon, Oxon OX14 4RN

Routledge is an imprint of the Taylor & Francis Group, an informa business

© 2009 Taylor & Francis

Typeset in Minion by Wearset Ltd, Boldon, Tyne and Wear
Printed and bound in the United States of America on acid-free paper by
Edwards Brothers, Inc.

Library of Congress Cataloging-in-Publication Data
Designing socially just learning communities : critical literacy education
across the lifespan / Rebecca Rogers ... [et al.].

p. cm.

Includes bibliographical references.

1. Literacy. 2. Social justice. 3. Critical pedagogy. I. Rogers, Rebecca.

LC149.D424 2008

370.11'5–dc22

2008037894

ISBN 10: 0-415-99759-3 (hbk)
ISBN 10: 0-415-99762-3 (pbk)
ISBN 10: 0-203-88167-2 (ebk)

ISBN 13: 978-0-415-99759-1 (hbk)
ISBN 13: 978-0-415-99762-1 (pbk)
ISBN 13: 978-0-203-88167-5 (ebk)

Collectively, we dedicate this book to all of the courageous educators who give their lives teaching for social justice

and

To Patricia Rogers and Christina Rogers-Spang, my sisters
To Kim and Linda Mosley, my loving parents
To Kateri and William Chapman-Kramer ... with love from mom.

Contents

Preface

This book demonstrates the power and potential of educators working together to use literacy practices that make changes in people's lives. Since 2001, a group of educators, including K-12 classroom teachers, adult educators, university professors, and community activists have worked together to better understand the relationship between literacy and social justice in a teacher-led professional development group called the Literacy for Social Justice Teacher Research Group. This book joins these educators' stories with the history and practices of the teacher inquiry group, providing a twofold emphasis on critical literacy education. Based in teacher inquiry and action research, the authors present examples of classroom-based critical literacy studies that showcase teachers' reflective practice in action. Exploring issues such as gender equity, linguistic diversity, civil rights, and freedom and war, the authors provide insight into the possibilities and struggles of teaching literacy through a framework of social justice. The book also models how teacher-led professional development can provide the support and inspiration for courageous teaching and educational activism. The teachers' practices and actions—in their classrooms and as members of the teacher research group—speak loudly to the policy-makers, educational researchers and activists who wish to work alongside them.

Written in a collaborative manner, the lively narratives in this book blend the voices of dozens of members of the teacher-led professional development group, providing a truly lifespan perspective on designing critical literacy practices. Whether you are interested in critical literacy, lifelong learning, educational reform, professional development, teacher inquiry, or teacher activist groups, *Designing Socially Just Learning Communities* will provide you with engaging examples of teacher inquiry and professional development across the lifespan. This book provides an excellent model for educators and researchers who are seeking ways to transform educational practices.

Unlike other volumes that bring together critical literacy practices of educators working in different cities and even countries, our book focuses on the collaborative work of a group of teachers who are all involved with a grassroots teacher-led professional development group. In this way, we offer a model of radical educational reform that positions teachers as professionals, values their activist spirit and sends a loud call for the conditions necessary for designing socially just learning communities.

Format and Chapter-by-Chapter Organization of the Book

This is a layered book of teachers talking, teaching, reflecting, and acting. Each of the chapters is authored by teachers involved with the Literacy for Social Justice Teacher Research Group (LSJTRG). In each chapter the author(s) share their process of designing critical literacy education. Additionally, each chapter discusses the role of LSJTRG in their professional development. The concluding chapter is a conceptual one that theorizes about learning from teaching and research as a form of professional development and the implications of critical literacy education across the lifespan.

A few words about the structure of the book. We have tried to make the book both theoretically and practically rich so that the reader can dip in and out of it for different purposes. Conceptually, we have laid out the chapters in each section so that readers will read their way through the lifespan. Each case study chapter includes a "Rethinking Practice" section that invites the reader to explore other literature and websites, and offers suggestions for self-study. In addition, photographs of the teachers in each chapter provide another layer of interpretation. Because our framework for critical literacy education includes both individual and group dimensions, we have layered the book so that the reader moves in and out of teachers' classrooms and the LSJTRG. Each section ends with a response chapter written by LSJTRG participants that reconnects the teachers' case studies with the teacher-led professional development group—creating a dialogue between the chapters and teachers' voices. We have also made efforts to move back and forth between local, national, and international threads and themes and issues that unite educators around the world together in struggling for more just communities. Text boxes in each chapter make connections to national and international actions, advocacy, and solidarity. The purpose of these text boxes is to cause the reader to pause and reflect on the actions of advocacy and solidarity that occur around the world in the name of more socially just educational practices.

The book is organized into five sections. Part I includes Chapters 1 and 2. Chapter 1 provides an introduction to our project and an overview of theories and research in the areas of critical literacy education and professional development. Departing from other frameworks of critical literacy education, our framework attends to the role of learning and is structured by dimensions that are applicable both to individuals and to groups. At the heart of critical literacy education is the power and potential to hold both critique and hope together, alongside of each other, in a generative way.

Chapter 2 is a case study of the Literacy for Social Justice Teacher Research Group that shares the history, timeline, and processes of the teacher-led professional development group. This chapter is structured around the dimensions of critical literacy education and also includes the "tools" as they apply to the LSJTRG. We hear the voices of past and present LSJTRG participants as they come together to explore social justice education. This chapter sets the backdrop for the case study chapters that follow.

Parts II, III, and IV each present a group of chapters that are set across the lifespan—including elementary, secondary, and adult education (e.g. GED, higher education). Each section includes chapters portraying the complexity of teaching critical literacy across the lifespan. A "Rethinking Practice" section at the end of each chapter offers ideas for critical literacy education. Parts II, III, and IV conclude with a multi-vocal cross-case analysis chapter written by several members of LSJTRG (who also represent diversity across the lifespan) that draws out key themes, connections, and patterns across the chapters in the section. The dimensions of the critical literacy framework—building community, developing critical stances, critical inquiry, and analysis—are further developed using the voices of the chapter respondents. In each of these cross-case study chapters, we include a section on action, advocacy, and social change.

Part V includes Chapter 16 and Appendices. In Chapter 16, "Designing Socially Just Learning Communities Across the Lifespan: What Is and What Might Be," we reflect, as a group, on the connections that can be made across the lifespan as we teach and learn for more socially just classrooms, schools, and communities. We lay out an argument for a model of critical literacy education across the lifespan that situates learning as a product and process of working the hyphen, the in-between space between what is (reality) and what might be (possibility) (Anzaldúa, 1987; Collins, 1998; Palmer, 2007). We conceptualize the space between what is and what might be as the place where learning occurs, as we move back and forth between two contexts of learning. The first context, the schooling spaces in which we work, often do not look, sound, or feel just to us, nor result in socially just outcomes for students. On the other hand, the contexts of the learning and actions that we engage in through LSJTRG feel like spaces of possibility, the places where our own critical literacy learning thrives. We know, however, that engagement between these two spaces is a borderland where we can try on different practices and identities, with the constant reflection and dialogue that is at the center of democratic processes.

Throughout the book we present a range of classroom-based, school-based, and community-based projects initiated by teachers involved with the LSJTRG. Each of the chapters explores the themes of critical literacy education and teacher-led professional development. We believe the chapters presented in this book represent our process of inquiring into our own teaching practices individually and within the collective of LSJTRG. As we brought data from our classrooms in the form of student writing samples, videotapes, and transcripts to the group to collaboratively analyze and discuss, we started to think about learning and teaching for social justice across the lifespan, rather than just in second grade or just in a GED classroom. Consequently, we started to examine how what happens in second grade might impact a future GED student and how what a GED student learns might impact a second grader. This type of questioning has caused us intellectual unrest because some of our long-held assumptions about teaching and learning are challenged.

Part I

Beginnings

This section provides an introduction to our project and an overview of theories and research in the areas of critical literacy education and teacher-led professional development (Chapter 1). We introduce you to the theoretical frames we are working in and against. For example, we share a framework for critical literacy/popular education that has been developed within educational contexts that are age level and context specific but show how we envision these models expanding to include learners across the lifespan. We move from a description of practices to attention to the role of learning for both individuals and groups. We reframe the practicing teacher as a learner and activist, a person who continues to become critically literate through experiences with participation across contexts. Here, we depart from the dichotomies that often characterize our talk about teaching and learning, in which one is either a teacher or student, oppressed or oppressor, novice or expert, and so on.

In Chapter 2 we present a case study of the Literacy for Social Justice Teacher Research Group that shares the history, timeline, and processes of the teacher-led professional development group. This chapter is structured around the dimensions of the critical literacy/popular education framework (building community, developing critical stances, critical inquiry and analysis and action, advocacy and social change) and also includes the "tools" as they apply to the group. We hear the voices of past and present LSJTRG participants as they come together to explore social justice education. This chapter sets the backdrop for the case study chapters that follow.

We invite you to join in thinking critically about where our experiences intersect and do not align with your own. As a group, we are constantly in this position of being faced with new ways of seeing literacy education, experiencing democratic practices, and generating new learning. We look forward to sharing our story with you.

1   Introduction

On the steps of the Old Courthouse in downtown St. Louis, Missouri, a crowd of people gathers at a rally in support of public education. The Literacy for Social Justice Teacher Research Group (LSJTRG) and the ABC's of Literacy Group[1] have organized this rally to voice concerns about the privatization of education in St. Louis as it affects the rights of all people (locally and globally) for equal access to quality education. Across the street from the Old Courthouse a national conference of adult educators (Commission on Adult Basic Education) is taking place. We leaflet at the conference for attendees to join us at the rally, knowing that our struggle for education includes both K-12 and adult education.

> We are here today to reaffirm the importance of education as a civil right — as the cornerstone of a strong democracy—not as an entitlement program or as a commodity in the market place. We are here today to call for a democratization of public education—not a privatization of public education.

Rebecca Rogers, co-founder of LSJTRG (with Mary Ann Kramer), opens the rally with comments that frame the importance of educators across the lifespan uniting around principles of democracy and civil rights. "The idea for this rally emerged out of a series of dialogues and actions around literacy education that have taken place in St. Louis. Educators across the lifespan have been working on realizing the connection between literacy and freedom."

Ora Clark-Lewis, an adult education teacher and member of LSJTRG, makes the connection between the struggle for equal education today and 200 years ago when Freedom Schools were created in St. Louis in resistance to a state law forbidding enslaved African Americans to read and write.

Donna Jones, elected school board member, gives an update on the court case over the state take-over of the St. Louis Public Schools: "We are taking our case

---

1. ABC's of Literacy stands for Acting for a Better Community and includes a group of adult education teachers and educators who organize around literacy education for freedom. At different points, the paths of LSJTRG and ABC's cross, such as in planning this rally (Acting for a Better Community Organizing Team, 2008).

to the state Supreme Court and we will be heard later this summer. The fight is not over and we are asking that you stand and you fight with us."

A local high school teacher and a student share the song they wrote called "Democracy Anthem" to protest the state take-over of the public schools. Between speakers the crowd claps and cheers.

Extending to a global focus, Cynthia Peters from *The Change Agent* states,

> We need nothing less than all of our minds to solve the problems we are facing today. We need broad based social change movements with deep roots in all communities. This means that educators need to work with anti-foreclosure, environmental justice, immigrant reform and peace groups. Together we can stop the militarization and corporatization of our daily lives. We need education but we don't need just any kind of education. We need an education that empowers and that frees our mind and helps us unfold as human beings.

An adult literacy student and intern reads the Declaration Statement—a statement that calls for united action among advocates for public education in the face of unjust educational reforms. Over 200 signatures were collected on the declaration statement, including participants at the conference, and will be sent to local, state, and national elected officials (see Appendix 1). Other speakers, including national adult education advocates, make connections between the ongoing wars and the privatization of public services, including education.

On the sidewalk, people gather together holding signs that read "Books not Bombs," "Literacy is a Civil Right," "Our Schools are not for Sale," and "Defend Public Education," to listen to the speakers and music, and to participate in the symbolic actions. They wave their signs at the rush-hour traffic and receive honks of support. The rally ends with the drumming of Thunderheart, a traditional Native American drumming group, accompanying the posting of the mini-protest signs on a public display board. Later, the nightly news reports, "A group gathers in downtown St. Louis to voice their support for public education."

This is a gathering of teachers—across the lifespan, of community activists, of union members, of candidates running for political office, adult learners, parents and elected officials. Despite the pressures of silencing of teachers, outsourcing of curriculum, high-stakes standardized tests, reduced education budgets owing to the war in Iraq, teachers, parents, and students are standing together to call for justice. On the steps of the Old Courthouse, the boundaries between traditional grade levels, between teacher and activist, and between the school and the street disappear. Here, teachers use their voices to defend public education and stand in solidarity with educators across the nation and world.

Several weeks before, members of LSJTRG and ABC's gathered to plan the rally following Meredith Labadie's workshop on Teaching for Social Justice in Reading and Writing Workshops. During this and subsequent meetings we brainstormed slogans for the signs, generated a list of speakers and musicians, designed fliers, wrote a press release, obtained a permit for the rally, and circulated announcements and leaflets. We thought of ways to make the rally interactive and participatory, including circulating a declaration calling for education to be considered as a civil right and having mini-protest signs available where people could pen their own message.

The rally captures the essence of the LSJTRG—the power and potential of a group of educators working together—inside and outside the classroom—to use literacy and language to make changes in society. Many of the teachers who planned and participated in the rally are members of LSJTRG. Many of them appear in the pages of this book. These teachers work in different schools and in different districts. Their students vary in age and range from working-class European Americans to middle-class African Americans to adult immigrants. Whether in or out of the classroom, these teachers are committed to educational practices and outcomes that contribute to freedom and justice—in short, critical literacy education. While exploring social class, gender, sexuality, race, the environment, or human rights with their students and collaborating with other educators to plan a workshop or rally, these educators draw on a set of tools to interrogate social practices, sort through multiple agendas encoded in texts, and to collaborate on ways of acting in more socially just ways.

The LSJTRG is a grassroots, teacher-led professional development group dedicated to exploring and acting on the relationships between literacy and social justice. The intersecting stories of this group of educators are told in the pages of this book. Along the way we set forth a lifespan perspective on critical literacy education, one that draws on popular education and can be utilized across the lifespan.

This project—both the book and the ongoing cultural work of our group—was conceived in the spirit of engaged scholarship. Since 2001, we have been organizing, holding public meetings around social justice issues, conducting inquiry in our classrooms, sharing our analyses, and participating in social justice events. We believed there was something unique about our work together. It was not until 2005 that we learned that other teacher activist groups like our own were springing up all over the United States in cities such as New York, Chicago, and San Francisco. We were busy building a space where educators could network, learn, and grow with each other. When we looked up, we realized we were not alone in the journey.

We believed there was something very generative about our work together that could serve as a model for other educators, researchers, policy-makers, and activists who are also involved with grassroots educational reform. We decided to formally document our process of working together for educational change. We extended an invitation to people involved in the group to a summer institute to explore the process of writing a book to document our experiences, as individual educators and as a social justice group. Several of the teachers at the institute had already conducted inquiry projects in their classroom that they wanted to write about. Others had not begun the process yet. The institute was a place for us to brainstorm, share, and organize our thoughts.

Many drafts later, we arrive at a book that offers a snapshot of our journey—as individuals and as a group. As educators and citizens who believe education is vital to a healthy democracy, we embarked on this work as a form of praxis—

Photo 1.1 LSJTRG participants at the Defend Public Education Rally.

theory, practice, reflection, and action (Croteau, Hoynes, & Ryan, 2005). Our research allowed us to delve more deeply into the public domain; our activism inspired our writing and provided us with a grassroots perspective. This book joins these educators' stories with the history and practices of the teacher inquiry group, providing a twofold emphasis on critical literacy education.

Literacy Education, Freedom, and Democracy

In our work as literacy educators—with GED, high school, elementary, and teacher education students—we are constantly reminded of the importance of guiding our students as readers, writers, and thinkers while at the same time educating towards social responsibility. Children, adolescents, or adults who have had, or are expected to have, the most difficulty with literacy are commonly the most oppressed by literacy. It is these students and their teachers who stand to benefit the most from developing critical literacy practices within socially just learning spaces.

Critical literacy education takes many shapes and forms (for reviews of critical approaches to literacy see Collins & Blot, 2003; Janks, 2000; Luke, 2000; Muspratt, Luke, & Freebody, 1997; Street, 2003). When critical frameworks guide literacy education, they are referred to as critical literacy or participatory literacy education. Critical literacy education has deep roots in the struggle of historically marginalized people to gain literacy and political power (e.g. Clark, 1990; Freire, 1970a; Horton, Kohl, & Kohl, 1997). Because of the links between literacy and freedom, access, and economic mobility, literacy has always been political and central in struggles for freedom (e.g. Monaghan, 1991; Moore, Monaghan, & Hartman, 1997; Prendergast, 2003). Critical literacy education includes practices that disrupt or critique dominant knowledge–power relationships that perpetuate unequal gender, race, and class relations and instead center dialogue, debate, and dissent, features of a democracy. We envision critical literacy education as the vehicle for building more democratic communities.

There are many good introductions to the theory and practices of critical literacy (e.g. Lewison, Leland, & Harste, 2008; Stevens & Bean, 2007; Vasquez, 2003) and demonstrations of critical literacy in classrooms (Cowhey, 2006) and out-of-school spaces (Comber, Nixon, & Reid, 2007; Morrell, 2008). We have accounts of how children in elementary classrooms practice critical literacy (e.g. Comber, Thomson, & Wells, 2001; Henkin, 1998; Lewison, Flint, & Van Sluys, 2002; Powell, Cantrell, & Adams, 2001; Sweeney, 1997; Vasquez, 2004) as well as accounts of critical literacy in middle and high school (e.g. Morrell, 2008; Myers & Beach, 2004; Rogers, 2002), adult education (e.g. Brookfield, 2005; Degener, 2001; Rogers & Kramer, 2008), and teacher education (e.g. Comber, 2006; Dozier, Johnston, & Rogers, 2005; McDaniels, 2006). Our work departs from earlier work in our dual emphasis on critical literacy education—within classrooms across the lifespan and within the context of a teacher-led professional development group. Here, we sort through what we mean by critical literacy education—discussing each of the terms associated with the concept in turn, "critical," "literacy," and "education."

Critical

> I am linking the struggle of men and women of color as a common struggle—and teaching implicitly that feminism is a set of issues and actions that is relevant in the lives of men as well as women.
>
> (Carolyn Fuller, Adult Education and Literacy Teacher)

What does the term "critical" mean in critical literacy education? We use the construct of "critical frameworks" to refer to the myriad ways in which educators practice critical literacy to create socially just learning spaces. There is no one critical framework or set of methods or approaches that characterizes a critical teacher. A critical framework includes an analysis and critique of systems of oppression and the tools for social action. See Table 1.1 for a list of the social justice issues that are explored throughout this book.

Critical frameworks start from the assumption that literacy learning includes a struggle over power and knowledge (Edelsky, 1999; Freire, 1970b; Janks, 2000; Luke, 2000; Richardson, 2003). In Carolyn's voice above, we see that struggle is a common theme in society, and is therefore in our educational frameworks. In the sense that knowledge is never neutral but is defined by those who have access to resources, critical education practices seek to redistribute

Table 1.1 Critical Literacy Education: Infusing Social Justice in the Literacy Curriculum

Chapters	Author	Grade Level	Social Justice Topic	Strategies for Literacy Teaching
3	Melissa Mosley	Second grade	War, patriotism, freedom	Book clubs, discussions
4	Rebecca Light	Fifth grade	Codes of power, student voice	Reflective writing
5	Sarah Hobson	High school	Gender inequity, sexual violence	Socratic dialogues, literature discussions
6	Carolyn Fuller	Adult basic literacy/GED	Self-respect, equity, politics, African American history	Book, clubs, discussion of current events
8	Melissa Mosley and Margaret Finders	Sixth grade	Leadership and cultural capital	Literature discussion, role play
9	Mary Ann Kramer and Rhonda Jones	Adult basic literacy/GED	Civil rights and African American literature	Literature discussion, writing for political action
10	Jacquelyn A. Lewis-Harris	Teachers	Racial literacy	Examining artifacts, discussions
12	Liesl Buechler and Kate Lofton	First grade	Monocultural classrooms, organizing	Class meetings, culturally relevant instruction
13	Janet DePasquale	High School	Heterosexuality and homophobia	Writing for political action
14	Sarah Beaman-Jones	Adult basic literacy/GED	Popular education, organizing	Community action groups

power/knowledge relationships. This redistribution means recognizing, challenging, and rebuilding relationships that are fundamentally constructed out of the fabric of oppression. To do this, we need multiple frameworks to notice and name oppression. Thus, we recognize the multiplicity of critical perspectives from anti-racism, class-based instruction, culturally relevant instruction, multicultural education to feminist teaching. Our stance is that they all add to the struggle for human liberation.

Underlying each of these frameworks is a set of values that conflicts with the values of dominant institutions. For example, underlying culturally relevant instruction is the purpose of recognizing the values and perspectives and the ways of knowing of people who historically have been silenced. When such values become part of the curriculum they often conflict with the values of the institutions themselves. Structuring a curriculum where the stories of people of color are elicited and heard, without interruption and critique, conflict with the Eurocentric norms and values of dominant institutions. Similarly, structuring a classroom that is community centered rather than centered on the individual runs counter to the dominant values of individualism, authority, and competition that comprise society.

Thus, engaging in instructional practices from any of these perspectives, we would argue, is engaging in a form of resistance and struggle, a struggle that opens space for traditionally marginalized voices and, at the same time, restructures the institutions themselves. Thus, the action component of critical literacy is essential in the movement towards designing socially just spaces (e.g. Bomer & Bomer, 2003; Comber, Thomson, & Wells, 2001; Heffernan & Lewison, 2005; Van Sluys, Lewison, & Flint, 2006). Action often occurs at the local level, as a response to the conditions of day-to-day life, but critical educators constantly move back and forth between the local and the global.

Critical frameworks recognize the politics of literacy in society, the struggle for power inherent in literacy movements, and centers action. In the present society in which we live, oppression is perpetuated by globalization, the distribution of wealth, and war. Literacy frameworks in a global society cannot remain too local, in other words. Often, in order to change local conditions, conditions of oppression and injustice across the globe come into play. A "critical" framework takes us beyond immediate circumstances to the larger structures that limit our ability to make change. Critical frameworks bring awareness to heightened world conflicts, increased international connectedness, and the need for solving common world problems.

Literacy

> Yes, indeed, among other topics, my journalism students were writing some stories that dealt with homosexuality.
>
> (Janet DePasquale, High School English and Journalism Teacher)

What does *literacy* refer to in critical literacy education? As others have convincingly argued, a more apt term to capture reading and writing practices is "literacies." Literacies are conceptualized as situated social practices, imbued with power and ideology and used to accomplish certain social goals. Literacies refer to the myriad social practices that purposefully use language and texts. Texts, then, are any social artifact that produces meaning. Texts include literature, web pages, instant messages, advertisements on the sides of buses, a concert schedule, a parking ticket, and so on.

Literacies not only refer to the writing and reading of texts in the traditional sense, however. Conceptualizing the multiple dimensions of literacy broadens the edges to include multiple modalities and the concept of designing (Cope & Kalantzis, 2000). The New London Group (1996) considered the ways in which critical literacy education might reshape how children and youth come to know the ways in which literacy can be powerful. That is, people learn literacies by examining both the construction of texts and constructing new texts. The focus shifts from the individual user to the collaboration between users with the idea of design, drawing on the notion that learning happens in the social interactions around the decoding and design of texts.

More and more, people represent themselves and others in ways that break boundaries, from web pages to MySpace and Facebook pages to multimedia sharing sites such as YouTube. The concept of multiple literacies is particularly important for adults, who read and design multiple types of texts because of work and life experiences. We rely on a conception of designing texts that considers how people draw on tools at hand in this design (Kress, 2003; New London Group, 1996). Tools can be literacy practices such as writing, design of a web page, or blogging, *or* critical literacy practices such as questioning social practices, seeking out information from diverse sources, or organizing for a rally.

Different social practices are comprised of different types of texts and literacy practices. Schooled literacy, as Hicks (2002) and Street (2005) have argued, often consists of functional approaches to reading and writing that are decontextualized from the lives and realities of learners. Family and community literacy practices, on the other hand, consist of the literacies that people use in their everyday lives to accomplish social projects. These include reading directions, negotiating a play station, skimming a new magazine, and finding the correct forms needed to apply for an identification card. Many studies have shown that people considered illiterate in school settings are often quite literate in their homes and communities. At stake is what counts as literacy and who defines what it means to be literate.

Literacies are political. In the quote above, Janet writes that her students were writing about gay, lesbian, bi-sexual, and trans-gender issues (GLBT), in the context of a journalism class with a public project, the school newspaper. The students were writing news stories, a traditional literacy practice. Imbued in Janet's statement is the recognition that the practices of the students were not politically neutral. In fact, Janet foregrounds the students' work as intentional. Further, literacy has always been deeply enmeshed with privilege and oppression. The continued legacy of denying people access to literacy education based on race, language, and ability continues today as high-stakes tests, punitive state laws, and prescriptive curricula are put into place for children living in poverty including linguistic and cultural minorities. Such tests and curricula continue to secure and preserve literacy education as a right for the privileged, white classes in society. As a result, linguistic and cultural minorities have restricted access to the political, economic, and educational structures necessary to gain equitable outcomes in society. However, movements have also used literacy as a tool to construct more complete notions of the intersections between literacy, language, schooling, and power. Movements for bilingual education, for example, talk back to the No Child Left Behind Act in order to advocate for the rights of English language learners in U.S. classrooms.

Education

> We are the people and so we do have the power to make changes. We need to own our power. This is what I learned long ago from the women's movement.
>
> (Sarah Beaman-Jones, Literacy Program Developer)

What does *education* refer to in critical literacy education? In the quote above, Sarah draws from her experiences in the movement for women's rights as a tool towards educating, in her case, adults working towards empowerment through literacy education. Sarah brings her understanding of how knowledge and power is constructed as well as how leadership emerges from her participation in a social movement to her work as an educator. Both contexts share the belief that to realize the goal of democracy, all people must have both equal access and opportunity for social, economic, and political power. Education has also been described as a vehicle realizing democratic ideals. Indeed, many philosophers have argued that it is in education that people can realize the multiple possibilities and positions that exist around any question (Dewey, 1966; Greene, 1988; Palmer, 2007). The women's movement also worked towards the idea that each person holds a standpoint that is essential to understanding. Education, as well, involves taking up positions and finding one's voice and perspective.

Education is the process of naming one's experiences and world and, in the process, transforming these experiences. Education, then, is a dialogue between participants- -positioning both students and teachers as learners. Dialogue plays a central role in an education that is liberatory. The teacher's role is not, to use Freire's (1970b) metaphor of a banking approach to education, to deposit information into the students' heads but rather to "mine" resources and knowledge that students have at their disposal. People of all ages have linguistic and cultural resources for solving problems and generating new ideas. In this view of education, any cultural worker who is informed in the construction of knowledge—from social activist, political revolutionary, seventh grade math teacher, university professor, religious worker—is an educator.

Education is the process of designing spaces for resistance and problem posing, especially through the process of dialogue. Dialogue around critical issues is what makes a theme into a problem. For example, globalization and the outsourcing of jobs is a theme. But "what is the effect of globalization and outsourcing on the economy of the community" is a question. People move from themes to questions through dialogue, and through dialogue, begin to understand how local problems exist. When education is conceptualized as a process

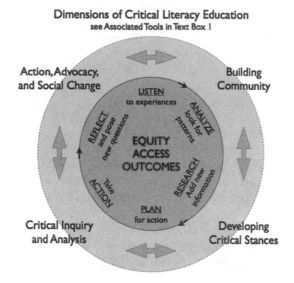

Figure 1.1 Critical literacy education framework.

ot dialogue it becomes apparent how similar education is across the lifespan. Education as a process of dialogue is learner driven and based on authentic problems that come from everyday life.

Critical Literacy Education: A Framework

At the heart of this book are educators working with students and other educators/activists to use literacy practices in ways that make changes in people's lives. Critical literacy education has most often been applied in adult literacy education in the name of popular education (Clark, 1990; Freire, 2001; Horton, Kohl, & Kohl, 1997). To address our concern with a lifespan perspective, we have joined a framework for critical literacy education with the popular education model to illustrate how we conceptualize learning. Figure 1.1 visually represents our framework for critical literacy education across the lifespan. This framework emerges from the individual and collective actions and practices of members of the LSJTRG and reflects the tools used by both individuals and communities to practice critical literacy.

Intentions of Critical Literacy Education

At the center of the figure we have printed the words, "equity, access, and outcomes" but we envision that depending on the short-term/long-term goals and intentions of individuals or groups, the center of the framework might be "human rights," "democracy," or "social justice." We keep intentions at the center of the framework to emphasize that "so what" of our critical literacy practices. Between the intentions and the critical literacy practices is a cycle or process of popular education (Freire, 1970a; Horton, Kohl, & Kohl, 1997; Horton, Freire, Bell, Gaventa, & Peters, 1990).

Popular Education

It is through the process of popular education that the intentions and outcomes of critical literacy are realized. At the root of the popular education model is the belief that people hold the answers to their own problems and worries. These answers are not the product of the individual but the accumulation of the knowledge of all of the people in the community. Beyond sharing answers, there is an element of research in which gaps in knowledge are filled by going outside of the group. On this point, Horton (1990) said, "Once you get the people talking about a problem and there's no solution within the group, which is often the case, then you go outside the group and introduce ideas and experiences that are related to the problem" (Horton, Freire, Bell, Gaventa, & Peters, 1990, p. 169). The popular education process relies on horizontal relationships between people, "experts" who provide other information, and organizers who keep the cycle of popular education moving. After gaining all of the information and looking for patterns, the group has the needed knowledge to plan for action. Finally, the cycle ends with action and then reflection towards the posing of new problems.

Learning occurs as people follow this cycle. Horton spoke on this in a conversation with Paulo Freire: "We based our whole thinking on the premise that people learn what they do. Not what they talk about but what they do. And so we made our speech about social equality without saying anything, but by doing it" (Horton, Freire, Bell, Gaventa, & Peters, 1990, p. 164). The process of popular education is the very model of participation that creates democratic spaces and teaches democratic processes.

Critical Literacy Dimensions and Associated Tools

The four dimensions of the critical literacy framework are: (1) building a community that is sustained over time, (2) developing critical stances, (3) critical inquiry and analysis, and (4) action, advocacy, and social change. Along with each dimension come tools (see Text Box 1.1) that we have seen enacted and developed as people learn to implement critical literacies in classrooms, organizations, and in LSJTRG. Within the dimension of building a community over time, for example, are the associated tools of establishing routines and norms and learning to listen. The dimension of developing critical stances contains the tools of placing information from multiple sources in historical and political contexts, for example. In the dimension of critical inquiry and analysis, we see individuals using the tools of inquiry such as finding patterns between sources and critically examining information gathered from multiple sources including the World Wide Web. As part of the fourth dimension of action, advocacy, and social change, we see the tools of building alliances outside of the group, or using the Internet to organize people from different organizations to think about

Text Box 1.1 Tools for Building Socially Just Learning Communities

I. Building and Sustaining a Learning Community
The following set of tools is designed to help build and sustain a learning community, particularly for groups.

- Establishing routines and norms
- Celebrations
- Balancing individual and collective needs
- Learning to listen
- Recognizing and naming struggles
- Open invitations to participate
- Collective decision-making
- Opportunities for leadership.

II. Developing Critical Stances and Multiple Perspectives
The following set of tools is designed to broaden and deepen the content knowledge of people within the group, recognizing that each educator brings a wealth of resources into the group setting.

- Reading widely and deeply
- Making local/global connections
- Placing information in context
- Finding relationships between sources
- Seeking out multiple, non-dominant perspectives.

III. Critical Inquiry and Analysis (Systems of Oppression)
The following set of tools is designed to equip educators with the methods for engaging productively in a problem-posing/problem-solving dynamic in their classrooms, community, and within the group itself.

- Reflecting through multiple modes
- Considering histories of participation
- Finding patterns and generating theories
- Planning for action
- Critically reading and evaluating information from web-based sources
- Engaging in inquiry processes
- Reflecting on group processes and dynamics.

IV. Action, Advocacy, and Social Change
The following set of tools is designed to support individuals and groups who are moving from dialogue and reflection to action.

- Recognizing incremental change
- Building alliances
- Appreciating different roles in activism
- Drawing on previous experiences
- Developing skills of activism/advocacy
- Using technology to organize for social action.

actions together. The list of tools that we have generated here are necessarily flexible and the list is in no way exhaustive of the tools that we know people draw on to design critical literacy education.

People and groups can enter into critical literacy practices from different entry points. The dimensions and tools are also intertwined. Part of constructing a critical stance is to explore one's potential to apply tools of critical inquiry and analysis to the problems that emerge in local contexts and to consider their global connections. Critical educators recognize that their viewpoints are part of who they are and embody those viewpoints through their actions. They listen to their students and colleagues, who represent many viewpoints, beliefs, understandings, languages, practices, and worries. They spend focused time thinking about how their literacy instruction and the practices they encourage are a form of action. They also consider how the conversations about social class, race, stereotypes, difference, justice, and equity that occur in classrooms and professional circles infuse their personal lives and actions. The bi-directional arrows in the model designate this feature of the framework. We see the critical literacy lifespan framework as a model of how groups of people (or individuals) create the dispositions to work towards social change through literacy practices.

Contribution of the Framework

The theories and methods of critical literacy education through a popular education framework (for example, Morrell's (2008) work with youth in participatory community action projects) are becoming more common in K-12 education although hesitancy still exists about integrating these types of projects into primary grades. Less often, however, do we hear about the tools needed to support educators as they continue to broaden and deepen their own critical literacy practices. In our work with educators who teach across the lifespan—from primary grades to adult education—we have found it necessary to broaden our lens to consider critical literacy education from cradle to grave. As we will demonstrate across the chapters in this book, many of the processes and conditions for critical literacy education are the same, regardless of age, grade, or experiences. As we move between the case studies of classrooms based in teacher inquiry and the examples of collective action and practices through LSJTRG, we will demonstrate the dimensions of the critical literacy framework. In the next section, we discuss the importance of critical literacy education in professional development settings.

Teacher-led Professional Development

This lifespan approach assumes that educators who teach any grade across the lifespan can engage with critical literacy education and that, as teachers, they must themselves experience the process of learning to be critically literate. However, given the strict requirements of state and federal standards, professional development is more inclined to focus on the details of literacy instruction, including standards, testing, and designing instruction that prepares children, adolescents, or adults to do well on tests. Indeed, in the era of neoliberal education reforms, opportunities for teachers to focus on cultural and linguistic diversity, anti-racist instruction, and social justice are rare. Further, professional development offers few opportunities for teachers to construct their own understandings around critical literacy that emerge from their local contexts.

There are limitations to current models of professional development for teachers. Cochran-Smith & Lytle argue that periodic staff development days do not support learning for experienced teachers. Most effective professional development occurs over time, rather than in isolated moments of staff development (Cochran-Smith & Lytle, 2001). In *Learning from Teaching in Literacy Education*, Rodgers and Pinnell (2002) describe "what is and what could be in professional development" (p. 2). "What is" for professional development includes district-based professional development, conferences, school-based teacher education and school-based professional development early interventions. They ask, "what if we had the power to buy whatever we need to improve literacy education? What would we want?" (p. 5). They argue that "what could be" needs to be based in broad and systemic-wide approaches to professional development. Examples might include integration of research and practice, and long-term professional development with clear parameters. To this list we might add ongoing teacher-led professional development focused on problems that arise out of teaching, which span traditional grade-level boundaries.

Teacher networks, inquiry communities, and other school-based collectives in which teachers and others conjoin their efforts to construct knowledge can become the major contexts for professional development in this model (Cochran-Smith & Lytle, 2001; Fecho, 2000; Picower, 2007). On the power of teachers working together, Atwell (1998) writes, "one teacher can do great things, a community of teachers can move a mountain" (p. 20).

As learners, teachers are not often asked to think seriously about matters of inequity (e.g. Delpit & Kilgour-Dowdy, 2002; Fecho, 2000; Lewison, Flit, & Van Sluys, 2002). Nor are teachers who focus on creating socially just spaces likely to get the professional development and support that is needed to sustain their teaching (Picower, 2007). And yet, inquiring into how literacy and social justice are linked is important because teachers often expect their students to be similar to them as mainly white, middle-class females (Delpit, 1995). Many of the teachers' notions of literacy, language, and development are based on their own ideologies formed by the theories of a predominantly white male academia and administration, and therefore their teaching reflects gendered, raced, and classed behaviors. Further, white teachers often believe that racism has nothing to do with them because they do not consider themselves to be racist or prejudiced (Cochran-Smith, 1995, 2000). Teachers must first explore issues of race in their own lives (Howard, 1999; Stokes-Brown, 2002; Tatum, 1994). However, it is difficult to accomplish such sensitive interrogations in traditional professional development forums.

Photo 1.2. Aleshea Ingram leads a workshop on using socially responsible literature in the writer's workshop.

Teacher Research

Teacher research offers educators a space to experiment with their practices, theorize about patterns, connect their learning with professional literature, and reflect on their practices in deep and meaningful ways. A review of the literature suggests that inquiry is embedded throughout various phases in an educator's life. Many collaborative groups, for example, are connected to teacher education programs (Cook-Sather, 2002; French, Garcia-Lopez, & Darling-Hammond, 2002; Nieto, 2003; Picower, 2007; Wiedeman-Ramirez, 2002). Other collaborative groups comprised teacher educators studying their own practices (e.g. Cochran-Smith, 1999; Cooper, 2006; Hyland & Noffke, 2005). Hyland & Noffke (2005), for example, report on a long-term action research project that investigated the teaching of an elementary social studies methods course for pre-service teachers within a social justice framework. Teachers may come together to inquire into literacy practices without a specific focus on social justice. Or, other inquiry groups arise out of collective needs or mutual interests or concerns of practicing teachers (e.g. Duncan-Andrade, 2005). The Mapleton Teacher

Research Group and their inquiry around spelling development is a prime example of a longitudinal form of professional development within the context of one school (Chandler-Olcott, 2001; Chandler-Olcott & The Mapleton Teacher Research Group, 1999).

Teacher Activist Groups

"If your aim is to change society," as Myles Horton wrote, "you have to think in terms of which small groups have the potential to multiply themselves and fundamentally change society" (Horton, Kohl, & Kohl, 1997, pp. 57). Teacher networks, inquiry communities, and other school-based collectives in which teachers collaboratively construct knowledge can help develop professional development models whose aims are to fundamentally change society (Abu El-Haj, 2003; Cochran-Smith & Lytle, 2001; Fecho, 2000; Fecho & Allen, 2003; Powers & Hubbard, 1999).

When educators are given the space to determine their areas of strengths and the areas of their practice where they need support, genuine learning and development can occur. While there is abundant work on the importance of teachers working together, we know less about teachers working together to design socially just learning spaces. Picower (2007) describes the support of critical inquiry groups in a multi-racial group of first-year teachers teaching in the New York City School system. Lewis and Ketter's (2003) study of a longitudinal professional development group describes how white, middle-class teachers learn to discuss sensitive issues in children's literature through a community of practice in Iowa. In Massachusetts, a critical literacy inquiry group that conducted teacher research projects included practicing teachers enrolled in a graduate level course (Luna, Botelho, French, Iverson, & Matos, 2004).

In summary, educators need support systems to continue to work towards social change. Around the country, teacher activist groups are emerging to support social justice education and socially just policies (Miner, 2005/2006). Many of these groups are located in cities where teachers are increasingly under attack and silenced in the name of accountability and standards. We have listed several of these groups here that we have come into contact with through our participation in a national coalition called TAG—Teacher Activist Groups (See Text Box 1.2). We know that there are additional teacher activist groups around the country. Teacher activism nourishes the design of critical literacy education in the classroom. It takes us closer to the struggles we explore with our students.

Engaged Scholarship

At the heart of our teaching, research and activism is a commitment to the potential that literacy practices can build a more socially just society. We take responsibility for uncovering, building, and advocating for the types of social practices that can be used to make the world a better place. We side with scholars such as Palmer (2007) and Collins (1998) who advocate for a "visionary pragmatism" that integrates the possibility of acting in the world as it is (unjust) without losing sight of the world as

Text Box 1.2 Teacher Activist Groups

Many of the groups included below were cited in a *Rethinking Schools* article (Au, Bigelow, Burant, & Salas, 2005/2006):	
New York, NY, The New York Collective of Radical Educators	www.nycore.org/
San Francisco, CA, Teachers 4 Social Justice	www.t4sj.org
Chicago, IL, Teachers for Social Justice	www.teachersforjustice.org/
Oakland, CA, Education not Incarceration	www.ednotinc.org/
Portland, OR, Portland Area Rethinking Schools	http://web.pdx.edu/~bgds/PARS/
Louisville, KY, Progressives Engaged in Struggle Support Network	http://pressnetwork.blogspot.com/2006/07/education-action.html
St. Louis, MO, The Literacy for Social Justice Teacher Research Group	www.umsl.edu/~lsjtrg
Harlem, NY, Education for Liberation	www.edliberation.org/
Boston, MA, Education Action!	www.ed-action.org/
Atlanta, GA, Atlantans for Better Schools and Social Change	https://www.student.gsu.edu/~jsauer2/teachers/Teachersforsocialchange_index.htm
Los Angeles, CA, Association of Raza Educators	www.razaeducators.org/
Washington, DC, Save our Schools	www.saveourschoolsdc.org/
Milwaukee, WI, Rethinking Schools	www.rethinkingschools.org/
Milwaukee, WI, Educators Network for Social Justice	www.ensj.org
Teacher Activist Groups	www.teacheractivistgroups.org/

it might be (just). This means that we flexibly take on roles as teachers, researchers, and activists, transforming ourselves and society in the process.

We intend for the narratives of each of the teachers and the group (as well as the dialogue between teachers and the group) to be read as an example of "engaged scholarship." Engaged scholarship looks very much like the process of critical literacy education, but allows us to position our work within a tradition of scholarship about our work as knowledge builders. Engaged scholarship is a problem-posing process (Freire, 1970b; Morrell, 2004), taking us from our observations and dialogues to broader understandings of cultures, institutions, and societies. The tools we have outlined in the critical literacy education framework cut across our work as teachers, researchers, and activists.

As people committed to social justice, we seek to enter into teaching and research relationships that are consistent with the way in which we make sense of the world. The theories and methods of our engaged scholarship draw on the overlapping traditions of teacher research (e.g. Cochran-Smith & Lytle, 2001), action research (Kemmis & Wilkinson, 1998), participatory action research (Morrell, 2004), feminist research (e.g. Brantlinger, 1999; Lather, 1991; Naples, 2003), and activist scholarship (Croteau, Hoynes, & Ryan, 2005; Guajardo, Guajardo, & del Carmen Casaperalta, 2008; Lipman & Haines, 2007; Urrieta & Mendez Benavidez, 2004). The thread that we draw on from all of the traditions is their engagement with social life, an emphasis on collaboration, and a deliberate focusing on the problems that face society. Engaged scholarship happens within and alongside our communities, at a local level, and is sustained over time. Further, as educators, the process of doing "engaged scholarship" reinforces the frameworks of critical literacy education that we seek to develop in our classrooms (Guajardo, Guajardo, & del Carmen Casaperalta, 2008).

Within each case represented in this book, and across the entirety of the book, the multiple authors straddle the traditional lines of teacher-researcher-activist. Each of the case studies were conceived in the spirit of more deeply understanding and changing a social problem through the tools of literacy education. We (Becky, Melissa, and Mary Ann) worked with each author, keeping the larger structure of the book in mind, to develop her understandings through the process of writing the chapter (from brainstorming, to analysis, to writing and reflecting).

Photo 1.3 Teachers hold signs at "Defend Public Education" rally.

The authors in each case draw on a range of methods including discourse analysis, narrative analysis, grounded theory, memoir, and document analysis. The projects span a school year, unit of study, multi-year project, or a single day. Some drew on data they collected in their classrooms and others are of the variety of educational memoirs, where the teachers reflect critically on their experiences and practices. Often, in the process of researching and writing the chapters, the authors redesigned their practices, another form of social action.

We looked at the teachers' case studies individually and as a group to analyze patterns and threads about critical literacy education across the lifespan. We moved back and forth between the teachers' cases and the research literature in an iterative manner. In order to conduct cross-case analyses, we intentionally asked participants in LSJTRG to read each of the chapters and look for patterns, themes, and connections across the chapters. In this way, other teachers were put in the position to theorize about the teaching and learning in each of the chapters. This analysis and discussion helped us to build the critical literacy education framework.

Similarly, we view LSJTRG as an ongoing action research project that cycles through various stages. We document our group's processes through fieldnotes, audiotapes of meetings, analysis of structures, and processes. We present and write about our group. We notice how elements of our roles as teachers-researchers-activists are present in both our classrooms and in the groups we participate in out of school. Through the practice of constructing this text, we also built useful skills such as writing for publication, presenting at conferences, advocating for best practices, and developing tools of advocacy and organizing. Telling our stories of resisting injustice is a form of social activism and advocacy.

Members of the LSJTRG have collaboratively written this book. As you might expect, the book is filled with the unique voices of teachers working towards social justice through critical literacy education. There are, needless to say, many voices from LSJTRG that have not been included in the book but whose inspiration can be found on every page.

2 A Framework for Critical Literacy Education Across the Lifespan

A Case Study of the Literacy for Social Justice Teacher Research Group

Teachers and students throughout the world are searching for avenues to exercise resistance to oppressive educational mandates. The resistance takes place in the classroom and on the streets. Educators are finding strength in numbers, power in collaboration. In St. Louis, Missouri, a city in which the public schools have a long history of struggle for racial equity, a group of educators in 2001 formed a professional development group called the Literacy for Social Justice Teacher Research Group (LSJTRG) to learn from each other, study our own teaching practices and build socially just communities. Our group follows a recursive process of reflecting on authentic problems in our classrooms and communities, designing and carrying out inquiry projects, sharing data with the group, strategizing and planning further classroom and community actions, and disseminating our research and actions.

There are several unique aspects to our group. The first is that we consist of educators across the lifespan—including early childhood, elementary grades, middle and high school, adult education, community education, and higher education. Second, the group consists of teachers across the professional development lifespan. There are teachers who have been teaching for 60 years, for six years, and who are preparing to become teachers. The group is racially, religiously, and socioeconomically diverse. All teachers volunteer to participate because they are committed to their own learning and socially just forms of instruction. Third, the group reveals a longitudinal portrait of professional development.

In this chapter, we share a case portrait of our group through a framework that supports critical literacy education across the lifespan (introduced in Chapter 1). Drawing on seven years of fieldnotes, archived notes/plans and agendas from meetings and transcripts of group discussions (much of which may be found on our website www.umsl.edu/~lsjtrg), we demonstrate how we integrate the content and processes of critical literacy education into the lived practices of our group. We share vignettes from the group, at different points in time, to illustrate each dimension.

Dimension 1: Building a Community

Mary Ann Kramer and Rebecca Rogers co-founded the Literacy for Social Justice Teacher Research Group in the fall of 2001 to attend to the needs of critically oriented teachers across the lifespan, rather than focusing on K-12 *or* adult education. During our discussions the previous year we shared our sense that there was a lack of community for educators in the St. Louis area who were committed to designing socially just learning spaces. Rather than lament this absence of community, we created our own group. We have a core leadership team of seven people that makes decisions about the direction of the group and helps with the organization, outreach, and recruitment. Approximately 12 to 15 teachers regularly attend our meetings and workshops throughout the year and our base consists of over 200 people who participate, in various ways, in our group's events and actions throughout the year.

Dialogue is at the center of building a community, because dialogue is necessary to share experiences, divide tasks for completion, and make decisions democratically. At the heart of our group are the tools associated with building and sustaining a learning community. There are logistical elements that are important to the life of the group, routines, and norms of how things work. Our group meets every two weeks, generally at the Adult Learning Center in the city, although we have met at various community sites and universities. We meet for two hours, and our meetings begin with introductions and sharing celebrations (personal or professional)—both set the stage for building community—and then announcements of activities occurring in the community or at a national level. Some weeks we invite speakers (both local and national) to share their research/teaching with the group and facilitate a discussion. Other weeks we problem-pose and problem-solve based on critical social issues that arise in our teaching and in the community. Still other weeks we might watch and discuss a movie that relates to social justice and education or plan an interactive workshop (See Text Box 2.1).

Text Box 2.1 Partial List of LSJTRG Workshops from 2001 to 2008

For a complete list see www.umsl.edu/~lsjtrg/summaries.htm

Highlander Center and the Popular Education Model
African American Literacies
Teachers for Social Justice Group, Chicago, Illinois
Race and the Death Penalty
Leaving Children Behind: The Untold Story Behind the Federal NCLB Law
Jobs with Justice & Workers' Rights
Talking about the Iraq War in Classroom
Multimodalities in the Classroom
Social Class and Ruby Payne in the High School English Class
State-takeover of SLPS and Anti-war Protests: What are the connections?
Implementing Gay and Lesbian Themed Literature in the Curriculum
Ritual, Culture and Transformation: An Interactive Workshop for Teachers
Teaching about Jena-6
The Impact of Neoliberalism on Schools and Society
Teaching for Social Justice in Reading and Writing Workshops

Table 2.1 Timeline and Overview of LSJTRG

Year	Focus	Major Accomplishments
2001–2002	Readings: multiple definitions of literacy, culturally relevant pedagogy Inquiry: case studies of student learning, problem-posing, problem-solving	10–12 participants at meetings, locations for meetings, developing cur name
2002–2003	Readings: culturally relevant pedagogy, social and political contexts of literacy, teacher research Inquiry: teacher research, several classroom studies conducted	10–12 participants at meetings, several visiting scholars: JoBeth Allen and JoAnn Kilgour Dowdy conducted workshops on teacher research and adult literacy education, participated in African American Read-In (NCTE)
2003–2004	Readings: critical literacy, African American Language Book club discussions: Betsy Brown and No Disrespect Inquiry: teacher research in classrooms, building leadership within the group, LSJ participant attends Highlander Center and shares popular education with the group, outreach and recruitment	10–12 participants at meetings, email distribution list grows to 50+ people Disseminate teacher research at conferences, participate in African American Read-In (NCTE) Summer Institute with Elaine Richardson and Jesse Senechal from Chicago Teachers for Social Justice Group
2004–2005	Readings: Rethinking Schools Inquiry: teacher research in classrooms, building leadership within the group, writing up teacher-research projects, outreach, recruitment and networking Summer Institute: Book writing retreat	First Educating for Change Curriculum Fair (100 participants): anti-racist, pro-justice education. Participated in workshop with Bob Peterson from Rethinking Schools Development of our website (www.umsl.edu/~lsjtrg/) 75+ people on email distribution
2005–2006	Readings: Rethinking Schools Inquiry: connecting and building alliances, inviting community leadership to share their projects and organizing, publishing several articles on the group, building leadership in the group	Second Educating for Change Curriculum Fair (150 participants): racial justice in the context of immigrant and refugee rights Summer Institute: LSJ strategy session 100+ people on distribution list Included in a Rethinking Schools article on teacher organizers

2006–2007	Readings: Edison schools and privatization of public schools Focus: counter-assault on public education, develop curriculum about privatization Activism: demonstrations, letters to the editors, forums	10–15 participants at meetings, participate in public demonstrations against state takeover of SLPS. Development of a listserv with 200+ people on list Develop a brochure, open a bank account for the group, design a logo for the group
2007–2008	Focus: Privatization of public education Activism: Stop School Closings! Position Statements, Rally for Public Education	Third Educating for Change Fair (150 participants): peace education San Francisco TAG meeting, Social Justice Night at Saint Louis University, Mid-TESOL table, Citizenship Education Day, School Closings
2008–2009	Focus: Educating for a Democracy Readings: Dibels, immigrant rights Activism: Counter-narratives about Dibes, Read-In of Banned Books	Fourth Educating for Change Fair (200 participants): Defining Democracy Campaign for Education as a Civil Right Joined TAG (Teacher Activist Groups) www.teacheractivistgroups.org/

Photo 2.1 Participants after a LSJTRG meeting.

Our meeting structure is flexible and has changed over time, based on the needs and interests of the group. In the spirit of popular education (Freire, 1992; Horton, Kohl, & Kohl, 1997), we believe the answers to many of our problems lie within the expertise of the group. Our process begins with dialogue, to learn about people's experience, but also assumes that we often have to bring in outside resources for help. Together, group members and our allies from other community organizations use the knowledge that is constructed around problems posed by the group towards planning and taking action. We often plan actions within our group meetings and try them out in the community. We come back together to reflect on the process and to pose new problems and next steps. See Table 2.1 for an outline of LSJTRG's history, key events as well as changes and development.

We keep membership open, and encourage members to bring friends and colleagues. Among the group members we inherently embrace struggle rather than sweeping it under the rug. Horton and Freire (1990) talked about conflict being a meaning making opportunity. Even if a focus or topic has been pre-decided for a meeting, we will spend some time allowing people to share their frustrations or struggles—whether it is in the classroom or in the community. It is through the recognition of struggles that we may decide to go more deeply with our inquiry. For instance, as we discuss later, when the issue of linguistic variation came up over and over again in our discussions, we knew it was a place we needed to return to, to deepen our collective and individual understandings. Therefore, collectively agreed-upon readings, discussions, videos, and guest speakers address our needs as teachers and activists.

Dimension 2: Developing Critical Stances

The leadership team of LSJTRG tries to balance what can be competing needs and interests that exist within the group—between novice and experienced teachers, teachers/activists, and elementary and adult education teachers. We listen for patterns in the topics or questions and respond by choosing relevant readings, workshops, or experiences. These readings often represent multiple points of view and the implications across the lifespan. Our common theme is developing critical stances and bringing multiple perspectives to the table, which is essential for critical literacy education. In the following vignette we illustrate how we developed critical stances and multiple perspectives around the issue of linguistic diversity in the group.

Language diversity was one of the issues that surfaced as important to the learning and development of the group. As a group we watched and discussed a short movie called *My Brown Eyes* (Koh, 1994) about the experiences of an immigrant boy's first day at school. The video documents his resourcefulness at home and how his cultural and linguistic resources are not valued at school. After discussing the movie, two of the adult education teachers (one ESOL and one AEL teacher) shared the movie with their class and discussed the importance of making connections between school and home, and valuing the language and literacy practices of students. After showing the movie to their class, they came back and shared the discussion with the group. The group discussed when and how to integrate people's home language or primary discourse into the classroom. During this time, Rebecca Light (Chapter 4) was sharing aspects of her teacher research with the group. Her research focused on integrating funds of knowledge—cultural and linguistic diversity—into the fifth grade curriculum.

There were different points of view about the value of standard English and non-standard dialects, and in what contexts each should be used. During one of these discussions, Dorothy Walker, an 80-year-old African American adult education teacher who had been teaching for adult education over 20 years, entered the conversation with a narrative from her teaching experience.

One time, in my adult education class, we were diagramming sentences in order to bring out the verbs, nouns, and this one girl, she was angry. She came up to me and said, "Mrs. Walker my grandmother said that the way you teaching us about the language, well we don't need that, and that's just for other people to talk like that and use that kind of language." This is what she said. She didn't understand why we talked about verbs and how we used them. So I said to her, "You know, I tell you what, ask your grandmother why you are in school. I said just ask her." I then shared a story with my students about a researcher who was advocating for Black English. This was at the same time when I was teaching, you know, during the 1970s when people started to talk about Black English. My students thought that I should be letting them use Black English in the classroom instead of teaching them the standard forms of English. I told them to call this researcher and if the researcher answers the phone and talks with them in Black English then I will let them go with Black English. Well, they called. And they all came back and said that he didn't talk Black English. Then we had a conversation about who could speak Black English and where.

(Transcript, 5/02)

Dorothy's narrative put the issue of linguistic diversity, standard and non-standard codes into a historical context for us. She emphasized the relationships between language, power, and social identities. Howard (2006) argues that we cannot expect to understand dominance and its impact on education until we explore the process of knowledge construction. Each member of the group brought a history of participation with schooling, formal education, race, class, and gender that shaped the stances by which we read, interpreted, and challenged practice, and acted in our classrooms and communities. For example, Dorothy, who had grown up in the segregated South, earned a teaching degree and then was not allowed to teach because she was married, lived through civil rights demonstrations, and taught for over 30 years, had different beliefs about language and literacy education than Rebecca, a Jewish college student who was transitioning into her career as a teacher. The different stances of our group caused us to take on multiple perspectives, to re-examine long-standing truths, and to *reconstruct* the stances through which we constructed knowledge.

Dorothy's comments reflect a theme that surfaced for many teachers in LSJTRG during this time; that is, the power of language and the language of power. Our interest in examining multilingual and multicultural as well as the linguistic and discourse features of African American Language (AAL) began to deepen at this time. During this same time, Carolyn Fuller's students (Chapter 6) were participating in book club discussions around the book written by black activist and feminist Sister Souljah (1996) called *No Disrespect*. The book presents a complex array of narratives of African American life and counter-narratives. At once the book includes stereotypical images of African American women and men *and* provides a meta-narrative through the author's foresight on her own experiences and how her decisions are rooted in the systemic racism that exists in society.

As part of the research in Carolyn's classroom, we videotaped the discussion her students had around this book. She shared the videotaped discussion with the group. In the discussion, the adults in her classroom debated whether or not the language Souljah used in the book was "slang" or "language." They reflected on *why* they appreciated reading Sister Souljah's book, a discussion that led to the topic of AAL. One student, Chaz, used an example that included double negatives and a syntactic pattern that is associated with AAL—"momma said nobody better not let, you better not let nobody jump on your brother"— and that includes a reference to "your momma" which is often associated with African American discourse patterns of "playing the dozens" (Morgan, 2002; Smitherman, 1977). Chaz pushed against the everyday representation of AAL as slang and instead argued for a view of his "mother tongue" that is rule governed (Rogers & Fuller, 2007).

To deepen our discussion and understanding of linguistic and cultural diversity, we decided, as a group, that we would together read and discuss *No Disrespect*.

During our book discussion, we explored the oppression and agency of black women including housing conditions, violence, and poverty. Part of the discussion included a discussion of the term "projects" and the history of low-income housing in St. Louis. We learned about the historically racist roots of the term "project" and how this term could be viewed as offensive to African American people. We discussed the history of the projects in St. Louis and their connection to the residential segregation of the city.

Sara, a European American adult education teacher, decided she wanted to use the book in her class of all African American adult education students. While Carolyn used the book in a book club format, Sara would read it aloud. Sara brought back her observations to the group. Before she read the story they talked about racial positioning, including Sara's position as a European American woman teaching African American students. They talked for a long time about the sociopolitical history of the word "projects" being used to describe housing for low-income people. Sara explained, "even though it wasn't part of the plan, it led them to asking for more information the following week, and it fostered more questions. They were happy to see that it was relevant to their lives." Sara shared with us that, had she not read and discussed the book within our racially diverse group, she might not have taken the risk to use the book in her classroom.

What was interesting for us as a group to observe is how Sara and Carolyn used Sister Souljah's book *No Disrespect* in their adult education classrooms in different ways. While they both used this book to engage their students with literature, to open up multiple perspectives, and to evoke discussion, there were differences in the role each educator took up in the discussion. When we were done reading Souljah's book, we gave the books to Carolyn for her classroom

Through our discussions, we contemplated what each of us was positioned to know and how we might best design a curriculum that reflected the diversity of our students' cultures. Such opportunities for analyzing others' teaching practices provide a window for us to look through to theorize about our own teaching experiences. Serendipitously, Sister Souljah gave a talk at a local university soon after we finished reading and discussing the book. Several members of the group attended the talk as well as Carolyn's students. Souljah talked about the relationships between local and globalized forms of Hip Hop, thus extending our knowledge and making local and global connections.

We also read more about African American language and culture (e.g. Delpit & Dowdy, 2002; Richardson, 2003). We watched a documentary about AAL and another on Hip Hop culture. We invited Elaine Richardson, author of *African American Literacies*, to conduct a workshop for our group to deepen our understanding of the historical roots of AAL. She discussed the historical and linguistic roots of AAL, dispelling the myth that non-standard varieties of English were "slang." It was a powerful workshop because several of our colleagues—both African American and European American—expressed that they never realized the grammatical elements of AAL nor did they really think about the relationships between language and identity and the importance of recognizing this in schools.

In this way, we explored the area of African American language and culture widely and deeply; reading multiple sources of information, drawing on outside resources and each other's experiences. We placed the arguments around language in a historical context. We also connected the dots by looking at the role of the media in representing AAL and the ways in which language connects people not only in St. Louis but throughout the world. Throughout our inquiry and discussions we were careful to make connections across the lifespan so that our discussions were relevant to elementary teachers as well as to adult education teachers. During a summer institute, Sarah Hobson (Chapter 5) designed a critical literacy text set that included the titles of books about African American language and culture that is available as a mini-library for other educators.

Not all of the teachers who participated in these deep discussions around linguistic diversity are still present in the group. Some have retired, others moved away to go to graduate school. But some of the teachers have remained in the group, and when the conversation turns to issues of linguistic diversity, we have a shared history with texts and resources. One of the most important aspects of developing critical stances as a group is that our process leads us to see ourselves as knowledge constructers with expertise, not just reproducers of knowledge. This fundamental shift in position vis-à-vis knowledge has implications for how we understand teaching and learning in our classrooms.

Dimension 3: Critical Inquiry and Analysis

We also draw from a set of tools designed for engaging productively in a problem-posing/problem-solving dynamic in classrooms, communities, and inquiry groups. Teacher inquiry is a disposition in which dilemmas are reframed as questions, and data are collected and analyzed for patterns and answers (e.g. Cochran-Smith & Lytle, 2001; Hubbard & Miller, 1999). These processes are not new for teachers. We constantly observe our students, analyze their needs, and adjust the curriculum to better meet their needs as learners. Teacher research places us in control of the questions that are asked and answered in the classroom. It is often easier to inquire into questions that relate to strategy instruction and comprehension. However, when the questions lead to matters of social justice, the stakes are higher. We often worry about the responses we might receive from parents, students, administrators, or colleagues. During these times, it is especially important to have a network that can encourage and challenge us to think critically about matters of teaching and learning.

Teacher inquiry is a cornerstone in our work as a group. Over time, we have built our capacity as teacher researchers through institutes where we learned the tools and skills of developing good questions, collecting data, analyzing data, changing practices based on the data and reflection, and starting the cycle anew. At different points in time, teachers carried out formal and informal teacher research projects in their classrooms. Sometimes these inquiry projects were carried out in a collaborative manner among several people within the group (see, for example, Chapters 8, 9, and 12).

Some of the steps in conducting teacher inquiry include posing questions, collecting data, and looking for patterns in the data. Throughout the book, we hear the types of questions being asked and answered: How do I teach about race, racism, and anti-racism with white second graders? How do I negotiate the traditional space of student teaching and my commitment to social justice? In what ways can critical literacy practices be embedded within the adult literacy curriculum? The common ground between all of the projects is that they arose from genuine questions that plagued teachers, concerns and issues that nagged at us. To answer these questions, we collected data such as students' work samples, newspapers and media reports on the surrounding community, audio or video-tapes of interactions, surveys, transcripts of classroom interactions, teacher observation and notes, test results and attendance measures, interviews, lesson plans, fieldnotes, and teachers' journals. Data collection and analysis often occurred in a recursive manner. Teachers would bring data into the group, for example, students' writing, and together we would analyze the data. See Text Box 2.2 for a list of some of the tools of inquiry we have used in our research.

As teachers wonder about how their practices might be better and how they might more fully make a difference in their work, they begin the process of inquiry. The habits of inquiry do not always result in fully developed teacher inquiry projects as they are represented in the chapters in this book. In Janet and Sheila's cases, shared below, for example, they started with the desire to make their curriculum more relevant and socially just. They each brought this desire to the group, collected ideas, and redesigned their practice. This, too, is a form of teacher inquiry. The tools that we draw on in conducting teacher inquiry are characteristics that many researchers have used in participatory projects with youth and university students to build knowledge alongside communities (McIntyre, 2003; Morrell, 2006). We are building the capacity to engage in inquiry with our students.

Text Box 2.2 Tools of Inquiry

Discourse analysis
Analyzing recordings of oral readings (e.g. running records)
Analyzing students' writing samples
Mining strengths, funds of knowledge, and counter-stories
Taking anecdotal notes
Taking fieldnotes
Analyzing multimodal texts (e.g. illustrations and children's drawings)
Case studies
Video analysis
Analyzing narratives
Co-generative dialogues
Focus groups
Interviews
Analyzing children's literature, young adolescent literature, or adult literature
Writing curricular plans
Writing autobiographies, reflections, and literacy timelines.

In 2002, Sheila Carves, an African American third grade teacher who had been teaching for three years, brought her basal literature book and a question to the group. Sheila explained that she and her third grade students would be reading a new story—*Tony's Bread*—written by Tomie dePaola (1996) from the district-mandated basal reader the following week. She stated that she wanted to "make the literacy curriculum more relevant to the kids." She referenced Rebecca's presentation at the previous meeting where Rebecca had shared the ongoing project of integrating funds of knowledge into the fifth grade literacy curriculum (see Chapter 4). Rebecca and Sheila looked together at the standards for communication arts in third grade, which suggested an exploration of the Hill (Italian section of St. Louis) as a model for studying culture and community and then looking at the different restaurants and traditions.

REBECCA: I think the Hill would be as foreign to your students as any other place. Maybe you can look at their traditions first as far as food and recipes and then connect it to the story.

SHEILA: We could start with their traditions and then go from there, bring them in, write about them, and talk about them.

BECKY: I think it is key to start with their culture first and use that as a bridge to another culture. But a big idea might be something like, "Traditions are power in any community." I started to go through all of my books this afternoon that have to do with food and traditions.

Sheila opened the discussion by posing an authentic problem, from her classroom, to the group, expressing her desire to make the story *Tony's Bread* (dePaola, 1996) more relevant to her class. After exploring different options, including researching local Italian culture and bringing in their own family recipes, the discussion made a more critical turn to address the politics and business of food and hunger.

MARY ANN: It can help us to understand the social and political. I don't know how much third graders will understand in terms of what is impacting their lives but all of these things are interconnected. It sounds like anyone can grow up and open a restaurant but it doesn't happen that way. You might pick how food is political and how three-fourths of our world is starving to death and what does it mean that we all have food.

This transcript provides a window into the group's problem-posing/problem-solving dynamics. Sheila left the discussion with many different options for teaching this piece of literature in her classroom. She sent a note home to the parents letting them know that they would be learning about the politics of food. Other people brought in resources that they thought Sheila could connect with including *Rethinking Globalization* (Bigelow & Peterson, 2002) and a movie called *The Business of Hunger* (1984) about how in many countries cash crops are exported while the poor go hungry.

We rotate the responsibility for tools of inquiry with the group. For example, Rebecca Rogers shared her process for taking fieldnotes in classrooms, Mary Ann

Kramer and Phyllis Thomas shared how they analyzed classroom dynamics through a feminist lens, and Earline Scott conducted a workshop on taking and analyzing running records which helped everyone become more sensitive observers of literate behaviors. Similarly, the tools used in the context of collaborative inquiry are not used just to gain more information but to solve socially important problems. Along the way, we have written articles about our inquiry projects (e.g. Kramer, 2005; Pole & Rogers, 2007; Rogers, Mosley, & Kramer, 2005). The articles along with this book serve as a vehicle for promoting and supporting our voices as educators.

Dimension 4: Action, Advocacy, and Social Change

Developing critical stances through critical inquiry and analysis often leaves us with the question of: Now what do we do? Over time, we have struggled with the space and place of action and advocacy in critical literacy education. We have wondered: Where is the action located in the classroom? What is the best use of our limited advocacy time? The fourth dimension of our framework is *Action, Advocacy, and Social Change*. We have identified a set of tools that move us from critique of injustices to productive social action that builds more socially just classroom and community spaces (e.g. Croteau, Hoynes, & Ryan, 2005).

Drawing on Past Experiences with Activism

As teachers, we advocate for our students on a daily basis. Yet teachers often express many reasons why they are not working more actively towards social justice. Our educational system often teaches people to feel disempowered ("I can't change anything, I am one person"), complacent ("I don't have time to change anything"), hopeless ("We've tried and nothing will ever change"), or scared ("I might lose my job") (Hackman, 2005). Part of the problem is that when we advocate on behalf of our students we do so as individuals. The other part is that the general public does not view teachers as activists; consequently, we learn to not see ourselves in this way.

When we took stock of the experiences with activism among participants in the group, we learned that there was a wealth of collective resources for us to draw on in our work together. Participants in the group have participated in many movements including the civil rights movement, the feminist movement, the peace movement, the environmental movement, and the immigrant rights movement (See Text Box 2.3). We have learned the strategies of picketing, leafleting, non-violent demonstration, building networks and alliances, connecting with legislators, and taking actions outside of the political process. Each of these strategies is a tool that can be harnessed for education. Many of these tools for social action include literacy and language, and can be put to use within the critical literacy curriculum. The range of social action tools that participants bring to the table strengthens our collective problem-solving. It is also important to point out that there are other teachers who participate in LSJTRG who have not participated in community activism. The mixture of activities and events

Text Box 2.3 Activism Experiences within LSJTRG

Community housing movement
Educating for Change Curriculum
Fair
Women in Leadership Training
VALUE training (student advocacy)
Neighborhood stabilization
VISTA program

Refusal of privilege
Organize with migrant workers
Picketing
Counter-recruitment
Organizing for women's rights within
the Catholic church
Protest at Union Station
Civil rights activist
Voter registration drives
Author
Questioning the status quo
Commitment to process of social
change
Living values in personal and
professional life
Feminist majority
Women's choice
Rallies and marches in D.C.
NAACP

Free speech movement
Civil rights movement
Committee on Racial
Equality
Student leadership movement
Feminist movement
Mothers Day for Peace
Environmental movement
Anti-nuclear movement
Child Assault Prevention Program
Campus Acquaintance Rape Education
Dismantling Racism Institute for
Educators
Participation in political campaigns
Reauthorization of NCLB
National Organization of Women
Jobs with Justice
Immigrant rights rallies
Recycling

Literacy for **SOCIAL JUSTICE** *Teacher Research Group*

that LSJTRG provides often draws in educators who might not otherwise participate in a social justice-focused event. We intend to be inclusive and also broaden the community of people working for equity.

Developing Skills of Activism and Advocacy within the Group

An important tool for social change is developing the skills of activism and advocacy within the community of a group. People learn how to become activists when they work towards finding solutions to problems they care about. Educators concerned with matters of social justice understand the links between cuts in education and a wartime economy, between privatization of health care and schools. Activist activities are rooted in issues that people care deeply about and can be part of authentic and meaningful professional development.

All too often, educators worry about whether or not they will get into trouble for their activism and social justice work. Hackman (2005, p. 106) writes,

> Educators need to disrupt the notion that silence is patriotic and teach students that their rights as citizens in this society carry responsibilities—of

participation, voice, and protest so that this can actually become a society of, by and for all of its citizens. Students (and teachers) need to learn that social action is fundamental to the workings of their lives.

Advocacy and action are routines in our group processes. From advocating for students, to holding fundraisers for a classroom library, to organizing a public rally, to writing the results of teacher inquiry projects, to writing letters to the editor, to leafleting at public forums, our social actions are ongoing. We often focus on local issues that demand immediate attention. A few examples will illustrate the process of how, as we work on solving problems collectively, we also develop the skills of activism and advocacy.

The beginning of the 2003 school year was marked by an outbreak of strikes and protests about public education in St. Louis. The school district hired an independent financial consultant. To reduce the district's debt, the consultant embarked on a number of money-saving tactics including selling school buildings (some that were in use), outsourcing janitors and food preparation workers, and eliminating instructional positions. There were articles in the newspapers, protests at school board meetings, and parents who kept their children home from school to protest. This was the backdrop of our discussions, readings, and actions.

We focused our meeting on the sale of an in-use adult education school building that was marked as "unused" because it was not being used by K-12 education. One of the teachers explained that the students were upset because it was their neighborhood school and they had no other school. We wondered how the teacher might structure the literacy events in the classroom so that the students could exercise agency. We discussed options including writing a letter to the editor, the real estate company, or writing a petition. The students in the adult education classroom chose to write a letter to the editor, which was published in the locally owned and operated African American newspaper. The school building was taken off of the real estate list (see Chapter 9).

We continued to be concerned about the ongoing attacks on public education. To provide us with a more global perspective we watched and discussed *Granito de Arena* (Freidberg, 2005), a documentary of the Mexican teachers' struggle against the privatization and neoliberal effects on education. We invited Pauline Lipman, scholar and activist from the Chicago area, to talk with us about the Chicago Teachers for Social Justice Group's struggle against Chicago's plan for privatization, called Renaissance 2010 (e.g. Lipman, 2003; Lipman & Haines, 2007).

Three years later, in the same chain of events, we began the 2006 academic year studying the charter school movement and Educational Management Organizations (EMOs) to understand the relationship between EMOs and privatization in schools. Rebecca and Melissa developed a workshop and curricular unit that explored privatization of public education with a diverse text set ranging from politicians' campaign materials to photographs in the newspaper to advertisements from Edison's website. As a group we analyzed the materials and developed a resource guide for talking and teaching about privatization in education. Then, we came face-to-face with an assault on public education when it was announced that the Missouri legislature was considering bills to increase spending for charter schools, tax credits for private schools, and vouchers. Before we could blink, the St. Louis public schools began to face the loss of accreditation, leading again to the mayor's plan for increasing "alternative" options rather than choosing to make a plan to save existing schools. This was followed by a state take-over of the St. Louis public schools and the closing of more public schools and the ushering in of more charter schools, many of the for-profit variety (Rogers & Pole, in press). We followed these lines of attack on public schools and acted in solidarity with parent and community groups as well as other teachers to create a united front on behalf of children and schooling. We attended public forums, rallies for public education, and wrote position statements on the deleterious effects of school closings.

We continue to link what is happening in St. Louis to larger trends in the privatization of public education in cities such as Chicago, New York, Philadelphia, and Washington, D.C. What global and national historical, political, and economic forces have contributed to the privatization of public education? And on a micro level, how are my classroom practices impacted by globalization and privatization? How might my personal consumer patterns impact these trends? What does research say about the performance of charter schools? What will be the impact of these decisions in 20 or 30 years' time?

As we participate in this type of inquiry, we are also modeling good teaching. We sifted through different sides and arguments so that we could hear multiple perspectives on the same issue. We developed critical literacy text sets that included newspaper articles, federal reports, political cartoons, and political campaign materials. We also developed a curricular guide for teaching about privatization. Through observing and practicing activism with other teacher/activists, people learn how to become activists. Good activists are good educators and organizers. They are able to meet people where they are; be responsive; design strategies and actions that move the cause forward.

Appreciating the Different Roles in Activism

Moyer (2001) in the book *Doing Democracy* argues that there are four different roles that activists and social movements need to play in order to successfully create social change. These roles are: *the citizen, the rebel, change agent,* and *reformer.* Each role has different purposes, skills, and functions within different points of social change. Social justice advocates need first to be viewed by the community as responsible citizens who believe in the fundamental principles and values of a good society. Social justice advocates also have to be willing to protest social conditions and institutional policies that violate core societal values and principles. These people might be considered to be rebels. It is not enough, however, to express disapproval and reject current conditions, regardless of how unjust, if the activist does not work towards changing those conditions. Therefore, social justice advocates also need to be change agents who work to educate, organize, and involve the general public to oppose current conditions and imagine more just practices. Social justice advocates also have to be able to work within current social and political systems. As advocates work with elected officials they can incorporate solutions into new laws and policies.

As educators, we are better at some of these roles than others. The public tends to see teachers as the epitome of the good citizen. Often overworked and underpaid, teachers play an instrumental role in our society and are seen as important and respected citizens. Because, as teachers, we work within educational systems, we are prepared to work as reformers, more so than rebels and change agents. Over the life of LSJTRG, we have witnessed that many of the people who are attracted to LSJTRG are teachers who either have the inclination or history of working towards social change. Somewhere in the life course of becoming a teacher—whether it is in teacher preparation programs or in the first years of teaching or in negotiating the ever-increasing demands of policies and tests—teachers bury the activist components of themselves. LSJTRG recognizes that the tools needed for each of these roles—citizen, rebel, reformer, and change agent—are as important in the profession of teaching as they are in organizing social movements. In LSJTRG we try to recognize the tools that people bring with them and put them to use at the classroom and community level but not every person will play the role of rebel. Certainly, in our experience we have seen some people who do not feel comfortable with educational policy or at pickets and protests. An assessment of the group's actions and activities reveals that, as a group, we have moved in and out of these roles at different times and for different reasons. We have spent much more time in the citizen role—building credibility as a group, building up our own content mastery, gaining name recognition, and building alliances. As teachers, we work as change agents in the day-to-day lives of our teaching practices. Moyer (2001) states, "social movements can only achieve their long-term vision by incorporating it into their everyday practice" (p. 23).

As a group, we educate citizens and promote dialogue around critical social issues. We have used "extra-parliamentary means"—methods outside of normal political channels including community education in the form of meetings, leafleting, public rallies, and mass distribution of emails. These methods are most likely associated with the role of the *rebel*. Much time is spent nurturing people in the group to become actively involved in the leadership process. For instance, when Melissa attended Highlander, she conducted a workshop with us on popular education. When Rebecca attended the International Reading Association's legislative workshop, she brought back information on the reauthorization of No Child Left Behind. Mary Ann and Phyllis's workshop on feminist strategies in adult education taught us to facilitate discussions in a dialogic manner. We deliberately draw from the resources of the group.

Building Alliances and Noticing Incremental Changes

There is no shortage of social injustices that warrant protest. When we look across the political and social landscape we see the efforts of the peace movement, the labor movement, the immigrant rights movement, the health care movement, the GLBT movement among other efforts for social justice. Each of these movements has a set of targeted issues that they are working on and yet the issues of one group impact all of the other groups. The underlying systemic issues of greed and profit unite all of these movements. It is important to build alliances among these groups—recognizing that each group (and each person) is working on resisting and transforming unjust practices. We may not all work together at the same time on health care or the war or education but the work of each of us is important for building a strong base that is ready to come together at the right moment. Sometimes LSJTRG takes the lead in organizing a rally or writing a position statement. During these times, we rely on the organization of other parts of the social justice movement to lend a hand in support. Other times, other groups take the lead and LSJTRG does its part to get people out in support.

Each year we plan an Educating for Change Curriculum Fair to bring together courageous educators/activists who are designing socially just learning spaces for learners across the lifespan, in both formal and informal settings (Pole & Rogers, 2007). This fair represents an action step in our organizing as educators and it is our hope that it can be a conduit for building networks of justice in the communities in which we work and live. We stress that we have organized this day as a "fair" rather than as a traditional conference to emphasize dialogue and action. Figure 2.1 includes posters from past fairs.

The fair is a good example of a generative social action. The idea for the Curriculum Fair came to us when Jesse Senechal from the Chicago Teachers for Social Justice Group visited with us during our summer institute in 2003. Jesse shared the history and evolution of the Chicago group, including the details of the fair. That fall, we sent a handful of LSJTRG members to Chicago's Curriculum Fair. They came back and shared with us what they had learned and took the lead in planning the first St. Louis event. The process of organizing the fair is one of shared decision-making. People who do not regularly attend the school year group meetings help to plan the Curriculum Fair. Similarly, each year we bring together different sponsoring organizations.

Teaching for social justice in a conservative city like St. Louis is often a lonely act. What is so powerful about the fair is that like-minded educator/activists who might not ordinarily meet each other come together to share, learn from each other, and network. For instance, a professor at a university who is active in the efforts to close the School of Americas shared his experiences with this peaceful process. Several teachers who use peace education had never heard about the School of Americas nor thought about the connection between state-sponsored and U.S.-backed terrorism in Latin America and our current war in Iraq. After our first fair we heard positive feedback that encouraged us to continue with the fair. One teacher said, "I had no idea there were so many teachers in St. Louis committed to social justice!" Each year the fair feeds generatively into our next year's workshops, events, and actions as we begin again the cycle of popular education.

As we turn to the next sections of this book, which includes the projects from members of the group, we encourage the reader to refer to the framework presented in this chapter. As we move back and forth between individual teacher/activists and the group you will get a deeper understanding of the parallel practices that sustain both individuals and the group.

Figure 2.1 Educating for Change Curriculum Fair posters.

Photo 2.2 Table display of critical literacy text sets at the curriculum fair.

Photo 2.3 Table display of multicultural education at Educating for Change curriculum fair.

Part II

An Entry Point

Developing Critical Stances

Based in teacher inquiry and action research, the case studies throughout this book present examples of critical literacy studies that showcase teachers' reflective practice in action. Exploring issues such as gender equity, linguistic diversity, civil rights and freedom and war, the authors provide insight into the possibilities and struggles of teaching literacy through a framework of social justice. You also hear them reflect on the place of the Literacy for Social Justice Teacher Research Group (LSJTRG) in their learning. We invite you to think with us about new conceptions of critical literacy practice as we present four chapters and a response chapter that enter classrooms of teachers and students across the lifespan.

Educators who participate in LSJTRG embody a range of experiences. There are early career teachers and teachers who have been educating for years; teachers who are new to critical literacy practices and teachers who have participated in a range of movements for social justice; educators who work in formal K-12 settings and higher education, and community activists who provide literacy support for adult students and communities. Participants are racially, religiously, and socioeconomically diverse, and take up a range of positions on social justice issues. From the multiple positions these educators occupy, you will find some stories to be "like" your own, and others might bend and stretch your thinking. We encourage you to think about which stories do and do not resonate with you and to reflect on your responses.

In the following section (Chapters 3–7), you will meet four female educators who are committed to thinking and rethinking their classroom practices from the standpoints of equity and justice. Melissa Mosley and Rebecca Light are two early career teachers working to create socially just learning spaces with their elementary age students. At the high school level, Sarah Hobson, an English teacher, shares a deeply personal journey as an educator teaching in the Northeast, before her return to St. Louis and entry into the LSJTRG community. Carolyn Fuller represents an often-unheard voice, the voice of an adult literacy teacher in St. Louis.

We encourage you to consider the following questions as you read their narratives:

- First, in what ways did each educator design critical literacy education? As we discussed in Chapter 1, critical literacy education is linked to ideas of power, access, and equity, includes multiple literacy practices in which students and teachers together read the word and the world, and also builds spaces that are more socially just.

- Second, we encourage you to explore with each teacher how she engaged in constructing critical stances, one of the dimensions of the critical literacy framework (presented in Chapters 1 and 2) with her students.

  - How do you see tools such as reading multiple texts, connecting local problems to global issues, and seeking out relationships and patterns among multiple perspectives present in each of the chapters?
  - At another level, how did each teacher herself demonstrate a critical stance?
  - Finally, how do you see "action" enacted in each of the chapters?

- What are the possibilities in each chapter, the moments in which opportunities were open for learning but not realized? What are other ways in which educators might have imagined new possibilities for their students?

At the close of each section, we move into a response constructed by members of LSJTRG. We invited LSJTRG participants to respond to each section of the book. We intentionally asked people who had diverse backgrounds and interests, and who taught at multiple points on the lifespan, to design a book that was multi-vocal. Within each of these chapters, we continue to move back and forth between the individual case studies—the narratives of classroom practices—and the framework for critical literacy education across the lifespan.

3   Talking about War in a Second Grade Classroom

Melissa Mosley

The PEACE Project at Allan Elementary School in Austin, Texas, USA participated in Global Action Week in the spring of 2008. PEACE Project teachers, children, and their families are linked with a worldwide movement through learning and activities that allow them to exchange information and experiences. Teachers from the PEACE Project joined millions of other teachers around the world to participate in "The World's Largest Lesson Plan" that focused on issues of child labor. An estimated 7.5 million youth participated in the 2008 Global Action Week (www.campaignforeducationusa.org). The country with the highest recorded count in this year's action is Bangladesh, with 2.5 million people taking part in over 25,000 different locations across the country. Millions also took part in the lesson in Vietnam and in an impressive campaigning effort a million took part in the lesson in the Palestinian Territories

Introduction

During my second year of teaching in a public, suburban elementary school, as I entered the teachers' lounge one day, I noticed the din of a television set turned to a news report. As my teaching partners entered the room, we watched over and over again the reports reeling on the news station. Two, three, four airplanes were hijacked. We were in shock, but it was difficult to imagine at that moment what it would feel like later as the pictures became more graphic, more human, and less concrete and steel. The next spring, we again stared at this television in the small lunchroom and watched as one, two, three, four, and more bombs were dropped on Iraq's monuments and buildings. Again, it was unclear from these images of light bombs against dark sky, but there was a human element to this destruction. The words "shock and awe" describe not only a military tactic, but also the emotions I felt as a witness.

I am a native of the Midwestern suburb where Woods Elementary is situated. I attended a private university in a nearby city before accepting my first teaching job, where I felt very connected with the students and the community, including the parents. The grade level team I joined worked together to implement new curricula such as balanced literacy and constructivist math as changes occurred in the school. The administration was supportive of my creative teaching methods and classroom research.

Upon joining LSJTRG, I began to ask questions about the ways literacy instruction was implemented in the school. Teachers felt alienated when some were trained and others were left to try new curricula on their own. Practices were blindly adopted without discussion. Simply, a critical approach to instruction ran counter to the values and practices of the teaching community as I experienced it. Therefore, I brought these issues to the group that met at the university and several members helped me to understand the ways decisions are made in public schools. They also comforted me when I felt overwhelmed and frustrated.

When I thought about my participation as a teacher and researcher in this group, the most important part was the explicit critical literacy focus that helped me to reflect on my own teaching practices in a conservative community. To demonstrate how the group shaped my thinking over the past four years, I reflect upon the use of book clubs in my classroom as a mechanism to create a socially just learning space around issues of freedom, war, and justice.

The History and Context of this Classroom

Reflecting on the history and context of this classroom is not an easy task. Four years after the completion of this school year, I understand I was early in my journey towards critically literate teaching practices, and for each opportunity I embraced for critical teaching, there was an opportunity lost. Here, I reconstruct the ways I thought about literacy teaching at the beginning of the United States' war with Iraq.

At 8:25 in the morning on a spring day, 19 7- and 8-year-old students stand around desks in a square, concrete block room. The door is closed and above it is an American flag. The children are reciting the Pledge of Allegiance. As they finish the Pledge, several students look at each other and smile, anticipating what's next. It's Friday morning, which means a song will play over the intercom. The school year before, in the months following September 11, 2001, this song played each day. This year, the principal of the school has decided that only on Fridays will the children sing, in unison, *I'm Proud to be an American* by Lee Greenwood. So they sang,

> I'm proud to be an American, where at least I know I'm free.
> But I won't forget the men who died to give that right to me,
> So I'm going to stand up, next to you and defend her still today,
> Cause there ain't no doubt, I love this land, God Bless the U.S.A!

As a class we were drawn together by this song, which reminded us each day of the terrible events of 9/11 but also of the survival stories and bravery of Americans. As a nation, we were bound together after 9/11 by a sense of camaraderie and shared American identity.

Reflecting on the teachers' lunchroom and the classroom, there are differences between the two spaces. In the lunchroom I felt shocked, paralyzed, my eyes drawn to the images as my heart tightened. I wasn't thinking about my students in the lunchroom, who after lunch were allowed out on the playground to swing and play foursquare. They seemed to be protected, outside of the school. In the classroom, however, they were also protected: sheltered from images of airplane crashes and bombing light shows with images of patriotism through songs, pledges, reminders of safety. Certainly, these young people needed protection and reassurance, as did I. A year after the 9/11 attacks, a new group of students were experiencing a different piece of this story: a time when the U.S. government prepared to attack the country of Iraq and remove its leader from power.

I did not agree with the practice of playing this song each Friday, as it was inculcating the students with a particular way of thinking about freedom and war. "I'm proud to be an American" symbolized the passion we all felt for the lives lost on September 11. However, at this point, singing the song was intended to act as support for the war on Iraq, the "war on terror." Playing the song was a tradition this school felt was uniting and positive. However, now it symbolized more than a shared American identity and pride—it symbolized patriotism, which had different bounds and limits. What ideals was I supporting when I stood with the children to sing this song? What messages were we, as a school, sending to the children?

The school, along with its neighboring community, is an example of a working-to-middle-class American town, a place where families grow up together. Primarily white families with an average household income under $45,000 populate the city. Less than 18 percent of the city residents hold a bachelor's degree, although most have graduated from high school. A house can be purchased for under $100,000, which makes it an attractive place for young families to settle. It is a fairly stable, conservative community, which has faced a loss of manufacturing jobs. Most teachers claim to be politically neutral. There is a strong sense of white identity and patriotism across the economic, social, and religious sectors.

Intuitively, as I was teaching, I noticed the images and words that were circulating in the school, particularly "freedom." The message was loud and clear: terrorists threaten our freedom, and soldiers protect it. I wondered, what is the relationship between human rights, war, and freedom? Although this question was running through my mind, it was not yet circulating in the classroom. I did not know what my students felt about freedom, or how they understood this concept, but I was certain other teachers were *not* talking about these issues. In January, I began to think about how I could begin to ask some of these questions through my literary instruction.

Literacy Instruction

The literacy instruction in my classroom was based in practices such as guided reading, word work, and independent literacy centers; a primarily literature-based and student-centered curriculum (Fountas & Pinnell, 1996). I incorporated critical literacy into these instructional frameworks. Critical literacy is a set of practices used to analyze and interrogate texts that have had global appeal among subjugated populations as both theoretical and pedagogical tools of liberation (Freire, 2004; Luke, 2000). Critical literacy instruction has been implemented with emergent readers, adolescents, and adult literacy learners (Comber, Thomson, & Wells, 2001; Jordan, 2005; Moje, Young, Readence, & Moore, 2000; Powell, Cantrell, & Adams, 2001; Rogers, 2002; Sweeney, 1997). Critical literacy puts action and activism at the center of literacy instruction, and unveils and disrupts the naturalized discourses within texts.

I asked my students to read books about critical social issues such as human and civil rights, experiences of subjugated people around the world, and to talk back to the perspectives presented in these books. In this sense, my critical literacy pedagogy intersected with peace education. Peace education has been implemented in schools from the perspective of positive peace, emphasizing well-being, justice, racial and gender equity, and human rights (Reardon, 1988). Especially with young children, these perspectives are said to build a foundation for capacities needed for global responsibility.

Book Clubs

During the second half of the spring semester, the students in my class had many tools for talking about texts with their peers; they were able to make personal connections and talk with each other about these connections. They raised critical questions about the authorship of the texts and considering the identity of the author in how the book was written. I needed to release my support in order for them to take more control of creating meaning from their reading of texts. In book clubs, students discuss rich, meaningful literature after reading independently or with the support of a guided reading framework (McMahon & Raphael, 1997; Raphael, Florio-Ruane, & George, 2001). They also write in response journals, which often spark discussions. I emphasized to the students that talking about books was important because we learn more from a text when we question the author's viewpoint and interrogate the meanings of the text. When interacting with texts in this way, the book clubs became "critical book clubs," a useful tool for developing critical literacy. Often for young readers, who are problem-solving on both the word level and on the level of meaning, it is difficult to ascertain exactly what the author intended to say. In book clubs, the students were simultaneously interpreting the texts and the social practices happening in the texts.

Critical Book Clubs, War, and Freedom

Setting up a critical book club drew on critical literacy practices and fit into a larger theme of teaching about civil rights and freedom. Because of my association with LSJTRG, two of my colleagues collaborated in the data collection and implementation of a study of the students' book clubs. Rebecca, a university professor, was my co-researcher on an earlier study of peer learning in my second grade classroom (Rogers & Mosley, 2004, 2006). We worked together to plan units that would draw on students' funds of knowledge and support them in

Photo 3.1 Melissa describes her experience of talking about war with second graders to Cris Mann at the summer writing retreat.

connecting to the experiences of others (Gonzalez, Moll, & Amanti, 2005; Rogers, Light, & Curtis, 2004). We began with students telling family stories as an introduction to how to respond to the stories of other groups of people living in the United States and those affected by war.

The activities and texts we used in the literacy curriculum throughout the spring semester were focused on civil rights and justice. These materials included visual representations (photographs), music and recordings, storybooks, people's stories, and movies. The students read and responded to texts and took part in a dramatization of justice issues. This unit on African American history, civil rights, and human rights spanned most of the spring of the school year. We reflected on the timeline of enslavement and the civil rights movement, emphasizing that it wasn't until 100 years after emancipation when African Americans legally had equal rights. The children were amazed it was "close to now" rather than "long ago" when African American and white children were segregated in schools, theaters, and restaurants in the South. They read literature about how whites and African Americans worked towards justice.

Early Discussions of Freedom, War, and Justice

Beginning in January, I introduced the topic of freedom. An example from the classroom was a making words activity with the letters F-R-E-E-D-O-M. We worked with the letters, spelling known words with two, three, four, and five letters, until they discovered the mystery word. Each student arranged the letters until they discovered the word. When each student was finished, I asked the class, "What is the mystery word?"

I asked them to think quietly about what the word meant to them as they pasted each letter on to a piece of gray construction paper. Would they associate freedom with patriotism? Would they reflect on histories that tell us of people who have not been free in America? Around the world? Would they wonder about their role as children in a country that limits children's freedoms?

The students completed their pictures, and came to the carpet to hear a book about children's rights (UNICEF, 2001). I asked them about the rights they held and the rights we don't have. The students brainstormed conditional rights, such as the right to play with someone if they know the person. They mentioned that the president makes "good rules," that when followed keep people safe and able to exercise their rights.

It was common in this classroom for students to make connections across disciplines and topics during these carpet discussions. Freedom, in the context of African American history and the current war, quickly framed the conversation. Jerome made a connection between a discussion we were having about rights and his knowledge of the history of slavery. He stated, "Slaves didn't have the right to be free."

I chose to follow his lead but was a bit off guard, given we had not yet begun to discuss African American history. I followed up with a question, "Should they have?" to which Jerome replied, "Yes."

A few turns later, I brought the discussion back to the current war in Iraq. "So if somebody like a terrorist comes and tries to hurt people they take away their freedom. What did you think about what happened when the terrorists attacked?"

Pamela replied, "I thought that my freedom would be over 'cos something would happen to our state."

I responded with an affirmation, "Yeah, that was a scary time."

My statement about terrorists reinforced the popular notion—the war in Iraq was a war to protect the freedom of Americans in light of the recent attacks on the United States—a notion that was not critically challenged by the students or myself. Pamela responded in kind, that the terrorists threatened her freedom. Creating a critical literacy classroom raises awareness of how our language shapes the conversation. In retrospect, I might have prompted to explore more deeply about the relationship between terror attacks and freedom if I asked, "How did the attacks on the United States change the way we think about freedom?" or another open-ended question.

Later in the discussion, the children in partners described what they thought were their rights. Jerome and Sandra reported, "From what happened on September 11, we have the right to fight for our freedom and to pray for the people that died," again, making the connection between the attacks in the U.S. and the war in Iraq.

Colin added, "We have the right to protect ourselves."

Albert raised another issue, "To play with each other even if they say no," which was a throwback to the earlier conversation about civil rights.

Ryan raised a separate point, "You have the right to pray to God," which was textually connected to both the UNICEF book and the discussion about praying for those who died on September 11.

Finally, Katrina added, "To not hurt people and harm," which was taking a different position, of having the right to promote peace.

Throughout these discussions, we were on the cusp of approaching some of the questions. The children understood the connection between our rights and happiness, taking actions outside of one's immediate context, and certainly the connections between human rights and the current political context of the war. Therefore, I proceeded with the study of war. However, without a shared experience to speak from, our conversations remained on the surface. Responding to a need to delve deeper into the interplay of freedom and war, I implemented a book club study of Japanese internment in the U.S., which also led us into discussions about the current war and racial justice.

Japan, America, and Civil Rights

Japan was the topic of a unit I taught each year because the social studies curriculum required a study of a "non-Western country." In the past, my curriculum focused on Japanese culture, language, and arts. The students were talking about the war in the context of Iraq, so I designed a unit focusing on U.S./Japanese history and the internment of Japanese Americans during World War II. During the redesigned unit, the class explored the experiences of the Japanese and Japanese Americans during World War II through children's literature. Two main questions framed the literature study:

1. What was it like in Japan during and after World War II?
2. What was it like for Japanese Americans during and after World War II?

Students read and discussed texts in small and large groups, and we used community sharing to focus on large themes. The students read two books about the effects of war in Japan and two books about internment camps set in the United States, discussed below (see also Table 3.1).

All of the books were at the instructional levels of the students, meaning they could read the books with at least 90 percent accuracy and comprehension. Students moved from making personal connections to the text to questioning

Table 3.1 Timeline of Book Clubs

Theme: internment camps, war and peace, and global rights	
5/8/03	*Sadako* (Coerr, 1997) Teacher-guided book club
5/14/03	*The Faithful Elephants* (Tsuchiyu, 1951) Student book clubs
5/22/03	*The Bracelet* (Uchida, 1993) Student book clubs
5/28/03	*Baseball Saved Us* (Mochizuki, 1995) Student book clubs

others' interpretations. Finally, I observed intertextuality in which issues of fairness and equity from one context were revoiced in new discussions.

Moving from Personal Connections to Peer Questioning

I chose the texts in this unit based on the reading level and age appropriateness. Therefore, although there were difficult political issues in the text, I knew the students would make text-to-life connections when reading the books. The first book I chose was part of a second grade text set. *The Bracelet* (Uchida, 1993) is about a young girl who is sent to an internment camp with her family. Her friend gives her a bracelet to remember her California home. In the discussions, the students asked questions about the camp where Emi was sent and put themselves in her shoes. My colleague, Jane, said she had used the book before unsuccessfully because students had little background information.

My students, in particular the females, had a personal connection to Emi, the main character in *The Bracelet*. Katrina mused, "She [Emi] felt—I think she felt sad because she missed her friends and she didn't—and she wanted to move back home but she couldn't because she had to stay there where she would be safe." Katrina's statement indicates both her connection with Emi and a partial understanding of the function of internment camps: they were used to protect Japanese Americans. I picked up on this partial understanding and restated, "Oh, you think the internment camps were keeping them safe? Oh. What would be dangerous for them if they weren't in the camps?"

Larry interjected, "Can I respond to that?" He offered, "Well, actually, being in the house could be safer because not, because maybe people wouldn't know if you were Japanese American. But at the internment camps, some people died because ... they're both safe in a different way." Larry and Katrina had different perspectives based on their personal beliefs.

Over time, the students began to take on more of the critical questioning of one another's responses and connections. Students often read from the book to settle disagreements about meanings. In one book club about *The Bracelet*, students were discussing the student-generated question, "How does Emi feel about America?" This question was complicated because Emi and her family were forced by the U.S. government to give up their San Francisco home to move to a camp. However, Emi herself was confused about why a country she loved would do such a thing.

Kaitlin began, "She really likes it," indicating a partial understanding of the conflict Emi experienced.

Andrew agreed, and then Carl posed another possibility: "Actually she feels mad at America," another partial understanding.

Kaitlin disagreed: "She doesn't feel mad, she has her friends," which referenced Emi's best friend who gave Emi a bracelet to remember their friendship. Kaitlin put herself in Emi's shoes in the book club discussion, which she might have also been doing while she read the story.

This answer did not resonate with Carl, so he repeated his earlier comment, adding a bit of evidence: "Actually, she's mad at America because they're the ones that sent her to the prison camp."

Carrie was worried about this evidence because it disrupted her understanding as well. She provided counter-evidence to Carl's claim, stating, "But in the story it says she likes America."

At this point in the book club, Kaitlin and Carrie had come to one understanding and Larry and Carl had come to another. To resolve the disagreement, Larry referred to the book, "This is at the end of page one, the last sentence," and he read, "It was crazy because they loved America but America didn't love them back." The specificity of the comment allowed the rest of the group to get behind this answer.

This pattern repeated: the students were posing questions, constructing answers, and using the book as evidence, and they were learning with and from their peers. They practiced making connections to books personally and subjectively. In conversations with my colleagues at school, I would describe this as a tool to increase reading comprehension, interest in reading and discussing books, and other politically neutral terms. However, when I spoke with my colleagues in LSJTRG, I was able to express the greater purpose for doing this type of work with the second graders. I wanted them to move from personal connections to think about the sociopolitical implications of war.

Student Voices: Taking Positions on Internment and War

In another book club discussion of *The Bracelet* with a different group, the conversation did have a sociopolitical focus, indicating that the students were considering the motivations and consequences of the U.S.'s participation in wars.

Pamela raised the question with her group: "Do you think they [Americans] should treat them [Japanese Americans] nice or mean?"

Paul responded, "Mean."

The whole group was shocked. Quickly, Sam took a perspective, stating, "They should treat them mean," and then revoked, "Never mind. What I think is if they're in a war, they should be treated mean but they're not. They're in a prison camp, like Paul said, and they aren't going to be treated equally." Sam used the statement "What I think" to pose this as a possibility.

Brad added the notion that the fair treatment of Japanese Americans was at stake. He expressed his reasoning, "I don't see why they do that. That's the problem. They don't know if they [Japanese Americans] are going to try to help America. They don't know and it's a problem."

Sam continued, "The Japanese Americans have to make a decision. Okay, now on to my question." Sam silenced Brad's musings to bring the book club's attention to his question. He did not exactly pick up on what Brad posed as being one central theme of the book, that all Japanese Americans were hurt because they were not trusted, and further, in a time of war, people make unjust decisions. Sam made this move to gain the floor. Although we were talking about disempowering practices, the students often exercised the same types of practices on one another.

Prior to reading each text, I did a short book walk with the students (Fountas & Pinnell, 1996). For the book *Baseball Saved Us* (Mochizuki, 1995), I introduced the idea of an internment camp. Brad raised a question about the cover illustration, in which prison guards oversee a baseball game at the camp. "Um, do, are they allowed, I mean do they have to sneak and play baseball or do the soldiers just let 'em play baseball?" The prison guards hold rifles, which is juxtaposed with the images of the children's uniforms and baseball bats. The scene is a yellow-orange, dusty field. Brad noticed something awry between the images presented.

Sam posed another possibility: "I think that usually in baseball games, football games, any kind of games, there's this big screen where these two people talk. This is where I think the two people are probably talking about the game."

In a quieter tone, Brad responded, "Well, I don't think…" but was interrupted by my move to bring the group back to some of the tricky words in the reading. However, the conversation quickly shifted back to the question of what the guards were doing. Brad emphasized that the guns were for the guards to use if someone tried to escape, and Sam co-constructed along with Brad the benefits of having guards up high to oversee the situation. Neither boy questioned why guards oversaw a baseball game, and I failed to raise this important question. Five years later, it seems there is a strong parallel between the soldiers fighting in Afghanistan and Iraq and the guards with guns in this children's book. In Brad and Sam's co-construction, the guards were in a surveillance role. In Iraq, one viewpoint is that American soldiers protect civilians' freedom against tyranny—keeping the aggressors at bay. At the time, the nation was still united in an effort to fight terrorism, and there was not much room for opposition. Five years later, many more Americans question the move into Iraq, and there may have been more space for a critical conversation had the book clubs happened today.

An end-of-unit assessment illustrated varying positions students took up on social and political issues. I asked, "Japan and America have an interesting past together. What are some of the things that happened in history between these two countries?" The students responded:

PAMELA: The Japanese people had to go to a camp. The Americans treated them like slaves. Why don't you think they will treat each other equally? Are they mad at each other? Can they stand up for themselves?

COLIN: Well, for one thing, Japan has fought with us and against us. In World War I they were on our side. But in World War II they weren't. When they invaded China our friendship blew up. After World War II we were friends and we helped rebuild Japan.

These responses were reflective of the complicated history of war and racism, and were political. Pamela raised questions about justice and power in relation to the prison camps, while Colin illustrated the history of the relationship. He was cognizant that politically, interests can shift and relationships change. Pamela noticed an unequal balance of power, asking if Japanese Americans could stand up for themselves under the existing conditions.

I have mulled over the missed opportunities to bring issues of power and justice to the forefront of the classroom. In particular, through a project that

Rebecca and I did together (Rogers & Mosley, 2006), I worried about how children often silenced one another. Moving outward from the local to the institutional and global level, my conversations with colleagues in LSJTRG reminded me that this commonly happens in schools, school board meetings, and in state and federal legislation. One person often exercises the power to silence others in co-constructions of the problems and solutions. I wish I had been present in the book club discussions to highlight how taking counter-positions is useful in coming to deeper understandings. A critical book club requires that teachers and students are serious about, interpretive of, and emotionally invested in the stories they read. But like any other learning opportunity, critical discussions must be guided and protected, encouraged and fostered, knowing there are always powerful discourses that can stifle our conversations.

Looking Back: Lessons about Literacy Teaching and Learning

Many of my frustrations were rooted in my partial understanding about the role of a teacher in using critical literacy to interrogate social and political texts. It was very important to listen to the students and understand their positions as part of a larger context. I think I was focused more on the "correct" (liberal) interpretation of the story as I guided their discussions. However, I would have learned more by reading their responses in the context of the literacy practices of the larger community.

Listening to my own stories and the stories of my colleagues in LSJTRG, I find that teachers' practices are influenced by immediate worries. My worries began when I noticed the danger of the situation of the U.S. in Afghanistan and Iraq and the a-critical response in the community. Because we were riding on a wave of patriotism, championing freedom, it became confusing when the tables turned and America became the aggressor. I worried about students, who thought to be proud to be an American meant supporting unjust actions. The children worried about their freedom and safety, which were threatened. The children also worried about the members of their family who were in the military and might be in the center of an impending war.

The first response to any crisis is to remove the danger, to help children feel safe in their classroom, community, and society. However, I was not comfortable with leaving these worries uncomplicated in the waves of patriotism, waves that brought us to our feet to sing songs each Friday morning. I believed that in the book discussions of Japanese internment, the students would come to realize that we cannot always trust our government to act in the best interest of the global society. However, there were many roadblocks to this outcome. Through my work with LSJTRG, I have found that peace education holds many possibilities for shaping literacy education in the United States. The capacity for global responsibility can be constructed through education. Discussions around texts were highly influenced by the literacy practices of the family, community, and classroom. Most of the peace education curricula for the early grades, in contrast, are highly disconnected from real contexts.

When placed into a model for participatory education, peace education could be centered within real events and problems, even with young children. There is a visible tension between whether peace education should be primarily focused on positive peace (i.e. well-being and recognizing fairness and equity) or recognition and critique of violence at the personal (i.e. terrorism, institutional (i.e. war) or structural (i.e. racism)) levels. However, how do you infuse peace education and critical literacy within a book club with young children? If I had a repertoire of strategies available from peace education, such as language to think about the building blocks for global responsibility, I might have been able to move students into discussions of peace and violence with more ease. However, one of the critical aspects of the book club was that students put their responses on the table and critique multiple perspectives. The language for critique of war was simply unavailable in this context, and therefore the possibilities of book clubs to address freedom, justice, and the war in Iraq might have been limited and better accomplished with other pedagogical literacy practices.

Bringing peace education into critical literacy practices for young children promises to be an area for further teacher research and exploration of some of the tensions mentioned above. Today something has to be done, within schools, to educate and raise awareness of the alternatives to war and violence available to us. I plan to continue this exploration in my work with classroom teachers in LSJTRG and my own teaching.

Rethinking Practice

Doing peace education and critical literacy with young children in particular raises the big question of a teacher's role. Many teachers feel they must address the violence and injustice occurring in the global and local world we share. But the question often arises: What social issues should a teacher bring to the classroom? How do we make space for students to bring social issues into the classroom? In addition, when social issues emerge in the classroom, how can we be poised and ready to share tools with students for critical reflective practice? Finally, how do we both acknowledge and appreciate multiple perspectives even when they conflict with our own values and beliefs? Discuss with your colleagues, and then explore resources for peace education and critical literacy together for new ideas and strategies. Begin with an exploration of www.un.org/cyberschoolbus/peace/index.asp.

4 Writing our Way to Cultural Understandings

Rebecca Light

On December 19, 2007 nine members of the Progressive Teachers Union of Zimbabwe (PTUZ) were abducted for distributing leaflets about the country's education crisis. The teachers were speaking out against the state of public schools in Zimbabwe and were demanding that authorities act on the collapse of the education system. Earlier, the Educational International affiliate in Zimbabwe also protested the distressing situation of teachers and highlighted the fact that 8,000 teachers have left the country. So far, no charges have been laid against the PTUZ members. For more information go to Educational International (www.ei-ie.org/en/index.php).

Introduction

I entered the fifth grade classroom where I would spend the next four months as a student teacher armed with three and a half years of college coursework, a plethora of theory, an emerging understanding of culturally responsive teaching, a lined notebook dubbed my "reflective journal," and a healthy dose of nerves. My experience was unique because besides the students and my cooperating teacher supporting me in my reflective process, I had the privilege of being involved with the Literacy for Social Justice Teacher Research Group (LSJTRG) as I began to build my identity as a teacher. In the context of this group, I was able to inquire into and critically analyze my teaching practices through the lenses of equity and social justice.

LSJTRG provided a safe and honest environment filled with experienced professionals to help guide my reflection, challenge my theories, and celebrate my growth as a teacher. The sharing of power among professionals of different experience levels and the flexible framework of the group inspired the community I wanted to establish in my fifth grade classroom. This inspiration and constant support led to a classroom-based research project focused on designing a culturally responsive writing project using local knowledge to inform the writing content in my fifth grade student teaching setting. In this chapter, I describe this project and reflect on the process of learning to construct a culturally responsive fifth grade classroom.

Children clearly come to school with knowledge, ideas, and assumptions about the world around them and their place in it. They also have ideas and working theories about reading and writing. Gee (1996) defines these working theories as "Discourses." When a child from a low-income, African American background enters a classroom with curricula written by and based on white middle-class beliefs, there is a discrepancy in discourses which can lead to rejection of the student's own discourse as part of becoming a "literate" individual. Moll describes "funds of knowledge" as knowledge students have gained through experiences in community and home. One of the most important ways to explicate students' funds of knowledge is to ask them for detailed accounts of traditions and family stories (Moll, Amanti, Neff, & Gonzalez, 1992). These stories reveal what talents and skills are possessed within the family and how they are passed down and between family members. They position students as having useful knowledge, which changes one's own perception (Shor, 1996).

As a student teacher, I hoped to integrate all three of these theories into my teaching and the classroom community. I wanted to bridge the discrepancy in discourse by bringing in the funds of knowledge that students already possessed. However, it is important to note that my final goal was not simply to use this bridge to improve traditional reading and writing methods. I also wanted these students from a historically marginalized part of society to feel like powerful contributors and escape the "teacher knows all" mentality of traditional classrooms. Being involved in the LSJTRG with such a diverse group of teachers—both in experience and background—allowed us to commence the journey together, but we all had our own paths to follow to arrive at how culturally relevant teaching fits into our own personal teaching philosophies and assumptions about education and culture.

The Classroom, Teachers, and Students

The students who entered my fifth grade classroom in the fall of 2001 came from neighborhoods surrounding the school. One hundred percent of the students were African American. The majority of the students walked to and from school every day, while two took a bus provided by the school. Many of the students had been in this same school since kindergarten. One student was new to the school this year, but not to the city. Another student was in her second year at the school. Many of the students had siblings and cousins who attended the same school. Fifth grade is the oldest grade this school has in its building, so the siblings and cousins were younger than the students in the classroom. Most of the students knew Ms. Carver from prior interactions.

Ms. Carver is an African American third-year teacher who had previously taught fourth and fifth grade. She had a fourth grade class her first year, and looped with the class through fifth grade. This was her first time teaching most of the students in the class that this project is based on. She is the director of the drill team, and after-school step team for fourth and fifth grade girls. Ms. Carver is a science buff, as she told me the first day I met her, and was very enthusiastic about the new science textbooks and curriculum that were implemented this year.

I am a Jewish American woman who grew up in Cleveland, Ohio. Prior to student teaching, I spent a year in this elementary school observing in an adult education class and tutoring an adult education student and his son as part of my practicum course in literacy. I was familiar with the norms and routines of this community school and requested to carry out my student teaching placement in this school because I wanted to challenge current notions of urban schools perpetuated in the media, in the educational community, and even by my fellow peers in the teacher education program. I wanted to discover the literacy practices that were so different from the one I came from.

Aside from this experience, I had few experiences in environments where the majority of people were African American and of low socioeconomic status. Growing up in an almost all-white neighborhood and school, I had little exposure to those holding assumptions about learning and education other than my own. Being raised in an upper-middle-class Jewish family with two parents who held postgraduate degrees made school-based education of the utmost importance in my home. However, the ideas my family held about education were along the lines of traditional notions of education. Although the teachings of my Jewish background favor critical thinking and encourage one to always question, following conventions in order to succeed was also encouraged. It was assumed that I would go to college, possibly to graduate school, and that success in these areas as defined by grades would determine my success as an "expert" in my chosen field. To participate in this project, not only did I have to help the students challenge their notions, I had to spend much time challenging my own.

I began my teaching in the classroom with guidance from Ms. Carver, my cooperating teacher, in using the school's reading and writing curriculum. The curriculum was developed by Scholastic and consisted of a basal textbook with several short stories bound into a textbook form, a grammar workbook, and a teacher's guide with suggestions for writing activities to respond to/accompany the readings in the basal reader. From the start, I questioned how this communication arts curriculum was coming to life for the students—was it connecting school to their lives?

Designing a Culturally Responsive Classroom

While we had read a great deal about designing pedagogy that was culturally relevant and based on principles of equity and justice in my teacher education courses (e.g. Banks & Banks, 1995; Comber, Thomson, & Wells, 2001; Ladson-Billings, 1994), we had fewer examples of what this looked like within the context of a classroom. As a student teacher, I was eager to experiment with constructing a culturally relevant classroom. I realized I would have to find an entry point that began with the students themselves. I had to find ways to find out as much as I could about their lives, communities, values, and interests. In turn, my plan was to turn students into researchers of their own lives and communities (e.g. Mercado, 1998; Moll, Amanti, Neff, & Gonzalez, 1992).

I was also inquiring into my teaching practices using the tools of teacher research (e.g. Cochran-Smith & Lytle, 2001). I kept fieldnotes and reflective journals each day (e.g. Frank, 1999; Harste & Vasquez, 1998). I also tape-recorded and analyzed some of our whole group and individual conferences. I copied student writing samples. I gathered all of these materials into data packets for each student that became the basis for developing case studies of student learning (e.g. Johnston, 1997).

Timelines

I began by asking the students to construct a timeline of themselves—including important dates, events, and information that was salient to who they are today. There were a variety of types of timelines, as well as kinds of information each student chose to include. Some timelines were text, handwritten on a piece of paper, others were large poster boards with photographs and detailed descriptions of life events. Timelines included events such as church parades, trips, family reunions, championships won with athletic teams, and holidays celebrated. This project gave me a starting point to prepare some curricular designs that would speak to students' lives outside of school. However, there was another level of insight gained on my part through this experience. Distanced from these communities, the media often portrays the areas where the children live as places of despair and hopelessness. I realized that I had unknowingly fallen prey to these stereotypical descriptions of the "inner city." I entered this school, as a very sheltered 20-year-old college student, feeling a sense of sympathy for the members of this community, and thinking of myself as someone who could help these children have the same rich experiences that I did when growing up. Although my heart was in the right place, my assumptions were mistaken and misguided, and this timeline activity not only gave me insight into the rich lives of these children, but helped me to reflect on my own ideas about the lives and families in this community. I quickly realized that the goal in constructing a culturally responsive classroom was twofold: to help the students develop literate identities as readers and writers, but also to privilege the experiences that construct their identities outside of school. The students had already done this—it was just time for me to recognize its significance and help them see that all of their experiences and strengths can contribute to literate identities, and are as valid as anything they might read in a textbook.

Community Experts

To draw further on students' funds of knowledge, I designed practices for students to investigate their familial and cultural lives. I wanted to extend their thinking about family and community resources with a discussion and exploration of "expertise." Initially, I did not define the word "expert," but let the students' definition of the word "expert" come through in their inquiry, discussion, and writing. My goal was to help the class recognize how many experts (those who possess local funds of knowledge) were in their families and communities—and that the students themselves were experts.

Dominick, a young man with a delightful sense of humor who often gained his peers' respect through his humor and outgoing personality, was adamant that someone without a formal education could not be an expert. However, after conducting community interviews, the same student told the class that "[a]nyone can be an expert." This challenge to the traditional power structure and idea of who, exactly, can be an expert with valuable knowledge acted as the entry point to begin to empower students and lead them to access the codes of power. Students come to school with rich traditions and local knowledge that are rarely turned into privileged discourses in the classroom (Rogers, Light, & Curtis, 2004).

This discussion created a collaborative definition that acted as an entry point to a discussion of community experts. Students then went into their communities and interviewed people who they felt were experts to find out what learning processes were involved in these funds of knowledge. During a discussion when students brought their interviews back to the classroom, the class examined the proximity of the experts and what types of things they were expert at to see that the experts were right in their community and that they had a variety of skills, some learned in school, some not. Expertise varied from musicians to cooks to athletes. We discussed and shared the various forms of expertise in a whole group format. I felt that now that community expertise had been brought into the classroom, it was time to bridge this content to the classroom with a writer's workshop. We continued to examine funds of knowledge through writing about traditions in a writer's workshop format. We went through the writing processes of brainstorming and revision as a class and through individual conferences. I wanted to maintain the culturally responsive practice; we would be doing writing instruction within the context of the information they provided about their families and communities.

Writing About Our Expertise

To begin the writing process, I started as close to the known as possible: what students are experts at. This assignment would begin to uncover learning processes and interests that begin outside of school. I presented them with some guiding questions as prompts:

1. What are you an expert at?
2. How do you know you are an expert?
3. What are the steps you went through to become an expert?

I shared a piece of my writing, and emphasized that I had written it more like a story. Some of the students did expand their writing beyond answering questions, but many did not.

I conducted mini-conferences with students by walking around the room as they were writing and answering questions, hearing their pieces, and prompting students who were having trouble getting started. After reading the students' pieces, I felt that many were lacking detailed descriptions. I chose one that displayed understanding of the importance of detailed description and put this on an overhead. I tried to describe the importance of detail in their writing as relevant to their part of providing the content for instruction through their local knowledge. I explained that I was unaware of these traditions and everything involved in their execution. The students possessed this powerful knowledge, and in order to convey it clearly to me it was important that they add detail to their writing. As a class, we pointed out details that helped us imagine what a student's tradition must look like, as well as places where she could add more detail. Students were then given more writing time.

The next in-class writing assignment was following a large group discussion about who can be an expert and how we can find out what experts are in our communities. I asked the students to write down thoughts and questions after this discussion, because many important issues were raised. For example, some students thought anyone could be an expert, while others felt you need to have finished school to be an expert at something. The discussion was very heated and I thought the students would have much to write about. However, when I asked them to sit down and write their thoughts and questions, many were puzzled. When they asked me, "What's the question?" I was surprised—I thought they had so many things running through their heads at that moment that they would not be able to stop writing. However, I realized that the students did not have any experience with using writing to record thoughts and ideas. They were not accustomed to using writing as a tool to reflect and consider new ideas. They were accustomed to using writing to complete assigned tasks that answer a particular question.

I had to take a step back from my experience as a writer and consider theirs. I have been writing in journals ever since I can remember; I had infinite personal diaries growing up and always kept a journal in school. I can remember creating stories and using writing as an outlet for ideas as early as second grade. Throughout college, reflective writing has been a tool I have used to work through difficult issues and sort out my thoughts when I am intellectually challenged by complex issues. I was so excited to introduce this skill to the students, but I did not consider that their experience with writing may not lend itself to this type of reflective task. Reflective writing is a very different form of writing than writing to complete designated tasks. One must have fluency and comfort in writing, as well as the ability to write in detail. When I write reflectively, I examine issues in depth and come to new conclusions as I write. However, I realized that these students were so accustomed to writing in response to isolated and specific questions that the task of writing down "thoughts" was overwhelming.

The students needed a scaffold to reach this type of reflection in their writing. The thought processes were there; the students showed me from day one that given the right environment, they were able to engage in critical thinking and speak knowingly about issues of social justice and culture. As fifth graders, students seemed comfortable with how they fit into their environments and their complicated family structures. They knew their roles and were aware of how to perform them. With these complex thought processes, I was sure that the students would be more than capable of recording their thoughts, and merge their old ideas with new ones, as I have done so many times in my reflective writing. However, the students were not even aware of using writing in this way.

With support, the students started to write about their expertise. However, their writing tended to follow the structure of my questions. For example, one student wrote, "I am an expert at football because every day I go home and play football with my little brother. I know I am an expert at football because every time I play I beat my brother and he get mad and go in the house." Another student considered his or her expertise within the domain of the school and wrote, "I am an expert at reading. I can understand the words. I learned the alphabet." It appeared as though some of the children thought I wanted them to write about school expertise rather than expertise at home and in their community.

Moving Forward: Writing About Traditions

The students also came into my classroom with societal understandings about literacy from their family, the media, and faith-based organizations. They learn very early what types of language and literacy practices are valued and which are not. The fifth grade students in my classroom arrived in the classroom on their first day of school with preconceived notions about where their community knowledge fitted into this power structure.

One of the topics that came up in our discussion around "experts" was the idea of traditions. Earlier in the year, I had shared one of my Jewish traditions with the students—Rosh Hashanah, the Jewish New Year. Since I missed a day of school for the holiday, Ms. Carver asked me to explain about the holiday to the students, so I brought in some traditional Jewish holiday food and explained the Hebrew calendar to the students. At the time we did this writing assignment, I referred back to this experience as a model of a tradition. We had a discussion on what tradition means to them, and they all had a lot to contribute. They had some interesting ideas and very personal notions about what tradition was. For example, when I asked for comments about what "tradition" means, Jon said, "Like you have a family tradition like follow in somebody's footsteps." Mary added that traditions were "something like your family does like they do with their family, from millennium to millennium." James responded that he saw tradition as "…like something that listen to music and play cards." Later in the discussion, the students began to share some of their specific family traditions. Many of the students talked about family reunions that they participate in annually. Beth said that "The whole family there, they might have kids, barbecue." James went into even more detail: "My grandmother make sweet potato pies and she says she learned it from her mom." These comments began to uncover the exact type of information that Moll defines as "funds of knowledge." The students were going into detail about the local knowledge of their families and how it contributed to their lives. In addition, the students were getting into the processes of teaching and learning these skills. This was an ideal environment to initiate some writing that would be very personal to the students and provided them with a large bank of information to draw from to compose their pieces. The power and ownership over this assignment was shared between the students and myself. I provided the opportunity to write about local knowledge, and the students provided the "fund" from which to provide the content of the writing piece.

As for a prompt, following the discussion, I told students to "write about a tradition that you have with your family or your friends. Write a story that goes along with the tradition, how that tradition started, something interesting you remember happening when this tradition happened." My prompt listed several ideas, but I did not require that the students include all of this information. Unlike the expert piece, I listed different topics as ways to spark ideas, not to write down specific pieces of information. When I asked if there were any questions, there were not. The students were clear on what I asked them to do because it was not very complicated, and they were writing about something they were more aware of than I was, one way of disrupting traditional power–knowledge relationships in the classroom (Comber, Thomson, & Wells, 2001; Lensmire, 2000; Luke, 1995). As I was walked around the room conferencing with students, a couple of students claimed they had no traditions. Ms. Carver quietly told me to ask them about church or Sunday dinner. I did this with three students, and it worked. This prompt reminded me of the importance of religion and culture as a significant fund of knowledge—for myself and for my students. It was also a gentle reminder of how I needed to continue to learn about culture and language as a teacher.

We shared examples of students' writing on the overhead. As they shared their writing, they were also getting to know each other and building the classroom community. Many students had developed characters and dialogue in their pieces. For example, Melissa wrote about a funny incident at her Sunday dinner:

> When my Uncle Pede started eating my grandma's dressing, he said, "Mom, you really put your foot in this dressing." When he said that, I said "Thank you for saying foot 'cos I smell some Fritos." That had got everybody in their silly moods. I said to myself "I've got something started that I can't end" and sighed.

Students also began writing stories with a beginning, middle, and end. Darren set up his story by describing the setting:

> My family and I were at my cousin house all our family was there. We had everything to eat from barbecue to fried chicken. When we really start having fun, a big storm broke out on us. I was cover with water. It was mud everywhere. So the children made mud houses. Then we went home.

Creating these stories enhanced their writing by making it purposeful and lending itself to not only explaining the tradition itself, but explaining how this tradition fitted into the students' identity as community and family members. The class as a whole began questioning their traditional notions of content for writing and schooled knowledge. They began to write about their own experiences and community knowledge while simultaneously beginning to take ownership over the discourse of writing.

Reflecting on the Process

Designing culturally responsive instruction felt "risky" to me as a student teacher. For one, I was not an insider to this classroom. As a Jewish, white woman I did not have the insider knowledge of African American culture and community norms that my cooperating teacher did. I had not thought about the dual demands of designing culturally responsive pedagogy and supporting my students as writers at the same time. An additional surprise for me in the process was that all of the students did not readily see the connection among their funds of knowledge, their expertise, and the classroom curriculum. As fifth graders, my students had not been asked to choose their own writing topics, nor were they given the chance to integrate their home and community knowledge into the curriculum. I knew this was important for the students' literate identities.

There were times during the project when I brought some of these issues to LSJTRG for discussion. I shared my ongoing project and interventions and invited feedback. Our group discussions were focused many times on how to be culturally relevant teachers, and how to engage our classes by creating a community of knowledge, rather than a "banking" method of teaching where the teacher "deposits" knowledge into the students, who are otherwise empty (Freire, 1970b). At the heart of this power sharing is the idea that the students bring important knowledge into the classroom before the teacher has spoken a word. This idea provided the essential assumption for my project. Most class-rooms function under the assumption that teacher knows best. The content of

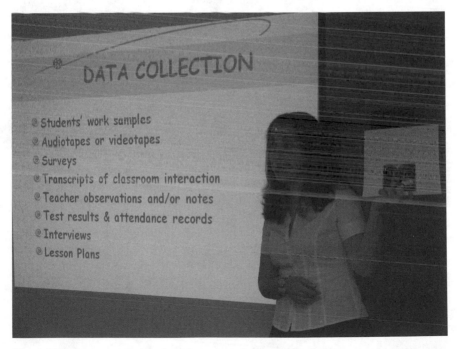

Photo 4.1 Rebecca presenting about her research.

the curriculum is all held within the textbooks and knowledge of the teacher and writers of those textbooks. Knowledge is power, but the powerful knowledge in school is one dictated by a chosen few—and is typically not the students. As a pre-service teacher, I was still developing my own teaching style and philosophy. LSJTRG provided a space for me to try out various identities.

This basic assumption exemplified the LSJTRG's frameworks. As I was bringing ideas and issues to the table about discourse and codes of power, I was engaging in just this type of format in a professional development setting. I gained knowledge into what access to codes of power and culturally relevant teaching "looks like" through participation in this inquiry group. By being a pre-service teacher, in this setting I did not have access to the codes of power (as they relate to being a teacher) as readily as experienced teachers and university professors. Not only could I learn from the content of the group discussions, but by the positive way we shared and extended each other's ideas. The form and framework of each session provided modeling of a socially just and culturally relevant discourse that I could bridge into my fifth grade classroom.

Throughout this process I brought ideas, reflections, and questions to the LSJTRG. One significant question I had was how to keep my values out of the classroom and privilege the knowledge and discourse of my students. Because I came from such a different background that represented those discourses that are normally recognized and privileged in school settings (white, middle class, formally educated) I felt that this was the only way to truly accomplish my goals for this project. However, the more experienced teachers in our group helped me understand that teaching is always value-laden. There is no such thing as leaving my values at the door when I enter a classroom. The key to culturally responsive teaching is recognizing and being critical of your own values, understanding where they came from, and revising them to include understanding your students' values. Only within the framework of this constant synthesis can true critical literacy and social justice teaching become the discourse of the classroom.

Rethinking Practice

Invite your students to study their own "localized" literacy practices by documenting the many literacy practices in their lives. You might ask students to consider the following questions: In what areas do you consider yourself to be an expert? How do you use literacies to accomplish this social practice? How did you learn these literacies? How do others regard these literacy practices? Do they function in parallel with "official literacies" or were they developed in opposition to "official literacies"? In what ways is this literacy practice part of a global network? What are the "flows of knowledge" that are connected with this literacy practice? Conduct your own "localized literacy" self-study alongside the learners in your class. Schedule time to share the inquiry.

---

5 Learning to Listen

Creating Socially Just Curricula for Middle and High School Classrooms

Sarah Hobson

In the Palestinian West Bank village of Deir Ballut, students used to take a school bus to class, but checkpoints and roadblocks installed by the Israeli military have now rendered vehicular transport impractical. Instead, students and teachers walk past snipers and barbed wire on their way to school every morning, showing their IDs and opening up their book-bags to be searched. In late 2003, Israel announced the impending construction of a Separation Wall through the village, separating local farmers from their livelihoods and destroying a new Palestinian schoolhouse in the Wall's path. In response, hundreds of villagers and their Israeli and international supporters set up a Peace Camp in the schoolhouse to non-violently prevent its destruction. Students at the Camp organized a protest against the Wall and the checkpoint. Villagers continued such protests for more than a year until eventually the Wall's path was changed and the village roadblocks removed, although the checkpoint remains (Baltzer, 2007).

Photos of the students' march are available at www.AnnaInTheMiddleEast.com/photos/demonstrations/deirballutdemos/db_childrens_march.

What is at Stake for Students?

Something had snapped in 18-year-old Kate, but no one knew how or why. Yesterday she had been fine, a regular senior, finishing up her final exams and dreaming about leaving for college in a couple of months. Today she had slipped into another world, a world her parents were desperately trying to access.

In the middle of a final exam, Kate, a dedicated student, had suddenly screamed and run out of the room and all the way home. For the rest of the day she would respond to no one. She paced vacantly around her home, passed her family. Her parents tried to comfort her, but she was too far removed from them to hear their love.

It took the rest of the week, multiple doctors, and the strong arms of her father holding and rocking her for the truth to begin to become coherent. After days of shock, Kate whispered her story to her father, a story he never could have imagined would ever exist in his neighborhood. Somewhere in the course of her senior after-prom party, a date rape drug had made its way into Kate's drink. It was not until she was in the middle of a final exam two days later that Kate's memory returned to her. She had been gang-raped by a group of male classmates.

I met Kate and her family because they were close friends of the family of my roommate Elizabeth. When Kate went into shock, I watched Elizabeth and her family grieve and begin the process of supporting Kate's family. The two families worked together to help Kate remember enough of what had happened to put the boys on trial. However, as is often the case with date rape drugs, parts of her story remained nebulous, and the boys were found not guilty.

Where Does this Leave Teachers?

Kate's rape coincided with a worry that had begun to invade my life as a fourth and fifth year high school English teacher. The worry began with September 11, 2001 in the middle of my first year of co-teaching a new Humanities World History and World Literature program. My students and I watched the towers fall, and their eyes kept searching for mine, looking for wisdom and hope. My world too had been thrown into confusion, and I had none to offer.

As the year progressed, books like Enrique Maria Remarque's World War I *All Quiet on the Western Front* were suddenly more real and present and possible. The books and characters were no longer people and situations from another period; they could happen again, and we now knew it. Thus, when at the end of my fourth year I learned about Kate's story, something in me also snapped.

Where were the words to express just what the boys had done? How could I process their actions and the influences in their lives? Why did the world I thought I knew seem to continue to fall apart in ways I could not fathom? What turned children into criminals? And most of all, how on earth could I teach students if I myself did not have the language I needed to understand these losses for myself? I began to talk with several of my female students, and what I learned about the sexual pressure they felt only deepened my worry.

Language. Language. Language. Where were the words that could protect my students and strengthen their personal power in the midst of the chaos and confusion of our culture and times? How could our classroom be a place where justice for Kate and others like her was possible?

Enter the St. Louis Literacy for Social Justice Teacher Research Group

These were the burning questions I brought to the Literacy for Social Justice Teacher Research Group between 2003 and 2006 just after I took a much needed break from teaching. The majority of the group were women of all ages, each one serious-minded about justice and dedicated to its rectification. The leaders created space for members to both enjoy one another and to focus on the task at hand, whichever piece of the St. Louis public schools or programs we would learn and discuss that day.

What I appropriated over the course of my three years in LSJTRG was the confidence and purpose each leader and member had. Each person had enough agency to see the vision and then to believe that together we would make it happen. The vision did not have to happen overnight. There was time to be new at organizing. There was time to stop and read and think together, and to see where our discussions would lead us as a group. I was welcome to choose how I wanted to participate, and anything I wanted to contribute was embraced with support and resources for my ideas.

Critical Literacy: Hope and Change in the Classroom

In the process of participating in LSJTRG, I can now see that even before I learned about Kate, there were several ways that I had focused on exposing my students to models of critical literacy. I would have called it critical thinking, and if asked to define critical thinking, I would probably have mentioned Bloom's *Taxonomy* and the thinking process building from understanding, to synthesizing, analyzing, and finally evaluating material (Bloom, 1984). Now, I can choose many aspects of critical literacy to explain what I attempted every so often as a teacher.

While I was only vaguely aware of what I was doing at the time and knew very little of the vocabulary I am about to mention, I created my own version of the Socratic Seminar that I still use with students today.

Socratic Seminars include a range of ways to structure classroom discussions with or without the teacher in the conversation so that students learn to effectively engage in dialogue together that helps them examine the sources of their ideas and their thinking processes, often in light of a provocative and engaging text. I took a tremendous risk which helped my students recognize some of the societal ways of speaking, acting, and interacting which they had inherited as a result of their gender, class, and race (Gee, 2005). In essence, I wanted them to know that each social discourse (Gee, 2005) they used shaped how they saw who

Photo 5.1 Sarah conducting a Socratic Seminar with students.

they were and could be in the world. I arranged activities in which they could see themselves as makers of meaning, as able to shape their identities by transforming societal discourses and patterns into new repertoires of being and acting (Hicks, 2002; Yagelski, 2000). I wanted them to find the courage to speak their real voices and needs, because I needed the same inspiration.

Due to large class sizes and my desire for all students to have access to group discussions, I leaned on Gloria Steinem (1995) to engender and support productive social interactions. We were just about to start *A Doll's House* by Ibsen, and I created a Socratic Seminar meant to deepen and personalize our readings of the play. The themes in the book include miscommunication between the main characters, Nora and Torvald. Torvald in particular degrades his wife daily by speaking to her as if she were a child, and while she appears to accept the identity of powerlessness he gives her, she proves herself capable of providing for her family, albeit behind her husband's back. When he learns she has forged his signature in order to take out the loan she has been working off that saved the family financially, he repudiates her for being immoral and deems her unworthy to raise their children. She begins to see that all along he has never really wanted her for who she is, but for how she helps him measure up to the outside world.

To interrupt the interactional styles that were disrupting true dialogue in my Humanities class, I decided to try out a seminar where the students would take notes and reflect on our group discussions. We comprised 44 students, all white, with the exception of a student of Indian heritage, mostly middle class, and two teachers, packed into a horseshoe of three to four rows. I sent a select group of ten students from the class out into the hallway. I passed out a photocopy to the rest of the class, which had a table with the names of the ten students at the top of the columns and several categories in each of the left-hand rows. The categories were the observations I wanted the class to make about the ten students who would sit in the inner circle. They included eye contact, initiating an argument, interrupting, making a joke, and time spent talking.

The 35 students who would be observing each other chose partners and categories, and knew they were not to say what they would be doing. I then went into the hallway and explained to the ten students there that I wanted them to choose a topic to discuss and that the rest of the class would get to listen to their discussion. They chose the topic of gun control and cheerfully entered the class and took their places.

The students I had chosen for the inner circle were two boys who were very bright and spoke the most in our class, two or three girls who were bright and popular and who spoke a regular amount in class, and several students who rarely spoke in class but who were smart and capable in their writing and thinking. Steven once again proved to be incredibly articulate on the topic, and Phil, almost equally articulate, began an attempt to undermine Steven's authority. I have re-created a possible version of their dialogue as I can only remember the dynamics and not their exact words. Steven led the discussion by setting the parameters of the debate.

"Laws are meant to protect us, and on the one hand how can we feel protected if people are permitted to purchase weapons? On the other hand, with or without gun control laws, people have been able to access weapons, and how can we protect ourselves if we are not allowed to carry concealed weapons?"

Phil responded by raising his tone of voice in attack as he looked for holes in Steven's argument. "You haven't thought this through. Carrying a concealed weapon is a separate issue from being permitted to own weapons."

Steven appeared undaunted and the rest of the circle watched as he calmly replied along the lines of, "I have thought this through. Owning a weapon and carrying a weapon may be separate issues, but ultimately anyone who is permitted to own a weapon can easily carry it on him, and what we have to determine is whether we are protecting ourselves by permitting the ownership of weapons or protecting ourselves by forbidding it."

Some of the other students attempted to join the discussion, but it inevitably landed back between Phil and Steven. I don't remember how or why, but their discussion shifted from gun control to advertising and the objectification of women, and when Wendy, one of the socially popular girls, vehemently entered the discussion saying, "I don't think that it's ever right to objectify a woman," Steven got a twinkle in his eye. There was only a slight raise in his tone on one or two words as he calmly replied. "A woman's body is often meant to be artistic and inspiring. A woman's body being revealed does not have to be just to sell a product or disempower her. It's the aesthetic nature of her body that brings men pleasure and keeps the world a beautiful place."

I knew Steven liked to play the devil's advocate, but he had spoken with such certainty and from such a potentially adult perspective that Wendy began to blush a deep red. She lowered her head and couldn't find a response. There was a momentary silence of awkwardness while each student grappled with Steven's position. Wendy's friend, Lisa, wanted to jump in, but each time a thought occurred to her she couldn't follow it through. The students who were regularly silent in class watched and listened but didn't dare to engage with their ideas.

After about ten more minutes of discussion, I turned the inner circle of students' attention to the rest of the class. I asked the 45 students to share what they had recorded. The students who had been timing each inner circle student's talking time shared the facts of their observations. Both Phil and Steven had spoken the longest. The student who had interrupted the most was Phil.

We discussed, as a class, what we had observed about whether or not the inner circle had made eye contact with one another or had looked down or around, and if they had directly responded to one another's points. We looked at how leadership changed, and we established the general body languages of the students, when they had leaned in or sat back, when they spoke, and how they had positioned themselves to listen. We also examined the content of their discussion, what their sources were, and their tones of voice.

To my delight, Phil and Steven were both comfortable with the spotlight and the feedback. I encouraged them to make room for their classmates. I mentioned Gloria Steinem and how she and other feminist writers have written about men being encouraged to discuss weighty political matters and to knock one another down in a one-upmanship way.

I then turned their attention to the interaction between Steven and Wendy.

"Wendy," I said. "Did you feel comfortable with Steven's idea that it's okay to objectify women as long as they are art that pleases men and makes the world more beautiful?"

Wendy was quiet. "Does it sound right to you?" I asked again. "Does it resonate with you?" She shook her head, but she was still uncertain. I then shared that the writers found that women are taught the exact opposite, to listen and encourage and get along, rather than to disagree and challenge, to put others first rather than themselves. If I knew then what I know now, I would have offered her words to say instead such as, "I don't have a response for you right now, but I also do not believe that I agree with what you have just said. Can you hold on to your point so I can research it some more and we can revisit it when I've had time to think it through?"

Walter Parker's (2002) version of a Socratic Seminar in *Teaching Democracy*, which I read this past year, would also have been a useful classroom model for identifying powerful underlying classroom dynamics. He would most likely identify Steven's didactic approach towards Wendy as not recognizing Wendy as an insider who has and should be permitted "epistemic privilege" where the topic of women is concerned (p. 89). Parker (2002) believes that outsiders have to be able to recognize when they have either committed or condoned discrimination (p. 90). Parker continues his societal model of power dynamics by defining Azizah Y. Al-Hibri's (1999) "the inessential other" as the minority who is "allowed into the discussion only through the voice and perceptions of the dominant 'I'" (Parker, 2002, p. 91). By speaking with authority, Steven did not recognize that he had silenced the exact person who could have helped him understand a woman's perspective. If he had begun by assuming her knowledge and asking her why she felt as she did, he would have gained ground, respect, and insider knowledge that might have shaped his understanding. Then, if he still wanted to present and examine his ideas about women and art, he could have considerately posed it as a question to be discussed by the group.

Parker's (2002) primary objective is to invite students into switching "loyalties from justifying positions and defending ground to listening intently, seeking understanding, and expressing ideas that are undeveloped and 'in progress'" (p. 129). As Freire (2004) states, the educator "is bearing witness to the educands as to how he or she studies, 'approaches,' or draws near a given subject, how he or she thinks critically" (p. 103). If my students had witnessed me sorting through various viewpoints and perspectives before landing on my own, I would have been a better model for them as a reader of discourses that construct my own meaning-making and identifying processes. Freire (2004) encourages me to see that I needed to structure my classroom in such a way that students could not only track my process of coming to knowledge but could put the process into practice for themselves.

Learning to listen across difference (Ellsworth, 2005) paves the way for mutual respect and social justice. Learning to listen and to respectfully challenge one another's ideas provides space for varied readings of the world (Freire, 1970b). Listening well opens doors for deeper levels of communication and deeper abilities to appreciate the diverse circumstances and thought processes that each of us has. Listening well invites students to be, as Susan Florio-Ruane (2001) writes, travelers "who have long been aware that cultural understanding involves making sense of the means by which others make meaning" (p. 27).

Parker (2002) states that Socratic Seminars offer a host of competencies: listening as well as talking, striving to understand points of view that are different from one's own, challenging ideas and proposals rather than persons, admitting ignorance, slowing the rush to decision so as to clarify or reframe the problem or gather more information, courageously asserting unpopular views, supporting claims with reasoning, drawing analogies, encouraging others to participate, noticing and seeking missing perspectives and arguments, even appreciating Voltaire's "I disapprove of what you say, but I will defend to the death your right to say it" (p. 88).

I would have loved to have worked more directly with my students to reposition themselves as makers of meaning who need the collective feedback of others in order to recognize and live their values and beliefs (Yagelski, 2000). We came closer to understanding a question I now value: "What is the lens through which I am reading and how did it come to be?" (Freire, 2004).

With the help of these theorists, I now see that being a teacher does not mean I have the knowledge my students need. As Freire (2004) writes, "educators who feel that they 'possess' content, hold it as their property—regardless of whether they have had a share in its selection—since they possess the methods by which they manipulate the object, they will necessarily manipulate the educands as well" (p. 96). In order to become a "progressive educator," I need to bring out the fact that there are other "'readings of the world,'" different from mine "and at times antagonistic to" my ideas (Freire, 2004, p. 96). I need to learn and appreciate what my students know and want and need to know (Comber, Thomson, & Wells, 2001; Freire, 1970b, 2004). I need to understand that it is not my task to teach and liberate my students. Instead, by learning from them what meanings they have come to make about their communities and the possibilities or lack of possibilities for their identities within those communities, I will be able to provide opportunities for them to read and write and deliberate with specific actions and goals for civic participation in mind (Freire, 1970b, 2004; Parker, 2002). Only then will I be able to be a part of unveiling "opportunities for hope, no matter what the obstacles may be" (Freire, 2004, p. 3). Only then will students be able to process alongside classmates such as Kate and Wendy the mental and physical silencing women have experienced.

My Silencing as a Female and a Teacher

Yes, I am an idealist again, but September 11, 2001 and Kate's story were the tipping points to a number of questions that had begun to emerge the longer I taught. Before I knew it I was grasping at straws, desperate to find my own hope as a person and as an educator. I headed into my last of five summers of graduate school eager to brainstorm with other teachers in my Master's program how to establish an after-school theater program which would help students share their process of finding their voice in the midst of confusing social, economic, political, and cultural influences (Hackman, 2005). I was eager to go to bat for Kate and to head off other date or gang rapes through drama.

I was so busy planning a way to save my male and female students from being raped that I hardly noticed I had stopped sleeping. To intensify matters, I entered my fifth year of teaching to find that due to a lower budget, and even though I had been promised smaller class sizes if I taught Humanities, with two classes combined, my class sizes were huge: 55 and 44 students in each section. It was getting harder and harder to get to students and their needs. I would lie awake at night for hours, wondering how they were receiving my teaching, if I was taking them too deeply into already heavy literature.

My department head came to the rescue and offered feedback here and there, but I just kept finding new questions about teaching. How was I to respectfully address and teach the language difference of African American language that my students experienced and playfully imitated while reading Zora Neale Hurston's *Their Eyes Were Watching God*? How could I help my students want to take responsibility for broken race and gender relationships in our country? Was I completely out of line to bring up pornography in the context of Charlotte Perkins Gilman's *The Yellow Wallpaper* as a parallel way that women are kept in a cage in today's society? How could I keep such a conversation balanced and how could I introduce the topic without completely embarrassing the students? Was I becoming an ultra-radical feminist? How on earth could I get the kids to read the actual book instead of Internet cliff notes and then to write without plagiarizing? How lenient or stringent did I need to be where grading was concerned? How could I build in time for the students to experiment with their drafts when I couldn't grade that many that quickly and keep new assignments coming?

By the end of the first semester, if I was fortunate enough to fall asleep, I would awake a short time later to terrible nightmares and horrifying panic attacks. When an angry student cussed me out one day, sleep no longer became an option. After crawling my way through to the end of the semester grades, I drove myself to school one last time. Shaking from head to foot, I told my teaching partner I was leaving and I did not know if I would ever come back.

Me First This Time

Most likely, Kate's gang rape touched on a growing fear of mine that my life and my work no longer belonged to me. As I struggled to relearn how to sleep, I realized that in the months leading up to my last day, I had been going through the motions of teaching and celebrating students but that I could no longer feel my own life or fully enjoy them.

Even when I returned to the classroom a month later, I would marvel that I was so thoroughly numb and yet so capable of going into automatic mode so that my students could hardly see my chronic fatigue. I had become so immersed in their lives, so ready to respond to everyone else's needs, that I ceased to fully exist. Where had I gone, and why had I left myself, I began to wonder. How had I gotten so good at pleasing everyone but myself?

An interesting phenomenon began to surface as I faced the truth of my physical powerlessness. I simply could not run hundreds of photocopies to keep students focused and on task and to answer the many writing questions that, as one person, I could not answer for all of them. I simply could not grade numerous writing assignments as I had before. I simply could not be on my feet for a seven-hour day. I simply could not facilitate 55-person debates and discussions. The only answer was to step back and let them do the bulk of the work.

As I had to put my own physical and mental needs first, and because I was in total survival mode, I stopped caring so much about what I was doing, and I started to listen and to observe more. I continued to implement group activities in response to the texts, but in order to keep them on task there would be a project or presentation or essential discovery for them to achieve together. Then, instead of focusing on keeping them on task, I would sit in the vicinity of one or more groups and watch them work. Because I had let go of the reins more than ever before, I even began to laugh more often with them over silly conversations. The more I stopped to just enjoy them for who they were, the more naturally I could link our reading to their lives and the more they took charge of their own learning. I realized that I had to learn how they learned, what their world entailed, what they were reaching for with their lives. As I got to know them, and as I let them know me a little more, I could hear their questions, recognize their journeys, and hear where they needed encouragement or inspiration.

One More Time, Why Critical Literacy?

Without a doubt, multicultural education and critical literacy need to be in place in all schools. Without knowledge of the sources of each of our beliefs, we fall prey to conscious and unconscious racism, sexism, and classism. Our misunderstandings and our unexamined actions can be deadly where our children are concerned. They are at risk for inheriting identities that do not serve them or others well. Emotional and physical violence against students penetrates every community. Becoming critically literate in our own assumptions, prejudices, actions, and misunderstandings is a way to pass on personal empowerment and agency to our children so that they can begin to protect themselves.

If teachers embraced critical literacy, when students encountered repeated story-lines and images in the media about the sexual and physical violation of women, they would be able to deconstruct the hidden messages there, the various representations of relationships between men and women and the potential reification of men as predators and women as objects to be preyed upon. They would begin to develop a critical frame, repeatedly asking themselves questions such as: Who is producing this show? Who is the audience? How are the characters being constructed? What representations of crime, criminals, victims or of relationships are being created? Why those representations and not others? What are the sources of these representations? What is being marketed and why?

Without critical literacy as a given in the history of our schools, is it any wonder that teachers too, an increasing majority female, and their intellect and passions are often silenced as they become conditioned to follow standardized curricula, to please state standards via scripted curricula instead of advocating for themselves, their own emotional, physical, and mental intellect and for their students? Is it any wonder that teachers remain isolated, often unable to collaboratively explore what would most equip them and their students for the world as, under No Child Left Behind, whole school districts become immobilized by fear of not making annual yearly progress, of losing federal funding and residents, of being shut down? Large class sizes, low teacher pay, societal inequalities, student language and cultural differences, a creative and entrepreneurial job market, new multimodal forms of communication, exciting student literacies, student purposes for reading and writing, all take a back seat as a one-size-fits-all, intellectually vapid education geared towards a one-yearly test continues to veer towards obsession with one form of performance (Willis, 1997).

Why do we live in a society that emphasizes harmful story-lines about gendered, racial, class, and sex roles for men and women? Why do we let that happen? Why are we tying the hands of our teachers with crippling policies for high test scores at all costs? If we do not leave room for teachers and schools to address the real world issues their students are already struggling with and will continue to struggle with for life, then what good are we to students? If we do not offer teachers across disciplines the opportunity to work together and to build collegial communities of practice (Cochran-Smith & Lytle, 2001), then in their isolation, prescribed curricula, and exorbitant class sizes, the good ones will continue to burn out. Too infrequently, we are neither listening to teachers nor students; we are not taking the time to take people and societal needs seriously.

Do we want to empower our students to become critically literate about how their world may be silencing them or punishing them for speaking their true minds? Do we want to empower our students to be able to discern the impact of public representations of harmful stereotypes on their interpersonal relationships? Or, like Torvald, do we want to keep trying to measure up to someone else's test or standard? Do we want to raise thinking and caring citizens who will advocate for themselves and others or individuals looking out for their own success, no matter what the personal cost? Our children reflect the practices and attitudes of adults in their world. Until adults and youth come together to stop and to understand the sea in which we are all swimming, the real needs and spirits of our children will be silenced.

Thanks to the collective wisdom of LSJTRG, I now have multiple models for who women can be in the world and what people who come together can do. It is time for teachers, parents, and citizens to join together on behalf of a relevant educational experience for our children, one that helps them understand and safely navigate their world. It is time for us to take sexual, intellectual, emotional, and physical violence against women and men seriously, to face it head-on, and to chip away at building curricula that address gender inequalities in a way that creates spaces for students to recognize how they have been positioned and constructed for marketing purposes. Only then will there be justice for young women like Kate. Only then will men and women stop to reflect on how they are seeing and enacting prescribed gender roles. Only then will missing voices find their way to the center of curricula. The battle ahead is risky, but not as risky as losing our children to teaching that does not do justice to their real lives, their real needs, and their real world.

Rethinking Practice

What are the multiple positions you occupy as a teacher? Make a list of all of the various positions you occupy—including race, class, age, occupation, gender, sexual orientation, language background, history with schooling, and so on. Which of these positions are privileged or hold "high status" in this society? Which are considered "low status" in this society? Why? How do you know? Share with other teachers. What did you discover? How is your teaching stance determined by your multiple positionalities? How does this intersect with your students' positionalities? Try this with the students in your classroom.

6 "No Disrespect"

Literature Discussion as Social Action in the Adult Education Classroom

Carolyn Fuller

In October 2007, teachers in Tokyo, Japan and San Francisco, California, USA gathered to protest the repression of anti-war teachers in Japan. Article 9 of the Japanese constitution is a "no war" clause that went into effect in 1947, immediately after World War II. The article prohibits Japan from developing a militarized society and educational system. Over 1,500 teachers were suspended or reprimanded for their refusal to sing a nationalistic, military song in classrooms and for demonstrating opposition to the militarization of schools. Once suspended, the teachers returned to school and demonstrated outside of the school building, explaining to students why they took action in the name of Japan's long history of opposition to war. Educators in San Francisco, in support of the teachers in Japan, gathered to defend the rights of freedom of speech and freedom of conscience.

Introduction

Sister Souljah is a black feminist, rap artist, and author of the book *No Disrespect*. Her semi-autobiography talks about her struggles and triumph to overcome negative stereotypes that have plagued African American people since the first slave ships landed. Her book employs African American people to become proactive and to find solutions for brainwashing and negative conditioning that confronts the majority of low-income African Americans locked into the cycle of pervasive poverty and disenfranchisement.

As an African American female educator, I had to consider many factors in deciding the various types of reading materials to present to my students. I would love for my students to understand Hemingway or Faulkner, Dunbar or Chestnutt. However, these writings are very foreign to many minority and low-income individuals who see no sense of connection. I see my role as supporting students as they arrive at new perspectives. My literacy curriculum is primarily literature- and text-based. I therefore choose culturally relevant readings. It is imperative that teachers consider the population when they are devising their literacy curriculum to help move disenfranchised people forward. I take an explicit and ethical stance on my social responsibility as a teacher and believe that as teachers, we need to support students as they develop and accelerate as readers and writers, but at the same time we need to encourage life skills.

I cannot recall how I came to read Sister Souljah's book *No Disrespect*. I do not remember if I stumbled by chance on this powerful piece of writing or if it was given to me to read. It really does not matter how I came to read the book, but what is more important is the indelible impression it left on me as an African American female and an educator. I see many similarities in Sister Souljah's background and the backgrounds of many African American women, including myself. Sister Souljah is deeply concerned with issues of black women's oppression and offers important perspectives on urban contemporary culture. Sister Souljah's book provides a mirror by which one can view and understand one's past mistakes and reshape the future by taking corrective action.

In this chapter, I draw on data collected in my classroom over a two-year period of time and reflect on my journey of designing culturally relevant learning spaces for students in my adult education classroom, using my own experiences and those of other educator/activists. I also examine the social conditions that create a need for the use of counter-narratives and mechanisms that aid marginalized individuals to succeed in life. Finally, I share how I have incorporated activism and advocacy into my curriculum—an important aspect of teaching within a social justice framework.

Old-fashioned "Home Training"

My mother would say Sister Souljah is advocating for old-fashioned "home training." In my upbringing, I can often remember my mother saying, "You have to act as if you have some 'home training,' when you go out in public and to school." I did not understand what she meant by this phrasing and I would question her about the use of this term. My mother would explain that "home training" means proper upbringing, refinement, educational attainment, and respect. My great-grandmother, who was born during the Reconstruction period following the Civil War, raised my mother, who is now 80 years old. Her great-grandmother used the term "home training." She could look at children who were misbehaving, acting unsophisticated, and say they have no "home training."

After the abolition of slavery, many African Americans migrated to the North. During this time they transmitted values passed down from traditional African families. While slavery broke down the traditional African family structure, African Americans were able to re-establish rules and morals that were unique to African American culture. In this value system the mother and father established certain rules of etiquette, proper behavior, and respect. These attributes reflected that the individual had proper upbringing or "home training." This home training was meant to counteract negative stereotypes created after slavery and to portray African Americans as being uncivilized and in need of guidance. Hollywood aided this stereotype by portraying African Americans as childlike. In many early movies of the 1930s and 1940s African Americans were portrayed as illiterate, foolish, and unsophisticated. After the Civil Rights Movement African Americans were no longer portrayed as childlike, but as unsophisticated buffoons and social degenerates with no "home training."

In Sister Souljah's book *No Disrespect*, Souljah is attempting to counteract these negative images embedded in the psyches of many African American people. Set in a contemporary context, her writing conveys a message of affirmation, respect, and appropriate behavior to many young people who were themselves raised by young people and never encountered this notion of "home training." She emphasizes self-respect, respect for education, and respect for African American culture. Individuals or students who lack "home training" will encounter difficulty in a society that judges individuals on how they conduct themselves. In one excerpt from her book Sister Souljah discusses respect and society's view. She writes:

> Our lives, beliefs, values, and rules were deeply rooted and clearly understood and respected by our communities. We celebrated life and encouraged and loved one another. We had strong families, schools, organizations, and nations.
>
> (Souljah, 1996, pp. xii)

A key aspect in Sister Souljah's writing reflects the significance of self-respect. Sister Souljah takes a critical look at the exploitation of African American females and sees her as the key to survival and architect of "home training" for her children as heads of households. Through her writing and activism, she emphasizes narratives of respect and empowerment. I do the same in my teaching and refer to it as "home training." Perry, Steele, and Hilliard (2003) refer to this same concept as "counter narratives." Perry et al. (2003) defined counternarratives as intentionally orchestrated and organized in opposition to the ideology of African American inferiority or lack of achievement. Counter-narratives affirm black humanity, black intelligence, and black achievement. Regardless of the name, all of these concepts mean the same thing: affirmation of African American values.

In my classroom, I weave the narratives of Souljah together with other powerful role models such as Frederick Douglas, W.E.B. Dubois, and Mary McCleod Bethune to help my adult education students create a social context by which they can see education as an important aspect of African American history. My instruction involves a two-prong approach; it allows students to study for their General Equivalency Diploma (GED), while promoting social activism at the same time. My goals for my students include obtainment of the GED, but I also believe that my role as a teacher includes teaching my students what I refer to as "life lessons" and how to be agents in their social worlds.

Context of the Adult Education Program

Before discussing the literacy experiences of the students in my adult education classroom, it is necessary to examine my background in order to determine how

I arrived at this juncture in my life. I am an African American female and was the primary teacher in the Adult Education and Literacy classroom. I do not have a history of participation with teacher education, nor am I a certified K-12 teacher. My background includes being a probation officer and working for the FBI. I have a Bachelor's degree in Criminal Justice and a Master's degree in Political Science.

I come from a background of humble circumstances. I was raised in a two-parent home. My father and mother migrated to St. Louis from Alabama, during the early migration of African Americans to the North in search of economic and educational opportunities. I cannot recall if my father could read or write, because his education never went beyond elementary school. My mother's education did not go beyond the tenth grade. However, in our household, education and literacy attainment were stressed. I can remember my father bringing my older sister books to read to my siblings and me. My sister would read to us at night, as we were preparing for bed. While my father was not an educated man he saw the importance of being literate and educated.

In addition to literacy being a part of my home experience, it also became a major part of my early school experience. I can remember always being singled out to read in class or being selected for major speaking parts in school theatrical productions. Even in our neighborhood, I was always selected to read. My mother was a member of a religious group called a "prayer band." Many members of the groups were my mother's age at the time and I was the only child sitting among adults reading the Bible. It later occurred to me that they used me to read the Bible to them. It was not until I was older that I realized they could not read and marveled at my abilities at nine years of age. Some of the women in the group suggested I become a teacher because of my reading and speaking skills.

Even though I possessed excellent reading and speaking skills, I never thought of becoming a teacher, I wanted to be a doctor or a lawyer. I went to college and started out as a biology major, and later switched to a major in criminal justice. It was not until sometime later in my life when I was in between jobs that I considered substitute teaching. During my first assignment, the principal of the school came to me at the end of a long-term assignment and said, "I'm going to recommend you for a permanent teaching position, because you are a natural." I was stunned by his response, because I had no formal training in education or practical experience. A similar situation occurred years later. After finding a job in my graduate major, I once again found myself in between jobs and someone suggested I apply with Adult Education and Literacy (AEL). I accepted a part-time assignment as an adult education instructor. I was in the position for three weeks when the Director of Adult Education called and offered me a full-time assignment at one of the large adult education and literacy classes held at King's Hall Family Support. These experiences have taught me that being an effective teacher is truly a "calling." I am on a path to make the most difference and to share the literacy practices I learned in my early childhood with other people.

The AEL classroom I was assigned to is in the basement of King's Hall Family Support Center. King's Hall is located in a high-poverty area of North St. Louis.

The area also has a high drop-out rate, and the majority of students enrolled in the program are considered "at risk." The majority of students in the classroom are African American, equally divided between males and females. There are numerous reasons the students cite for dropping out of school. Some are members of street gangs, others lack support systems to keep them involved in school, and others see no sense of connection between education and real-life events.

Literacy Experiences in my Classroom

In order to engage my students in the AEL classroom, I utilized many different types of literacy experiences such as silent reading, read alouds, interactive reading, rereads, writing, and discussions. I chose culturally relevant materials to stimulate critical discussions, and would encourage students to take action in their daily lives. Our society has become so diverse and technologically advanced that, as educators, we have to redesign our curriculum to meet the needs of the diverse literacies that students bring with them into our classrooms (Kellner, 2007). Throughout the literacy experiences in my classroom, I view my role as a guide or facilitator as students explore the critical social issues embedded in the texts we read. I provide whole group or individual mini-lessons on aspects of the reading or writing process.

Multiple Literacies

I used many different genres of texts in class—newspapers, speeches, literature, GED preparatory materials, and magazines. Speeches are one example of the many multiple literacies used by educators for teaching in the twenty-first century. I used Martin Luther King Jr.'s speech in class to analyze the content and the way in which the speech was delivered. For example, we looked at multiple speeches, not just the traditional "I Have a Dream" speech. We analyzed these speeches and talked about how African Americans have advanced our society. I used multiple literacies to develop the capacity of students to understand the monumental contribution Dr. King's speech had on reshaping social policy in the United States. Students were able to make the connection between the "I Have a Dream" speech and the creation of the Civil Rights Act of 1964 and the Voting Rights Act of 1965. In addition, students were able to see the connection between education, activism, and public policy. Multiple literacies are an essential component in engaging students in a multicultural perspective. Multiple literacies include many genres: media literacy, computer literacy, multimedia literacy, cultural literacy, and social literacy.

Whole Class Read Alouds

In reading aloud to the students I model the various aspects of the reading process and create a context whereby the students can have a chance to experience the literature. Many adult education students exhibit better comprehension of texts when they are read aloud than when they read the texts silently. Thus, listening to literature read aloud allows them the opportunity to expand their critical literacy skills. It also allows them the opportunity to hear fluent reading—reading with intonation and expressions. Often, adults have good comprehension skills but are not developed in their decoding and problem-solving strategies.

For many of my students this is the first chance they have had to see themselves in the text. I also think it is important to engage my male students in a feminist book. I invite them into the discussion and debate about life choices and structural conditions of men and women. I am linking the struggle of men and women of color as a common struggle—and teaching implicitly that feminism is a set of issues and actions relevant in the lives of men as well as women. I do this by making sure all voices in the classroom are heard. I ask my students to identify roles in the literature they read which they might then transfer to their own lives. It is what Oprah Winfrey would call an "Ah-ha" moment. The students see the connection between events taking place in the book and their own lives. If the character can move out of the circumstance, then they can do it too.

Book Introductions and Reading

I also encourage silent reading and shared reading in my classroom. Before I ask students to read silently, I provide them with a book or text introduction to debug the text they are about to read. A book introduction prepares students for the materials they are about to read and allows the instructor to create a context for the reader and to build prior background knowledge (e.g. Clay, 1993). Often, adult educators do not realize the power of book introductions to help students successfully problem-solve as they are reading the text. Sometimes I introduce a section of the book and then provide an ongoing book introduction as the students read. Other times I will provide a lighter book introduction when I think the reading material is familiar.

The following is a book introduction I used with a small group of students who were about to read a chapter from a book on the African Americans and their struggle for equality. Pamela struggled with the subject matter owing to limited prior knowledge. During my meeting with Pamela, I set the stage for the reading by previewing the Civil Rights Movement. I began the book introduction by explaining to Pamela that the 1950s and 1960s were an era of transition. During the Civil Rights Movement, millions of African Americans rallied in support of previously denied human rights and we made significant progress in the arena of social change. I countered the idea often presented in literature, that individuals worked alone to change unjust policies. I introduced the concept of organizing. At the same time, I introduced strategies for problem-solving multi-syllabic words, which had caused Ladonna problems in past readings. Throughout the introduction, I built on her prior knowledge and asked her open-ended critical questions such as: Why do you think the author represented Rosa Parks in that way? What would be another way of representing her? Who has power in this illustration? What do you think will happen next?

After the book introduction, the students read silently at their tables. I asked them to monitor their comprehension as they were reading and to ask themselves if the reading "made sense" to them after a few paragraphs. Other times, I might ask two students to share the responsibility of reading a text. Shared reading allows for peer review and allows students to share their ideas with a partner. It also allows students to re-evaluate the text and make connections between the texts and their lives. Ladson-Billings (1994) indicates that how each of us understands texts and language is grounded in our cultural, social, and historical backgrounds. In other words, educators have to capitalize on the realities brought by students into the learning environment.

Book Clubs

The book club concept, a common K-12 strategy, allows students to interact using oral and written language to construct meaning about what they have read. It includes the components of reading, writing a response to the reading, dialoguing about the book in a small group, and then sharing the small group's discussions during "community share" (Raphael, Florio-Ruane, & George, 2001). Many students in the class are familiar with the book club format from the Oprah Winfrey show but have never participated in one.

I learned about how book clubs could be used in the classroom through the LSJTRG. I chose to use the book *No Disrespect* in the book club format as an alternative framework for reading instruction and to explore this issue of counter-narratives. *No Disrespect* provides the students with a complex array of narratives of African American life and counter-narratives. *No Disrespect* is a book that the students in the GED classroom have read continuously. Sometimes I copy chapters for students to read, and at other times I read aloud from the book as the students listen. The following is an example of a discussion that occurred during the dialogue portion of the book club.

CAROLYN: [Reads aloud] Okay, you think you too good, these women have accepted the condition of the projects. They see men as rentals. When a woman got her teeth knocked out by the man she was sexing, they would tell her why she got her butt kicked and they would start sleeping with the same man.

After reading, I question the students about the motives of the character in the book. The students provide different commentaries about the character's motive.

CAROLYN: [Reads aloud] The services provided were made to make us feel inferior. We would wait all day to receive a tub of peanut butter.... [Student: That's true!] The basic assumption of welfare is that because you were on it, you had the time. What is she saying? It is a catch 22. Because on the one hand they want you to be honest and tell them but once you do get a job, you make $7.50 an hour.

This book club conversation was intended to demonstrate the inequity of the welfare system and how it creates a culture of dependence. While analyzing the text, students start to connect learning with real-life situations. I ask critical questions that demand the students articulate their taken-for-granted assumptions. From the dialogue, the students start to connect the dots about the socio-economic realities of their lives. The students think critically and become conscious of societal issues that impact their lives.

Rereads

Many adult educators do not think about the importance of rereading in the adult education classroom. I share with my students that, as a reader, I often reread if I have stepped away from a text for too long and need to refresh my memory, for pleasure (because I really liked a book), or if I did not understand the passage. Lipson and Wixson (2003) indicate that the point of repeated reading is simply to persuade and induce the reader to read a particular text several times so that he or she can improve fluency through increased familiarity. From my experience there is a correlation between fluency and the comprehension of the reader. For students who can read the text but may have comprehension or fluency difficulties, they gain multiple opportunities to make connections. The student population constantly changes in the classroom, so there may be people in the classroom who have heard sections of the book before, and they take pleasure in knowing a story that is familiar. The reread passages serve as anchors for discussion in the classroom community.

Current Events

I bring political issues and current events from around the world into my classroom teaching during my "current events" time in the morning or during the social studies part of the day. One of my goals is to make the political process and workings of the system transparent for my students. I discuss critical social issues that directly impact the communities where my students live and work. These issues include gay marriage, nightclubs burning down, federal policies, the war in Iraq, drugs and prison, Hurricane Katrina, and the significance of voting.

I actively encourage students to vote and participate in the political process. They often say they do not feel that their vote will make any difference. I remind them of the historical significance of voting rights. I remind them further of the sacrifice many African Americans made to ensure the right to vote. Along with the discussion about current events, they also read an article each day that relates to current events, one that that will connect to their lives and stimulate discussion. For example, one morning I chose an article on the controversy surrounding a local homeless shelter. The students debated whether or not homeless shelters should exist or whether people should go out and get jobs. The discussion continued for about half an hour and then I asked the students to write down their thoughts. Sometimes the students resist this type of reading, discussion, and writing because it does not remind them of what school should look and sound like. I will often remind my students that the GED is a reading test and there are lots of current event materials on the test.

In the adult education classroom there are many different perspectives and background experiences. Conflicting perspectives create a climate for lively debate. The debates allow individuals to voice their different views and see the big picture. In order to analyze, synthesize, and evaluate the reading it is necessary to see the big picture, develop essential questions, and create meaning from the text and their worlds.

Writing Practices

I teach writing in the classroom through a variety of means. I use several pre-writing activities to teach students the organization structure of essays. One of these pre-writing activities asks students to consider multiple perspectives on a topic, drawing on images that represent a critical social issue or a current event—a form of critical literacy. For example, I displayed a picture of Saddam Hussein in 2003 when he was discovered by the U.S. military hiding in an underground bunker. I asked the students to think about the picture. Why did the publisher decide to use this photo? From what was Hussein hiding? What are the implications of Saddam Hussein hiding in such a small hole in the ground? Then, I might provide students with the topic sentence of a paragraph and ask them to complete the remainder of the paragraph; for example, "Saddam Hussein was the dictator of Iraq, before the U.S.-led invasion." The students engage in a discussion on the military invasion and then complete the rest of the paragraph.

Another pre-writing activity I have used is the quick-write. Students are given a topic and instructed to jot down ideas and thoughts about the topic for two minutes. Students then write about the topic for two minutes and share their thoughts with the other members of the class. Prompts include questions that invite different perspectives that draw on the students' knowledge and experience, such as, "What qualities does a good leader possess?" Each student writes down his or her thoughts about leadership qualities. I ask each student to

Photo 6.1 Carolyn Fuller provides a timeline of events leading up to the Iraq War.

share an example of what he or she has listed on paper. As the students are talking, I write their ideas on the board. I then ask the students to formulate the main idea and provide supporting details to support the main idea. At other times, I ask the students to come up with their own topic and write down a main idea and supporting details. Another technique places students in groups where the same process occurs. Students write down their thoughts about the topic and then exchange it with the other group members. This activity allows students to discuss the topic and activate prior knowledge from each group member. Then, the group together composes a product of finished writing that again brings together multiple perspectives.

In these writing activities, I make the student's knowledge an official part of the classroom curriculum. I often do a mini-lesson on mechanics such as the use of punctuation (e.g. semicolons and colons) or spelling patterns (e.g. the "tion" affix) and give the students time to revise their writings based on the discussion before they get feedback from me. I always privilege their ideas before mechanics during writing time.

Many of the adult education students have limited exposure to formal essay writing. The techniques indicated above were a struggle for many students who had dropped out of school in junior high and never encountered formal essay writing. One student who I will call Ladonna made great progress using the techniques indicated above. When Ladonna first entered the GED program, the Test for Adult Basic Education (TABE) revealed a writing level of 4.0 and a reading level of 5.9. Ladonna had little experience writing in high school; she became frustrated when writing and would give up easily. Ladonna's writing was interesting to me as an educator, because she had excellent oral communication skills. Up to this point, many of the students I observed who had excellent communication skills also had very good writing skills. After studying Ladonna, I learned that she was an auditory learner. In other words, she had developed sophisticated listening skills and conveyed herself verbally without difficulty. I asked Ladonna to start off her writing by expressing herself verbally. I then asked her to go step by step and write down her thoughts in her log. She then organized each sentence into a paragraph that flowed logically. Ladonna's first GED practice test in writing was 380 and her score was raised to 450 in the span of one year.

Encouraging Activism and Advocacy

As an adult educator committed to teaching for social justice, I think moving from the classroom to real-world advocacy and activism is important for adult education students. During the spring of 2005, several of my students and I (along with students from many other adult education sites in the metro-St. Louis region) participated in a leadership academy in St. Louis led by VALUE (see also Beaman-Jones, Chapter 14). During the leadership academy students participated in a problem-posing, problem-solving workshop which helped them to learn how to effectively advocate for change and how to speak on issues that directly impact change in society. In addition to formal training such as the VALUE leadership academy, I also promote advocacy among my students in my classroom. When Sister Souljah came to St. Louis to give a talk, I encouraged students to attend the talk. Several students went to the talk and asked Souljah to sign their copy of her book after the presentation. I also invited a professor of political science to come to the classroom and talk with my students about their rights as voters and participating in the political process. In addition to voting, I also encourage my students to get involved in politics at the community level by regularly bringing current political events into the classroom.

In terms of my own activism, I am a member of LSJTRG. I value the work of this community of educators because it encourages people to see multiple perspectives on educational issues. The group also provides members with opportunities to engage with issues such as diversity, curriculum development, and multicultural perspectives, particularly in relation to literacy education. I think it is important for those working with children and youth to have the opportunity to dialogue with educators working with adults because many of the issues around literacy and social justice are similar. I can think of many times during a LSJTRG meeting when an adult education teacher learned about a literacy strategy from a K-12 teacher and when an adult education teacher educated K-12 teachers about the complexity of learning for adults.

One such example was when we read Sister Souljah's book *No Disrespect* together as a group because I was using it in my classroom. During the same time, another group member, Melissa, shared how she was using book clubs in her second grade classroom. After I learned about the book club process—reading, journaling about the reading, dialoguing about the reading, and then sharing ideas with the whole group during community share—I tried out the book club process in my own classroom. There is always a synergy of ideas that emerges when educators who work at various levels come together to build understandings of literacy learning across the lifespan.

Over the years of participating in LSJTRG, I have noticed many parallels between my teaching and the process of professional development in LSJTRG. LSJTRG attempts to meet teachers where they are—just as I try to meet the adults in my classroom where they are. Just as I expect the adults in my classes to transfer their learning and literacy to real-world contexts, teachers in LSJTRG transfer their professional development into classroom and community actions. Finally, in both contexts it is important that teachers continue to see themselves as learners alongside their students and to view themselves as lifelong learners.

In reflection, my experience in education has been different than the typical experience. In education you are taught theory first and then practically apply the theories that you have been taught. However, I engaged in the practical experience first and backed into the theory. I am now learning the terminology of practices that made sense to me. Sometimes I wonder if I should have gone into education early in my career, but as I indicated previously, I did not set out to be a teacher. Teaching chose me. Regardless of how I arrived at this juncture, it has been the most rewarding of all the experiences I have engaged in. Dialogue and exposure to ideas from my sister, schoolteachers, work experiences, and LSJTRG continue to transform me into the most effective teacher that I can become.

Rethinking Practice

Think about your own classroom. What are the purposes and goals for the literature you use in your classroom? What diversity exists in your classroom? How can literature be used as both a "window and a mirror" for students to see themselves and others' experiences in the curriculum?

Select three books that you think might be culturally relevant for your students. What, specifically, makes these books culturally relevant? Does one need to be an insider to the culture to use this book? What other information do you need? What are the possibilities and responsibilities for adult education teachers who are committed about teaching within a culturally relevant framework?

7 Response Chapter—Developing Critical Stances and Multiple Perspectives

Bridgette Jenkins, Mary Ann Kramer,
Meredith Labadie, Melissa Mosley, Kathryn Pole,
and Ben Yavitz

The chapters in this section of the book provide a window into how, in using the tools of literacy education, educators construct socially just learning communities. While we can see various aspects of the critical literacy framework woven throughout the chapters, we want to reflect more deeply on the dimension of "Critical Stances and Multiple Perspectives" in our discussion of this first section of the book. The educators who we hear from in this section reflect a process of developing critical stances and multiple perspectives as they take up important social issues in educational spaces. We hear how the tools of this dimension of the critical literacy framework are woven through each educator's practice: reading widely and deeply, making local–global connections, placing information in a historical context, seeking out multiple, non-dominant perspectives, and seeking out the relationships between sources.

Melissa, Rebecca, Sarah, and Carolyn noticed and named the intricacies of teaching for social justice in their classrooms. Melissa (Chapter 3) described a project in which second graders explored ideas about freedom and war during the U.S. invasion of Iraq through a study of Japanese Internment. Rebecca (Chapter 4) used writing with her fifth graders to create a culturally relevant classroom, examining the discourses in students' writing and scaffolding their use of writing as a reflective tool. Sarah (Chapter 5) wrote her way through the experience of her last year of teaching, finding that her need to step back provided a space for her students to take a more active role in constructing knowledge. Finally, Carolyn revealed in Chapter 6 the use of culturally relevant practices to help students to see reading as a powerful practice.

Also in these chapters, we see the importance of reflection as a tool for educators to build critical literacy practices. We get a sense that each teacher is using a mirror to look back at who she was within the classroom and view the moments, decisions, and interactions with a new perspective. They were looking behind them as a way to keep walking forward: reflecting on where they have been, the choices made, and the process of becoming a critical educator. As social justice educators, we constantly reflect on what happened in the classroom, our effectiveness as educators, and how our work impacts the lives of our students and society. These reflections happen in the car or bus ride to work, in the moments after a lesson is completed, or in the middle of the night when a worry awakens us. However, every once in a while we take the time to write down our reflections, and to describe how it is that we learned what we learned. The chapters in this section exemplify teacher researchers using the word to write their world, to articulate the process of developing a stance as a critical educator (Freire, 1970b).

We met together in late December at the literacy center that serves the adult community in St. Louis to discuss these chapters. Each discussant had previously read and taken notes on each chapter. We considered questions such as, "How do you see critical literacy defined and practiced in this chapter?" and, "What strategies and resources do each of the teachers use to teach for social justice?" Part of our praxis-oriented methodology was that the process of writing this book would, itself, be an act of building solidarity. Through the space of writing, revising, editing, reading, and sharing we would engage in reflecting, critiquing, affirming, challenging, and ultimately transforming our roles within educational spaces. In turn we were changing the spaces themselves. Kathryn (teacher educator) and Meredith (elementary teacher), who were both unable to attend, sent their thoughts to the group. Ben, Bridgette, Melissa, and Mary Ann discussed the chapters. Bridgette, a university educator with a background in counseling and multicultural education, also provided a perspective as the parent of a student in the local school district. Ben, a second year elementary teacher with a

Photo 7.1 (from left to right) Mary Ann, Kathy, Melissa, Ben, Bridgette, and Meredith discussing the chapters in this section.

background of college activism and advocacy, was also present. Melissa, a university teacher educator and former elementary teacher, was both an author of a chapter and a member of the discussion group. Mary Ann, also introduced previously, is a coordinator of adult literacy education in St. Louis Public Schools. Just as the chapters in this section represents different points on the lifespan, so, too, do our responses.

Using Literacy as a Tool to Explore and Build Social Justice

Literacy teaching practices such as book clubs, literature study, readers' and writers' workshops, and historical research are dialogic teaching methods compatible with critical literacy practices. For example, within a book club, multiple readers respond to a single text, honoring the voices that together build more complex understandings. In examining voices from the past, a historical perspective helps to ground social problems and inequities. Each of the authors of the chapters we read drew on the literacy practices that worked for them in the classroom to build social justice in the classroom. Here, we explore how each author constructed critical literacy practices as they built critical stances with students.

Kathryn, a teacher educator in our response group, pointed out that each author drew on literature as the foundation for discussion. Reading books in order to build understandings is a critical literacy practice, as it encourages the reader to engage with a narrative written from a certain perspective. Melissa and Sarah, for example (Chapters 3 and 5), drew on literature that would take a global issue (e.g. war, violence) and allow students to see the impacts of that issue on groups of people in order to *address* social inequality in the classroom. In Carolyn's chapter, she demonstrated that her first goal was to choose literature that appealed to students, literature that reflected their lived experiences, provided new (i.e. feminist) perspectives, and also literature which inspired discussion of perseverance in an oppressive society. Carolyn's use of book introductions in Chapter 6 was a type of reading support designed to bring students into texts with complex plot structures, vocabulary, and historical context. In their reading and responses, peers in each classroom provided support for one another—support that allowed for understanding—in both elementary and adult education. The social justice topics in this section of the book include patriotism, peace, student expertise, gender relations, sexual violence, and politics. Teachers, when concerned about an event occurring in the world, sometimes bring that event into the classroom to explore ideas of equity, justice, and human rights. Other teachers address topics as they arise from their students in the belief that students' concerns ought to drive the curriculum.

Carolyn's and Melissa's chapters both illuminate how, through literature study, social issues can be contextualized in a historical context, an important dimension of critical literacy learning across the lifespan. Both authors held an insider perspective about the goals, beliefs, and understandings of one's students. In Carolyn's work, she was able to bring literature to the students that reflected what her mother called "home training," perhaps based on her experiences as an

African American in St. Louis, past and present. Similarly, Melissa, teaching in the working-class town where she grew up, relied on her knowledge of how families approach discussions of work, education, and war to plan her curriculum. Educators who share cultural knowledge with the students, what Moll and others have called "funds of knowledge" (Moll & Gonzales, 1994), are well positioned to bring current social problems into a context that includes the history of practices such as segregation in schools and society, and competition for wages in working-class towns. During our discussion, Bridgette commented that there was a tension still in this point:

> But even she [Carolyn] had a little dilemma, because she said that she'd like them to read particular books, but she didn't think that they would be able to relate to those works.... I think that she wanted to connect to them and use the material that they would relate to, but she wanted to also move them beyond that.... She was in both worlds. She was inside and she understood the community, but had seen a lot more of the world, so she had to work within their worldview at least initially.

Even though Carolyn had an insider perspective, she also faced practical challenges that come about when teachers attempt to draw on culturally relevant practices. Her ways of situating social problems in a historical context were complicated. Her identity as an African American woman in St. Louis was also mediated by her age and past experiences. Similarly, Melissa reflected on how it was when she went away to college and returned to the classroom where the discourses of patriotism and competition arose. Each teacher found conflicts between what is, and what could be, and how to move with students from one space to another when addressing social issues.

Students read and compare perspectives that relate to a theme as a critical literacy practice. In Melissa's chapter, students questioned the texts and each other while they analyzed the characters and situations presented in their books. Meredith wrote, "I do not believe that Melissa's students would have thought about the book as deeply without critical literacy nor would they have had the same level of comprehension in their reading." Multiple perspectives are presented in both texts and in the connections that people make with texts from their unique experiences and perspectives. Meredith continued,

> Further, using these literacy practices in conjunction with teaching for social justice can raise the level of what students are capable of. In Rebecca's chapter, she brought in her students' funds of knowledge by encouraging them to write about their own culture, families, and traditions.

By exploring one's own culture, ideas, and then putting them out to the rest of the community, the students in Rebecca's class (as well as in the other classrooms) were practicing another form of critical literacy, dialogicity. Dialogicity, a term from the philosophy of language, refers to the multiplicity of voices in social interactions (Bakhtin & Holquist, 1981). When literacy education brings multiple voices into conversation with one another, students are often able to understand that their ideas come from somewhere—the church, family, peer groups—and recognize how their voice differs from others. Mary Ann reiterated, in our group discussion, that the positionality of the teachers allowed them to help their students to realize this part of social justice teaching. In other words, the women's insider status with their students—Sarah's knowledge of violence in the community and Melissa's understanding of the economic and ideological positions of the community, for example—allowed them to lead students to understand the ways their positions were socially constructed. Melissa and Rebecca opened spaces for students to take up multiple perspectives, paying close attention to the ways that children's take-up of the perspectives were gendered. As Kathryn wrote of Sarah's chapter, "students were led to critically examine the roles and value of women in society, and to speak out in the face of violence and injustice." Carolyn's focus on advocacy and the examples she sets for her students is also a powerful standpoint.

Because of the dialogicity of social justice teaching, multiple voices that often disagree, come into the same space. Bridgette, with her background in psychology, referred to the dissonance that students often experience when learning about social issues. She cited Melissa's chapter, "Talking about War" (Chapter 3):

> They were having cognitive dissonance and they didn't know what to do with it. I wrote down a couple, like, "Can you love something and still be mad at it?" To put that out for the children. Like, "I love my mom but I'm mad at her sometimes." Or how the Japanese might have felt, because they loved America but they were mad at them for taking away their homes and putting them in these camps.

Bridgette points to the internal conflict that students often face when dealing with critical social issues, namely that there is no one right answer to some of our hardest questions. Bridgette continued,

> I was thinking of Freire's book—*Pedagogy of the Oppressed* (1970b). A lot of what he talks about is writing questions and dilemmas so the learner has to grapple with that. And I thought that putting that in a language that the children could understand would help move them along; that they could be guards, but not all guards are protecting people, you know, and move it along as much as possible developmentally.

Freire's idea of the unfinished person was that we are all in the process of becoming critical thinkers, but that an educational approach should include space for people to pose problems, rather than only solve them (1970b). When posing critical questions, the teacher's role is to model the thinking process, not to lead the students into one way of seeing the world. In Sarah's chapter, she was scaffolding students to enter into Socratic dialogues in which problems could surface as a way out of directing the class towards one viewpoint or another.

Critical stances and multiple perspectives are built when student voices become central in the conversation, and the students become the question-posers. Ben, in our small group meeting, reminded the group that students do hold the questions that are often central to social justice teaching. He referenced an event in his own sixth grade classroom:

> Kids are interested in these topics. I was reading Patrick Henry's "Give me Liberty or Give me Death." . . . And some kid shouted out, "I would die for that!" And he was being serious! I thought, "This is an African American kid. So we're talking about what might have been his ancestors' liberty." And I thought, "teachable moment time!" We moved from talking about multiple choice questions to talking about, "What would you die for?" in a sixth grade classroom. And I didn't even bring it up! I was ready to shift, which was good. But I can see parents wondering why I was talking to sixth graders about what they'd die for, but they brought it up.

Ben's story illuminates that the introduction of a key text and a space where students' voices were centered together created a dialogic event, an event where the students became central. In this event, the students were active in posing questions, rather than answering someone else's question. Similarly, in Melissa's chapter, Pamela, in an end-of-unit assessment, used her writing to raise more unanswered questions about the war, Japanese internment, and freedom. She wrote, "The Japanese people had to go to a camp. The Americans treated them like slaves. Why don't you think they will treat each other equally? Are they mad at each other? Can they stand up for themselves?" Here, Pamela illustrated that inquiry does not end at the end of the curricular unit, but that she is still considering the issues around internment.

Challenges to Our Use of Critical Literacy Practices

Meredith made a comment on "how naturally critical literacy and social justice can be woven into their literacy teaching" which points to an issue that is often brought up by teachers who want to teach critical literacy but are unsure of how to begin. Even after observing teachers skillfully teach critical literacy or after reading books and articles on the theories and methods of critical literacy, there is a hesitancy to try out critical literacy. We see in the chapters in this section that critical literacy does not always go as planned. In Melissa's chapter, the students did not always "side" with the Japanese Americans, because as Bridgette mentioned, there was dissonance between their patriotism and understanding of the functions of the guards at the prison camps. In Sarah's chapter, Steven interrupted a female student during Socratic Seminar, silencing the very person who could provide an insider's perspective on women's rights.

Often, in our readings, we hear success stories of critical literacy—children who develop social justice projects in their school or community, adolescents who challenge the myths around military recruitment, teachers who advocate for change in policies. Less often do we hear when things did not go so well—when the students were not interested, when there was not enough time to work on an action, when the topic upset a student, or when someone resisted critical literacy. These are the areas that teachers worry about and in our experience teaching critical literacy, but there is no way to avoid such experiences. Rather, you build up the confidence to know you can handle the situations when they come your way.

One of the places that often lends itself to questions or resistance is around time. How will I find the time to explore this social issue? How do I balance this with what the district tells me I need to do? We discussed how teaching the details of literacy can be integrated into critical literacy. For example, Meredith suggested inquiring into the places where guiding students as readers, writers, and spellers overlaps with the places where teachers guide their critical literacy. This issue is a constant thread through LSJTRG meetings—balancing the demands of time and the details of literacy instruction with critical literacy education. As Meredith pointed out in a workshop she conducted for LSJTRG called "Teaching for Social Justice in Reading and Writing Workshop," it is often more commonplace to integrate socially responsible literature into reading time (guided reading, literature circles, read aloud) than it is in a writer's workshop. She took this absence as an invitation to explore the ways she could use socially responsible mentor texts; for example, using *A Chair for my Mother* (Williams, 1984) to teach descriptive language in her writer's workshop.

Text Box 7.1 Meredith Labadie's Lesson Plan for Integrating Social Justice into a Writer's Workshop

Writing for Change Unit
Unit Goals:

*   Students understand how authors write with a viewpoint and message in mind.
*   Students explore ways in which writing can be used to affect change.
*   Students write purposefully and with a specific audience and goal in mind.
*   Students focus their writing and revise to add additional support for their ideas.
*   Students develop a sense of personal agency.

Introduce Students to Social Issues Texts:

*   Read aloud several social justice themed texts on a variety of issues. Discuss them together as a class. Have students begin to think about the author and why he or she would have written the book. Chart what the theme/author's message is for each text. Ask students to write down topics from their own lives that connect in some way to each book you read.
*   Begin to focus in on change. Read books where the characters work for change. For example, read the book *Grace For President* (Dipucchio & Pham, 2008). Discuss Grace's plan for the school and what she changes. Shift students' focus to what they would change in their own school (and home,

community, and world). Chart ideas of what students want to change and ask them to keep a list of their own ideas in their journals.

- Focus on the topic of whether or not children have the power to change things. Ask students to keep a journal about what they think and then discuss as a class. Brainstorm together ways children might be able to change things. Read several texts that have a child affecting change as the main character and chart how the characters change things. In particular note the ways *writing* is used for change.

Begin Writing for Change:

- Ask students to look back through their journal and then make a list of the top things they would most like to change.
- Ask students to brainstorm with their writing partners how they could use writing to change the things on their list (this is a perfect time for mini-lessons on how to choose what topics are most important to you, how to choose a writing genre, how to choose a specific audience, and how to support your writing partner).
- Conference with students and decide which writing project they will start first. Ask students to start their first writing for change project. Possible mini-lessons to get them started include: how to plan using a storyboard, how to make an outline/list of reasons for your argument, how to research a topic and write down what you learn in your own words.

Possible Mini-Lessons to Support Students as they Write for Change:

- Mini-lessons specific to the craft of a specific genre (i.e. the parts of a letter, the different features in a non-fiction book, developing the characters in a fictional story, how to show not tell in a personal narrative).
- Mini-lessons on organization (developing a clear focus, adding supporting ideas, appropriate introduction/transitions/conclusion).
- Mini-lessons on persuasion (focusing on positives, giving ideas to refute possible negatives, using the right tone/voice for your audience, including *sufficient* and *specific* supporting ideas, making your writing more personal by including an anecdote).
- Mini-lessons on revision, editing, and working to help your writing partner make their piece better.

End of Unit:

- Ask students to pick their best piece to publish.
- After publishing, have a celebration for students to share their published pieces with the class.
- Ask students to share their published pieces with their intended audience (e.g. send letters, read aloud books to other classes, post signs).

From a fund of knowledge perspective, we want and need to know the ways in which students practice literacy in homes and communities and the history and reasons for such practices; but we also desire to change the quality of interactions that happen around reading and creating new texts.

Through the Author's Eyes: Developing Critical Stances

In our response group, we reflected on these challenges and also on the strength in the teachers' work. We also noticed that literacy practices that were enacted in each chapter, such as book clubs, were made up of sets of interactional practices that each educator has developed over time. In our group, we uncovered patterns between these chapters around the idea of dialogicity: practices that involve the micro-interactions between teachers and students.

Each educator, in her writing, found ways to enter into and outside of her participation in an event by describing and interpreting the interactions that occurred. Seeing and describing classroom practices in which one is a participant involves a great deal of reflection and a critical stance. Being a careful observer and integrating one's own perceptions are aligned with a feminist perspective, recognizing the knowledge and standpoint of oneself as an educator.

Along the way, each teacher encountered challenges such as cognitive dissonance and questions about the appropriateness of social justice issues in the classroom, parents' questions about why they were teaching for social justice, and struggles with time and logistics of teaching in this way. Meredith pointed to these challenges in her response to the chapters, coming from her position as a teacher in an elementary classroom:

> Even once you get past the hurdles of teaching for social justice in your school, there are the complex issues of how to appropriately scaffold the students, when to step back and turn things over to the students and when you need to step in, how to address the teacher/student power dynamic in the classroom, and how your own beliefs and values as a teacher fit in. In reading the chapters I was impressed with how each of these teachers were as deeply reflective of themselves as they were of their students. Clearly this reflection is an important component, in that it leads to not only student growth but also teacher growth.

Meredith was noticing that the teachers were using the chapter as a way to experience the situation again, and perhaps revisit some choices that were made along the way. Carolyn, perhaps, struggled with how to continue to introduce students to the powerful writing of black scholars who may or may not be accessible to the students. Melissa reflected that the students' ability to critically question unjust practices was trumped by a wave of national pride and patriotism.

Indeed, the teacher/authors' reflections indicate that teaching for social justice is not easy, simple, or always rewarding. Instead, we (teachers) often feel that we have failed at bringing our students to a new place. We see them leave the room and continue to treat one another with less than the respect that each human being deserves. We feel bogged down by what we just cannot possibly fit into our teaching day. And we worry about parents, who are sometimes less than thrilled with the choices we make. Bridgette realized through reading the teachers' reflections, the quality of "becoming" that the teachers were engaging in the writing of these chapters, that they were indeed writing their way into critical inquiry as a teaching practice. Bridgette noticed that the teachers in the chapter were using reflection as a way to become better at creating communities that do more than talk about issues; they move towards action.

Action, Advocacy, and Social Change

When each of these teachers held this mirror up, and gazed behind them at the process of becoming a critical educator, she identified a host of critical moves. Teaching for social justice is not an easy task, because many of our experiences with education tell us that learning should be a-political, the transmission of knowledge without a reconsideration of how that knowledge positions our students in the world. Sarah held this mirror and saw an image of the inequalities and violence in her students' lives, but also an image of a teacher disillusioned by the teaching situations in which she was put—teaching too many students without collegial and administrative support. It was when she gave up her ideas of what a teacher "should be" that she allowed the students' voices to address the critical issues.

Darder (2002, p 61) writes,

> wherever oppression exists are also to be found the seeds of resistance at different stages of expression. Hence, Freire firmly believed that the political empowerment of teachers functions to nourish and cultivate the seeds of political resistance—a resistance historically linked to a multitude of personal and collective struggles waged around the world in efforts to democratize education.

We hear In the voices of the teachers In this section how easy it is to become hardened by the dehumanizing restrictions on professional knowledge and the ongoing policies that impede the building of authentic bonds between students and teachers, teachers and teachers. Often, teachers committed to teaching from a place of critique and hope are positioned as subversive, radical, and not team players. Indeed, the high rates of teacher attrition and turnover, especially in urban schools where policies of domestication are the strongest, provide proof that the vision of public education that teachers went to work for is not what they find in many of our public schools. The authors in this section found unique spaces that were outside of the surveillance in order to construct social justice-focused literacy practices.

Bridgette came to realize the difficulty of teaching for social justice through the stories of teachers threatened to raise scores faster, and the effects of threats on students and administrators. She claimed, "the whole social justice movement arms the teachers, it gives them some support and the tools to be able to do what they've been doing for kids." Working towards social justice occurred in these chapters primarily within classroom walls. Melissa, Rebecca, and Sarah's chapters were written about practices they were using when LSJTRG was in its infancy, and we wondered if perhaps they would have a different story to report if the network was well developed while they were teaching.

Lingering Questions

In our discussions, we disagreed about whether the students in these classrooms would take their learning about social justice themes beyond the projects if, and in the likely scenario, their future teachers did not work towards social justice teaching. We also disagreed about what constitutes action, whether the students in the classrooms were working for social change. These remain as questions for us as we continue to think about our own teaching practices, but we were inspired to make use of the mirror that provides us with a look at our own process of becoming critical educators.

Part III

An Entry Point

Critical Inquiry and Analysis

Part III includes Chapters 8–11 that together help us to continue to think about the critical literacy education framework. This section is different from Part II, as the educators in this part take us outside of the classroom and outside of formal schooling contexts to focus on doing critical literacy with, again, students across the lifespan. Each chapter delves into the question of how experiences with literacy can provide students with a way to inquire into social practices and social justice. In Chapter 8, Melissa Mosley and Margaret Finders share their experiences of collaboratively planning a model program for sixth graders under the umbrella theme of "Writing Yourself into History," a program designed around the broad themes of American history, literacy and leadership, and including a set of four workshops focused on social justice. They interpret and reflect on the conditions of learning for the students who participated in the workshops, leading into a model for shared leadership that empowers students to act in their own communities. Mary Ann Kramer and Rhonda Jones, adult educators, initiated a Critical Literacy Lab at their school to promote the integration of literacy education and social justice with the teachers and students at their site, and also to serve as a model for other adult education sites within their school district. In Chapter 10, Jackie Lewis-Harris, Director of the Center for Human Origin and Cultural Diversity (CHOCD), describes the Center's role in educating pre-service and in-service teachers about and for cultural diversity. Jackie poses the possibility that in St. Louis, as in other U.S. cities, teachers may have limited experiences with diversity or with considering race outside of an individual difference model. As teachers and teacher education students participate in the CHOCD, they learn to integrate social justice and anti-racist concepts into their literacy curriculum in an integrated manner. We invite you to consider the following questions as you read each of their narratives:

- How did each teacher create a space for critical inquiry and analysis of social issues using literacy practices?
- How do you see tools such as reflecting through multiple modes; considering histories of participation; finding patterns and generating theories; planning for actions; engaging in inquiry processes; and reflecting on group processes and dynamics?
- How does each educator negotiate the space in between learning contexts?

8 Shared Leadership, Adolescent Literacies, and Social Justice Education in the "Third Space"

Melissa Mosley and Margaret Finders

Throughout the 2007 academic year, teachers and academic workers of Iran participated in a nationwide protest movement to denounce the distressing work conditions and livelihoods in education. The government responded to these protests with threats, beatings, arrests, dismissals, and suspension of teachers. Over 700 teachers who have been identified in the protests have had pay cuts, 86 teachers have been suspended, and 39 teachers have been banned from teaching.

In December 2007, nine teachers were sentenced to 91 days' imprisonment by a criminal court of the province of Hamadan in Iran. Nine teachers were charged with "disturbing social order, issuing announcements and holding illegal gatherings." The teachers have been sentenced for their participation in teacher union rallies calling for improved living conditions for teachers and respect of their right to form a labor association. For more information on conditions and issues impacting teachers around the world, visit the Education International website (www.ei-ie.org/en/index.php).

Introduction

Critical literacy pedagogy for adolescents includes the exploration of multiple viewpoints, the questioning of dominant perspectives, and engagement in critical reading and writing practices. In our work with students in middle grades, however, we find that students are often unlikely to assert viewpoints when their social relationships and egos are "on the line." Furthermore, schools often reject critical literacies as a part of the curriculum because of a focus on test preparation or perceived lack of time to address critical social issues. Third spaces, which are spaces constructed to engage students in meaningful, connected experiences, hold great promise for young adolescents because they exist outside of the regular classroom and allow for different thoughts, ideas, and actions to take shape. In this chapter, we tell the story of one such space, a two-day workshop we called "Write Yourself into History." The story of this workshop does not critically evaluate how the adolescents participated in critical literacy practices; rather it illustrates the beginning of an exploration of how such spaces might be created by members of professional communities who think outside of the box to come up with alternative spaces to practice critical literacies.

Darling-Hammond (1997) writes that the new paradigm for effective schools will be grounded on two assumptions: first, that teaching matters, and second, that relationships matter. We designed the "Write Yourself into History" program on these two deeply held beliefs. We brought 24 sixth graders from six urban middle schools to campus for two days. The students came from the St. Louis Public School District, both from the magnet school program and neighborhood schools. Melissa, Margaret (the authors), and four others, each bringing very different professional and personal experiences, planned the program that awaited these early adolescents. Traditionally, professional development for teachers, preparation for pre-service teachers, and programs for adolescents have operated as entirely separate entities, often in different academic contexts. The model of this program began with a rationale for a shared leadership initiative that unites teacher induction programs, professional development, and programs for adolescent literacy. Drawing from a culture of collaboration, this program was based on a respect for teachers' knowledge of their students and on professional relationships between pre-service teachers, beginning teachers, university faculty, and doctoral students.

The "Write Yourself into History" Scholars Program was specifically developed for the sixth grade students whose teachers were involved in a two-year professional development program with Margaret, a literacy professor at a private, Midwestern university. The students were selected to spend two days on the university campus with other young scholars and to learn more about American history, literacy, leadership, and college life. The students experienced an overnight, chaperoned stay in a university residence hall. A private donor who was committed to supporting urban initiatives for children funded the program, so there was no cost to the students or their families.

Components of the Program

The project included three components: an orientation meeting with families, a two-day workshop with an overnight stay on a college campus, and a year-long follow-up that included families and young participants. In this chapter, we focus on the July 2005 component of the program, the two-day workshop. The features of the workshop included a rigorous social justice curriculum by facilitators who engaged students in high-level, active learning. We expected that students would participate in collaborative critical thinking about social issues at a high academic level (Perry, Steele, & Hilliard, 2003).

The workshops were collaborative with students from different schools working together, which provided opportunities for multiple positive interactions with teachers, peers, and director. The features of the year-long follow-up included support from significant adults (teachers, parents, grandmothers, siblings) in an admission process (letter from teacher and letter from parent or guardian), the celebration orientation banquet, and explicit messages from powerful adults during the workshop. Finally, an orientation and follow-up sessions with the young people's families built relationships and allowed the facilitators to find out more about the students' backgrounds.

Background to the Project: Goals and Theoretical Connections

We designed the "Write Yourself into History" summer program because of our commitment to literacy for social activism. Our perspectives on literacy teaching and learning, in particular, include ideas from the New Literacy Studies (New London Group 1996), which focus primarily on the ways that literacy learning is situated in a larger web of social and cultural life. This type of literacy learning often looks like students reading a text in relation to other texts and personal life experiences. The purposes and goals of this type of literacy learning are that through social interaction, learners begin to understand how their literacy can change their futures by providing tools to critique and redesign the workings of their school, community, and world.

Several members of the LSJTRG worked collaboratively to plan a model program under the umbrella theme of "Write Yourself into History," centering on broad themes of American history, literacy, and leadership. We planned a set of four workshops focused on social justice. Melissa is a European American former second grade teacher and doctoral student in education and literacy who is interested in anti-racist literacy teacher education. She was one of the six workshop leaders who participated in the program. Margaret is a European American teacher educator and researcher whose interests include adolescent literacy and equity education. The other teachers, Gretchen, Stacy, Debbie, and Jamel, came with a range of experiences. We decided to focus on a period in history that would be covered in the middle school social studies curriculum: the Civil Rights Movement and its link to the theme of social activism.

Rationale: A Focus on Middle School Literacy

The program was designed to integrate best practices for adolescent literacy. Alvermann, Hinchman, Moore, Phelps, and Waff (1998) note that literacies in the lives of adolescents must be understood as "multilayered, shifting and relational" (p. xvii). In recent years, more attention has been given to the dichotomous nature of in-school and out-of-school literacies for adolescents (Alvermann, Hinchman, Moore, Phelps, & Waff, 1998; Hull & Schultz, 2002; Rymes, 2001).

A weekend workshop model held on a university campus might be understood as a "third space" (Gutiérrez, Baquedano-López, & Tejeda, 1999; Moje, Ciechanowski, Kramer, Ellis, Carrillo, & Collazo, 2004), a potentially productive site to bring together the intersections and disjuncture between everyday and school literacies. During a few high-energy sessions and a string of email correspondence, the group found that their goals and individual plans were highly aligned under the umbrella of social justice and critical perspectives on adolescent pedagogy.

Practitioners and researchers who work with adolescents express a growing concern that federal and state legislation that focuses attention on early reading programs will divert attention from the needs of adolescents and reduce expanded definitions of literacy. In a commissioned report, Alvermann (2001, p. 3) writes,

> More often than not in the United States, newspaper headlines and feature stories on national television networks focus on early literacy instruction and the so-called reading wars between advocates of direct skills instruction and those who favor more holistic approaches to teaching young children to read print text.

Unfortunately, adolescents and their specialized needs for literacy instruction at the middle level often go unnoticed by policy-makers and the general public. Although the neglect of older readers might signal that all is well in the area of adolescent literacy instruction, such is not the case.

Tantamount to the discussions of bridging in-school and out-of-school literacy practices is addressing the literacy needs of students of color and students who experience some form of perceived disadvantage that potentially affects their literacy development in America's schools. These students in the United States (1) are generally African American, Asian American, Latino/a, or Native American in ethnicity; (2) speak home language other than standard American English; and (3) come from poor working-class families (Finders & Tatum, 2005). Middle school drop-out rates are high, and as Finders and Hynds (2007) write, "Everyone enters middle school, but not everyone leaves. This is where we lose them" (p. 83). Given these grave concerns, the "Write Yourself into History" program focused on a group of energetic urban youth whose teachers, parents, and grandparents were determined to beat these grave odds.

Planning for the Weekend

The planning for this event began during a set of meetings between the facilitators, the teachers who were selecting students, and the project director, Margaret. Jamel, Stacy, Gretchen, Debbie, and the authors ranged in age from 50 to 22, in experiences in school setting from 20 years to four months. Yet their commitment to the students and the program dissolved any sense of hierarchy. Building on the wealth of knowledge and experiences, they began collaboratively planning for the July weekend. Each of us had expertise in a different area, including literacy, history, the arts, and leadership training. We chose a theme to bring together what we had to offer as well as to ground the experiences in a content and context of a historical event.

The workshop leaders were all concerned with critical approaches to pedagogy. What was interesting about this event was that the workshop leaders created a completely new learning environment without a dress rehearsal. We had no idea how all of our plans would come together, nor did we know the students and how they would shape the learning environment. We were all concerned with creating spaces for learning with the students that were empowering. Specifically, we wanted the students to choose causes to take up as young activists, build coalitions to support their continued academic success, identify role models and mentors, and perhaps come away with several specific tools to apply to texts, including media, written texts, and everyday conversations.

Collaboratively, we planned lessons around the theme of "Separate but Unequal": Focus on Brown v. Board of Education of Topeka, equality of educational opportunity, and the early Civil Rights Movement. We each brainstormed the major objectives for our session as well as related texts, activities, and questions and planned for the ways that the workshops would work together. Literacy was a major component of the plans, and the critical literacy workshop was the first the students attended.

Getting There is Part of the Challenge

On the first day of the "Write Yourself into History" program, we waited anxiously for the school buses to arrive at our university. Standing out in the humid July heat, two program leaders waited to greet the young participants while the rest of us organized notebooks, set out juice and snacks, and manned the phone. We were wearing red T-shirts that Margaret designed for the group, and held in our hands the T-shirts to give to the young people. The bus schedule hadn't accurately predicted the time for pick-up and the office phone was ringing off the hook.

"The bus was supposed to be here at 7:40 and it's now 8:15," one mother worried that her daughter had missed the bus.

"Just wait," we tried to assure them. "The buses are running late."

Trung called for a third time, "Miss Margaret, I'm waiting for the bus and it just went around the corner. I'm going back outside now."

By the time the buses and the 24 sixth graders arrived on campus, our anxiety was almost as high as Trung's. He had been calling periodically for two weeks, waiting for this day, making sure that he had done everything needed to attend, checking again on the paper work, on the bus schedule. Of Hmong decent, Trung's parents who were not fluent English speakers had not attended the orientation and so his teacher had hand-delivered the materials to his home. Mrs. Blue with Trung's help had explained the program and the need to sign all the necessary camp release forms. Mrs. Blue had been Trung's advocate throughout the selection process. As his sixth grade teacher, she saw great potential in Trung Nguyen, a mature and bright member of her classroom community. She made trips to his home to deliver and pick up the materials, and had written a nomination for him to attend the program. She wrote out the nomination form for his parents that included what they most admired about their son: "behavior, positive grades, and responsibility." The language barrier was broken by the deep commitment that she felt to provide this opportunity for Trung. She sat with his parents while Trung's older sister translated her questions. From the moment that the nomination was completed, Trung took over the responsibility to make sure he attended.

Similarly, Marianne, who after only a few hours on campus became known as Pink Slippers, took great initiative to come to the workshop. Like Trung, her teacher was a great advocate for her. Ms. Walker's nomination included a powerful commentary and ended with a plea: "Please include Marianne. She is really amazing. She doesn't have a home. She and her father live with friends and move often, but I really want her to attend. Please give MARIANNE your utmost consideration."

At the orientation, her father became teary eyed as he explained his pride in his daughter's selection into the program, stating, "She wrote her essay all by herself and never asked for any help in doing the work."

Once the students arrived (finally!) we began the first workshop. The students gathered in an air-conditioned classroom. We introduced ourselves and the program, carefully articulating the emphasis on leadership and strengths.

Critical Literacy and Building Alliances

In two sessions, critical literacy and building alliances for community action, we further defined the purposes and goals for the students. In the first session, based on critical literacy, Melissa introduced several concepts to the group that an author's perspective shapes the story they tell about a historical event, and that as readers, we question texts to reveal relationships of power and justice. In the building alliances workshop, Gretchen and Debbie helped the students construct and enact scenarios in which students were rewriting their worlds to act towards social change.

Critical Literacy

Melissa introduced the concept of critical literacy to the students, focusing on authorship and perspective in texts. To bring the students into a shared language and set of practices for approaching texts, and to activate prior knowledge, Melissa read aloud from Toni Morrison's (2004) picture-book *Remember: The Journey to School Integration*. The book tells the story of school desegregation with beautiful language and photographs. Melissa guided a discussion by asking the students to respond to themes and images as she read the book. The purpose was to set up reading as an interactive process in which questions come up, are explored, and new questions are generated by the reader.

Texts about schoolchildren were used to introduce Civil Rights because students can imagine their schools as segregated spaces and justice/injustice in that setting. All of the texts were non-fiction, and all were at or below sixth grade reading level to provide all students with decodable texts. After reading Morrison's (2004) book, Melissa divided the students into book clubs to read a chapter from an edited book, *Linda Brown, You Are Not Alone: The Brown v. Board of Education Decision* (Thomas, 2003). The individually authored chapters present school desegregation from multiple perspectives, for example, from the memories of a white woman who as a child had a live-in summer visitor from the inner city and from the perspective of an African American woman who recalls a high school graduation ceremony at her church.

Small groups completed the reading silently and then used a list of questions to critically discuss the text, which the team leader introduced before the students began reading. Building agency and leadership skills includes representing how authors share their messages through writing. Melissa emphasized that a text represents a story whether it is fiction or non-fiction, because an author gets to choose how to represent the subject, much like two people drawing the same object from a different place in the room will present a different two-dimensional representation. Similarly, no two people represent an event in the same way.

Because people see things through a lens of past experience, culture, race, and gender, along with many other aspects of their identity, part of critical literacy includes finding out who the author is, what their position is, and recognizing that the author's perspective reflects his or her race, class, gender, and other parts of his or her identity such as nationality. For example, in the *Linda Brown* text (Thomas, 2003), there are separate essays written by both European Americans and African Americans, representing experiences during the Civil Rights Movement. Students are able to see, within one collection, how people who live in geographically different places and have racial and class differences write history in different ways.

The next component of this workshop offered students the opportunity to "write themselves into history." Melissa provided this writing prompt for the students:

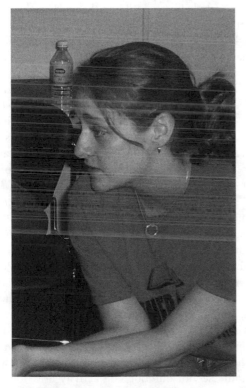

Photo 8.1 Melissa explaining the "Write Yourself into History" program.

Some people thought that desegregation, or schools no longer being separate for African Americans, had some problems. Here in St. Louis a woman named Minnie Liddell was upset because her children weren't going to a school in their neighborhood but had to get on a bus to go to a school that wasn't as good. This happened in 1972, several years after schools were desegregated. What do you know about this conversation now? What have you heard about schools in St. Louis? What do you think about these stories being left out of the books?

The prompt was constructed to move from critique to action within a critical literacy framework; to connect critical reading to conversation and writing. When the students were finished with the reading activity, however, there was little time left for discussion. In order to connect the workshop to personal experiences, Melissa asked the students to continue to think about how they make history by thinking, talking, and doing important things. These activities were used to practice core critical literacy strategies, namely recognizing that an author's perspective shapes the story they tell about a historical event, and that as readers, we question texts to reveal relationships of power and justice.

Building Alliances and Cultural Capital

Both explicitly and implicitly, we modeled alliance building throughout the two-day workshop. Gretchen and Debbie created a workshop focused on building alliances to enact change. Through a study of Rosa Parks and the Montgomery Bus Boycott, Debbie and Gretchen introduced the students to the concepts of cultural capital and alliance, focusing on how and why they were essential to the Civil Rights Movement. They didn't go into a highly theoretical explanation of cultural capital, a term coined by Pierre Bourdieu. They explained to the participants that cultural capital was any advantage a person has that gives him or her a higher status in society. They explained, using examples from the students' experiences, that cultural capital includes such things as social status and popularity. Debbie and Gretchen went on to explain that groups need to form alliances in order to advance their common causes.

Their work focused on two key issues: alliances and cultural capital. After explaining the key terms, the students read two very different versions of the Rosa Parks story, one in which she was characterized as a powerful member of the Civil Rights Movement and one in which she was portrayed as a somewhat accidental hero. Gretchen used the stories to model what cultural capital Rosa Parks had and how one story downplayed that. Together, the middle school students discussed the cultural capital Rosa had, what she needed from others, how alliances led to the boycott. Next, students were divided into small groups, each group given a hypothetical situation, creating a workable strategy for achieving the given goal, specifically focusing on who they need to ally themselves with, what help they would need, and their plan of action. For example, one group was given a prompt to develop a middle school outdoor safe activity area for the school. They first discussed how they had cultural capital and how that might be useful to further their cause. They then brainstormed who they knew who might be important allies to get this project off the ground. Each group was given a different prompt but were asked to discuss their cultural capital and who would be important adult and peer allies to help them. While the tasks were hypothetical, each group engaged in authentic ways, sharing their very real associations with faith-based, school-based and community leaders who they could call on for help.

By the end of the weekend, strong, real alliances had formed among all members of the program. In their program evaluations it was the ice cream, pizza, and staying in the residence halls that were the students' highlights. But when asked what was the most important thing they had learned, what appeared on their evaluations were comments such as "the importance of making alliances," "how cultural capital works," "how to make allies," "a leader listens," and "history is more than in books."

In another session, Stacy led the students through role play to take on the roles of one of the interested groups (students, parents, teachers, school board members) in a fictional school segregation debate (Centerville, USA). Groups created a statement of what they want, why they want it, and what they are willing to give up to get it. New groups were then formed, comprising one member from each of the groups, and were asked to create a plan of action that is satisfactory to all parties, for the integration (or not) of Centerville schools.

Finally, the students read from the Supreme Court of the United States Brown v. Board of Education, accessed online. While the text was beyond the comprehension level of most readers, they read brief passages and collaboratively unpacked statements such as "Segregation of children in public schools solely on the basis of race deprives children of the minority group of equal educational opportunities, even though the physical facilities and other tangible factors may be equal." They rewrote sections of this text, using their own words to explain what "tangible factors" might include. Throughout the weekend, we continued to engage in the practices of critical literacy to read and construct texts, in order to construct alternative texts and understand the complexity of social issues.

The curriculum was rigorous. It was July in St. Louis. The heat and humidity did not hamper the willingness of the youth to engage in complex historical and social discussions. They worked hard and long. They engaged in sustained workshops for each two-and-a-half hour session. But there were pizzas and malts and games. Jamel used his leadership skills to facilitate social activities throughout the two days. He might say his primary responsibility was to prevent the girls from sneaking on to the boys' dorm floor and to attempt to regulate the room-to-room phone calls throughout the night. But the rest of us would say that Jamel's participation was critical. He facilitated cooperative games that allowed the early adolescents to feel positive and competent about themselves and their new-found allies.

Pink Slippers concluded the weekend with a note to herself: "I am having fun. I am a leader and I will never give up on anything. I still want to be a vet. I've met a lot of new friends. love, me." Trung concluded the weekend with a hug to Jamel and a reminder to himself: "I will try to reteach stuff that I have learned here to my friends and families."

Conditions for Learning

Margaret and Melissa had a conversation just as the adolescents were boarding the buses on the last day of their university visit. We were remarking on how wonderfully the planning and execution of the workshops had just "come together." However, like all endeavors, there were certain conditions in place that led us to create a successful learning environment. The facilitators held a set of values and philosophies of education that were in alignment. We were modeling productive collaboration among people with different backgrounds and personalities in the way we planned activities and supported one another in the classroom. Further, we were working on a process that modeled the product we desired—to help students participate in thoughtful position-taking and to build alliances and lead from a collaborative model.

We were highly privileged in the conditions that were set up for learning in this two-day workshop. For example, the student-to-adult ratio in the room was 21 students to five adults. We had allies in the room, who were operating from the same social justice framework, to scaffold learning in the moment-to-moment orchestration of the lessons. As a result of the grant that funded the project, we had time and abundant material resources. These were luxuries that are most often unavailable to the teachers and students in a school setting. In addition, we had the privilege of working within a teaching schedule that could be modified at the moment of orchestration, which was responsive to the teachers' reflective tools to modify the structure of the workshop to support learning. Because we were not tied to other teachers' schedules, a bell or passing period did not dictate pedagogical decision-making. This is often the case for elementary teachers but not for middle school teachers.

There were interesting tensions within these conditions of learning. For example, we didn't have background knowledge on our students' cultures, competencies, families, or interests. We trusted the assessment of teachers who suggested that these students were leaders in their community. However, we all had the preconceived notions of the types of learning that happen (and do not happen) in schools in the inner ring of the city. Perhaps a lack of background knowledge hindered our planning of lessons and activities; we could not determine whether texts were at an independent reading level. However, we were also forced to plan activities that focused on critical conversations and making connections across close-to-life and historical contexts. We were not able to form a curriculum based on interests, competencies, and community funds of knowledge specifically, yet we were not constrained by any deficient thinking.

As outsiders of the school curriculum, we did not have a broader curricular scope and sequence from which we were working. We chose a content theme that was part of the middle school curriculum, but we had no idea of the prior knowledge that the students had when they came to us. Therefore, we were able to think outside of the box and shake things up by adding new perspectives and strategies for coming at a text or a social situation. We were not limited by a curricular scope and sequence, and we did not feel any constraints from a curricular framework or larger school culture, which might reduce pedagogical options.

The Weekend as a Third Space

The workshop, perhaps, was a third space because it did not carry with it a pre-scribed set of expectations and assumptions. Moje et al. (2004, p. 44) note,

> Third space can be viewed as a space of cultural, social, and epistemological change in which the competing knowledges and discourses of different spaces are brought into "conversation" to challenge and reshape both acade-mic content literacy practices and the knowledges and discourses of youths' everyday lives.

"Write Yourself into History" as a third space perhaps offers a productive model for both the early adolescents as well as the facilitators. Third space may offer a productive way in which to re-imagine professional development as well. As we noted in the introduction, traditionally, professional development for teachers, preparation for pre-service teachers, and programs for adolescents have operated as entirely separate entities, often in different academic contexts.

Only a Weekend: Lessons Learned and Next Steps

The small group of facilitators mirrored both the goals we had for our students and the LSJTRG group as a larger network of educators. We learned from this experience that a group of educators with common goals hold the potential to shake things up in their communities and schools. LSJTRG teachers who embark on projects such as this begin from a shared framework and set of understandings around critical literacy and social justice. We felt that the facilitators, along with other members of LSJTRG, are courageous educators, willing to take risks in the classroom and community to provide equitable and progressive literacy educa-tion for students. Gretchen, for example, is a leader in her school community in incorporating African American cultural and historical perspectives in her school. Debbie uses African American literature with contemporary social issues. These are bold moves in districts that often whitewash the curriculum.

However, to support one another as courageous educators, we must continue to complement each other's work by building alliances of educating for change, as well as noticing and naming our contributions in the larger education community. It is for this reason that we write this chapter.

We are not satisfied by the story of this workshop, because we see limitations and room for growth. We engage in (some of) the following tensions:

1. How do literacy educators design third spaces? How are these different than the third spaces youth create for themselves? What is the place of each?
2. How do we sustain these third spaces over time? Getting there is part of the problem, as is getting them back, securing funding, and time.
3. What is the tension between two-day workshops and critical literacy/social justice/action oriented pedagogy? How did we negotiate this tension? What was lost?

4.   What was diverse about the perspectives that were presented? How did the presentation maintain hegemonic viewpoints or perspectives?

Rethinking Practice

If the same workshop were conducted as a classroom reading workshop, a text set could be used, in which students read other texts individually, with partners, and in small groups. Text sets often include multiple texts at different reading levels, including picture-books, poetry anthology, non-fiction texts, biographies, and novels.

Text Box 8.1 Text Set on Civil Rights Movement Intermediate Grades

Greenfield, Eloise. *Rosa Parks.* New York: Harper Trophy, 1973.

Hughes, Langston. *The Dream Keeper and Other Poems.* New York: Scholastic, Inc., 1994.

Kelso, Richard. *Walking for Freedom: The Montgomery Bus Boycott.* New York: Steck-Vaughn Company, 1993.

King, Casey and Osborne, Linda Barrett. *Oh, Freedom!* New York: Alfred A. Knopf, Inc., 1997.

Lucas, Eileen. *Cracking the Wall: The Struggles of the Little Rock Nine.* Minneapolis, MN: Carolrhoda Books, Inc., 1997.

Martin, Lee Ann. *A March for Freedom.* Bothell, WA: Wright Group Publishing, Inc., 1999.

Miller, William. *The Bus Ride.* New York: Lee & Low Books, Inc., 1998.

Mitchell, Margaree King. *Uncle Jed's Barbershop.* New York: Simon & Schuster, 1993.

Morrison, Toni. *Remember: The Journey to School Integration.* Boston, IL: Houghton Mifflin, 2004.

Nevinski, Margaret. *Ruby Bridges.* Bothell, WA: Wright Group Publishing, Inc., 2001.

Polacco, Patricia. *Mr. Lincoln's Way.* New York: Philomel Books, 2002.

Rappaport, Doreen. *Martin's Big Words: The Life of Dr. Martin Luther King, Jr.* New York: Scholastic, Inc., 2001.

Ringgold, Faith. *My Dream of Martin Luther King.* New York: Dragonfly Books, 1995.

Rochelle, Belinda. *Witnesses to Freedom: Young People Who Fought for Civil Rights.* New York: Puffin Books, 1993.

Woodson, Jacqueline. *Martin Luther King, Jr. and His Birthday.* Englewood Cliffs, NJ: Silver Press, 1990.

9   Designing a Critical Literacy Lab in an Adult Education Center

Mary Ann Kramer and Rhonda Jones

Six teachers in Boise, Idaho, U.S.A. have ended their fast supporting education author and expert Jonathan Kozol in protest of No Child Left Behind (NCLB). Inspired by Jonathan Kozol, who had been on a partial fast since early summer, the Boise group members each fasted for one day a week. Their collective fast began on October 15, 2007 as a gesture of solidarity with Kozol's efforts. Kozol began his fast to draw attention to problems with NCLB and announced he would continue his protest until he was able to share his concerns with Senator Edward Kennedy. Kennedy chairs the U.S. Senate committee overseeing NCLB's reauthorization. For more examples of teacher actions go to www.ed-action.org/.

Introduction

We were privileged to observe Holiday, an African American adult education teacher and colleague at our Adult Learning Center, teach a unit on African American songs. This lesson was part of a unit on African American literature that took place within the Critical Literacy Lab (CLL). Holiday distributed the lyrics from the song "Lean On Me" to the adult education students in her classroom. She asked them to listen to the song first, without reading the words. The students listened, many of them singing along and swaying in their seats. She played the song again and asked her students to follow along with the words in their packet. The students followed with their pencils. They continued to sing along and dance in their seats. Line by line, Holiday and her students went through the song and talked about what the lyrics meant. The cultural knowledge they brought with them served as an entry point for their literacy learning.

HOLIDAY: What's someone's favorite line?
STUDENT: Just swallow your pride...
HOLIDAY: That's one of my favorite ones, too. What does that line mean to you?
STUDENT: It means to go forward in life.

As the student talked, Holiday recorded her words on the board, "go forward in life." Holiday asked another student what the phrase "swallow your pride" means. Drawing on real life experience, the student responded, "when food stamps came out that was embarrassing for some people ... we had to swallow our pride and go on up in there." Sitting in a chair, with her legs crossed, facing the student, Holiday carefully listened to her student's experiences. She immediately responded, "that's a great example."

Holiday demonstrates our collaborative attempt to integrate effective literacy instruction with a critical perspective. The idea for developing the lab grew out of the questions we initially raised through our involvement with the Literacy for Social Justice Teacher Research Group. Specifically, we asked: In what ways can "scientifically based reading research" and culturally relevant texts be integrated for adult literacy students? We then set about integrating the best practices based on the reading research available in the field of adult education (Kruidenier, 2002; Purcell-Gates & Waterman, 2000; Rogers & Kramer, 2007) with critical, culturally relevant and feminist perspectives (Allen Gunn, 1986; Freire & Macedo, 1987; Guy, 1999; hooks, 1994; Maher & Tetreault, 1994). We looked to the LSJTRG as a professional development resource as we pursued our efforts.

In this chapter we discuss the design and evolution of the Critical Literacy Lab. We designed the lab to be more responsive to our students' needs as readers and writers as well as their real world demands. In the process of collaboratively designing the lab we inquired more extensively into the areas of literacy, social justice, and integrated instruction. As a result, the design and implementation of the lab became a major source of authentic professional development for us and for other teachers who were involved with the lab.

Our Teaching and Research Context

Participants

Rhonda and I (Mary Ann) work together at the Adult Learning Center (ALC), the main center of operation of the St. Louis Public Schools Adult Education and Literacy (AEL) program. Founded in 1969, St. Louis Public Schools Adult Education and Literacy (SLPS AEL) currently operates over 70 sites in seven school districts in St. Louis City and St. Louis County (Ferguson-Florissant, Hancock Place, Jennings, Normandy, Riverview Gardens, St. Louis Public Schools, and Wellston).

Rhonda has been teaching Adult Basic Education and Literacy (AEL) for St. Louis Public Schools AEL since September 1991. Previously, she taught in secondary schools in the area of Alternative Education. She believes in quality education for all adults and the encouragement of lifelong learning. In her quest to be a better instructor, especially in the area of reading and literacy skills, she is always searching out professional development activities. When Mary Ann told her about The Literacy for Social Justice Teacher Research Group which had been meeting for a year and was a model of professional development, she quickly asked to attend. As a result, she increased her content knowledge about literacy education and social justice and has implemented many ideas at the Adult Learning Center.

Mary Ann has lived and worked in diverse communities and brings those experiences as well as her background in Women's Studies to her current role as Literacy Coordinator for the SLPS AEL. She believes that education, as a powerful means of socialization, is never value-neutral and should contribute to building a non-violent, just society. The idea for LSJTRG evolved from shared conversations with Becky Rogers and other founding members around this perspective. LSJTRG affords an opportunity for the caliber of professional development not readily available in the field of adult education, providing both a social justice and literacy focus as well as shared learning with K-12 and university educators.

Mary Ann was initially attracted to adult education because of its roots in liberation movements and through the influence of women with whom she worked at the Southside Women's Center in St. Louis. Her concern for the field's growing emphasis on testing, standards, and content based on patriarchal capitalistic values motivates her continuing interest in LSJTRG and the initiation of the Critical Literacy Lab. For Mary Ann, creating the CLL was a multi-purpose endeavor: it offered a proactive means for addressing social issues directly as participants developed the community, explicit skills, and confidence to do so.

The Program

SLPS AEL provides a comprehensive range of services including adult education and literacy, workplace literacy, family literacy, English for Speakers of Other Languages (ESOL), and services for special populations. The purpose of the program is to improve the literacy skills of adults, thereby assisting them in obtaining the knowledge and abilities necessary for employment and self-sufficiency; to assist adults in obtaining the educational skills necessary to become a full partner in the educational development of their children; and to assist adults in the completion of a secondary school education.

The heart of SLPS AEL is the Adult Learning Center housing administration, tutors, and master teachers while also providing classes for adult students in need of literacy development. All of those involved with the educational process at the ALC share the common philosophy that literacy is not a simple and elementary skill. Rather, it is a highly complex practice, a lifelong learning process. This belief has led us in search of research-based teaching strategies and professional development towards quality education. This search process has been enlightening, time consuming, and at many times frustrating as we came to see that quality professional development is definitely lacking and most times not offered to teachers who do not actively seek it out in the field of Adult Education and Literacy (AEL) (e.g. Wilson & Corbett, 1999).

We learned that some research did exist, but the only professional development offered to us at the time were three-day summer workshops and one four-hour in-service yearly. While many times these workshops and in-service choices mentioned research in the field, they did not give us a chance to participate or develop ideas, and were often taught by professionals with little background in AEL. It was indeed frustrating because we knew that professional development was necessary, that some research had been done in the field of Adult Literacy, and that to be high-quality educators we had to have access to it; but it was sometimes a challenge even for educators who were willing to search out professional development in their own time and at their own expense.

In our case, the predominance of sparse, dispersed teaching staff having multiple work locations and differing schedules, as well as limited budgets, makes organizing professional development difficult. Traveling to state or national conferences or required DESE workshops is usually the only choice for local professional development. Even those select few who have their travel or registration covered find themselves in the position of losing pay as they must close classes in order to participate. If teachers take part in professional development, it is most often done in their own time and at their own expense. Practitioners often depend on other AEL professionals to steer materials, workshop announcements, and other resources their way.

For years, AEL teachers have preferred interactions with their peers and yet this is the one avenue that is most closed to them. Teachers know that they gain the most from sharing experiences directly with others, discussing their successes and failures, and making sense of new information. The lack of this type of activity sets educators up for frustration. In addition, only a small majority of educators access print media and the Internet for information. The void we experience in our professional development has often led us as adult educators to create our own learning experiences.

As site supervisor and literacy coordinator, respectively, we share responsibility for students' instructional progress along with the master teacher. We drew upon Rhonda's previous experience in developing and teaching mini-courses and Mary Ann's interest in integrating critical literacy, accelerative practices, and social action in our process. In her role as master teacher on site and a vital contributor to the lab's formation, Holiday's creativity, insight, and exemplary instruction were invaluable. Most importantly, we enjoy working together and complement each other well.

The Design and Evolution of the Critical Literacy Lab

As adult educators we sought to create a resource that integrated the various dimensions we considered of value to our students and to expand our own knowledge and abilities as practitioners. As we implemented the "lab" we learned alongside our students, enriching ourselves personally and professionally. (See Appendix II for an outline of the principles of the CLL.)

In developing the Critical Literacy Lab we considered how to more effectively integrate the values identified with feminist teaching methodology (hooks, 1994; Maher & Tetreault, 1994), critical literacy and liberation theology (Freire, 1970b), popular education (Horton, Kohl, & Kohl, 1997; Purcell-Gates & Waterman, 2000) and guided reading instruction (e.g. Fountas & Pinnell, 2001; Massengill, 2004) into our teaching. As Literacy Coordinator, Mary Ann is responsible for addressing our students' literacy needs and she recognized that there was not a significant increase in literacy scores using one-on-one tutoring with traditional commercial texts. Engagement, relevance, and accelerated instruction were needed. The evolution of the CLL went through three phases: (1) Reading 101, a pilot program; (2) Introduction of the Critical Literacy Lab; (3) Mini-courses which included Real World Reading and Book Clubs.

In each phase, we chose multicultural or culturally relevant literature for students to read (Banks & Banks, 1995; Guy, 1999). Our decision was influenced by the perspective that the values of a culture are embedded within texts (Gunn Allen, 1986). It is possible to identify specific values of a people or culture and contrast these with those of the dominating culture. Reading culturally based texts affords the opportunity to identify specific values and keep them alive to address the conflict that exists between them and those of the dominating culture. The challenge that these values pose to the status quo is at the heart of the suppression/oppression of what are considered "minority" cultures. Using such texts then moves into a more critical perspective as people are challenged to consider the implications of the suppression of their cultural values in order to be assimilated into the dominating society. Using culturally based texts also allows scope for considering history from that cultural perspective.

We document the teaching and learning that occurs in the lab through keeping a "paper trail" of our lesson plans, instructional decisions, and students' writing. We also videotape and audiotape targeted lessons and have fieldnotes from these lessons. Our inquiry process is cyclical and involves discussion, planning, implementation of lessons, data collection, presenting at LSJTRG meetings, and reflection.

Critical Literacy Lab

Based on what we learned from our earlier teaching experiences, we initiated the CLL. We designated one of the classrooms as the Critical Literacy Lab and designed the first series as an eight-week course focused on African American literature. All of the students were African American and ranged in age from 17 to 70. Using students' scores of Test of Adult Basic Education (TABE) we set up two groups.

Our first course was structured each week thematically and included poetry, music, short stories, newspaper articles, and novel excerpts. We read materials including lyrics from rap and blues songs, *Women of Brewster Place*, poetry by Langston Hughes, and selections from *Oakland Readers*. Each group met for two hours twice weekly. Tutors were actively involved working with one or more students as necessary in the context of class and with follow-up assignments after group sessions. The course topic ensured relevant content and teachers facilitated discussions that afforded connections to current events.

In each session, we followed a flexible lesson plan that was informed partly by popular education reading methodologies (Purcell-Gates & Waterman, 2000). The lesson began with a generative word or theme that came from the students' experiences or from the text, followed by group discussion. A student-generated summary sentence was written on the board and copied by each student, who was then assigned to add two or more sentences. For the lowest level students, these language experiences were a primary source of fluency practice. Word work activities in phonics, phonemic awareness, or vocabulary used words from the text to provide explicit instruction. We used a word wall to help our students theorize between words and word families. The word wall also included infrequently used words such as "prejudice," "discrimination," and "strength." We connected each of these activities to the reading. Ideally, the text was read in the group more than once and specific comprehension-building strategies were targeted. All sessions included writing activities either directed or creative in structure. Throughout the lessons, we asked critical literacy questions such as "What makes you think that?," "Where is there evidence in the book for that?," "How does this relate to your life?"

The students demonstrated an engagement with the texts and made text-to-text and text-to-life connections. We also noticed that the students displayed evidence of empathy and caring for the characters in the texts and then generalized such caring to their communities. The following conversation was a part of the book introduction to *Women of Brewster Place*. Up until this point, I (Mary Ann) had used a word from the reading to generate discussion and a topic for the students to write about. I asked the students to think about the conditions of housing for the women in Brewster Place. Collaboratively, the students discussed issues concerning housing and racism in their own city—both historically and in the present.

MARY ANN: What are some other things in terms of housing not only being made to stay in certain areas but what were some of the other difficulties like if you were trying to buy a house?

ROCHELLE: You couldn't buy a house.

MARY ANN: Why not?

DARLENE: You couldn't afford it.

MARY ANN: You couldn't afford it and what else?

ROCHELLE: They were raisin' the process. = [students talking at once]

MARC: Real estate. They wouldn't sell it to you =

MARY ANN: Do you remember what that was called?

TUTOR: Red-lining.

MARY ANN: Red-lining. Exactly.

MARC: And really there weren't too many back then that could afford a home back at that time.

MARY ANN: Right, so things were connected. You couldn't get a job that paid much money, you couldn't get a job for a couple of, several reasons either discrimination [Marvin: right] or lack of education or the job wages were really low in a lot of places, um, so that it impacted the ability to buy a house [Marvin: right]. The inability to buy a house is one of those things that we see in our society as giving you some power, a base to work with. [At this point, Mary Ann is standing by the flip chart writing "red-lining" and "segregation," and other ideas that the students generate.]

TUTOR: I can remember my parents discussing sometimes with other neighbors they would have money to buy a house but then they couldn't move into the areas where they could really afford to buy the house. And then when they were red-linin' they would go up so high on the houses in the white neighborhoods.... And it was a problem because even if you had money you could not buy a nice house because all of the nice houses were in white neighborhoods with a lot of problems. My father said, "I don't care who lives there if they are black, white, yellow, green, blue, just let me buy my house and leave me alone." But it was real hard.

ROCHELLE: It was like impossible then.

MARC: When my dad came back from Vietnam. He was overseas and by that time you know how the Vietnam War he went over for the war, and that's what you wanted was a house. [Rochelle: And they faced the same thing. They couldn't get one]. Yeah = My dad said he was, you know, was in the military a veteran and had the money but still could not buy a house because they did not want to sell to blacks.

ROCHELLE: And they did not sell to blacks.

Such interactions encourage community development and recognize the relationships among participants as well as with the broader community. The use of students' language, values, and experiences facilitates an action dimension to the process not always realized in critical literacy classes but essential to social justice. As the students make text-to-life connections, they enter into the "text world" which allows them the opportunity to empathize with the characters, a necessary component of building and sustaining a community (McLaughlin & DeVoogd, 2004). A significant outcome of the CLL was movement to action based on text-to-life connections. We saw this as evidence that they were motivated to make social change that extended beyond the classroom.

For example, CLL participants along with the other AEL students on site were concerned because a "For Sale" sign had been placed in front of the Adult Literacy Center. This occurred during the 2004 school year when a costly management team was running the school district. The management team outsourced many of the jobs and sold school buildings to make money (e.g. Ayers-Salamon, 2005). When the students saw that their school had been listed as "for sale," they were upset because, for many of them, this was their neighborhood school. Responding to their inquiries, Holiday brought in multiple documents that discussed the sale of the school for them to read and discuss. She brought in a newspaper article that listed their school as "unused," she brought in a document from the real estate company, and another newspaper article that discussed the financial status of the school district. The class read and discussed these documents. They were concerned with the inaccuracies in the newspaper article that listed their building as "unused." The class generated a list of action strategies they could take in response to this inaccuracy. They decided to write a letter to the editor that exposed the inaccuracy and listed the reasons why they should not sell the school building. The letter appeared in the paper. Ultimately, the school building was not sold.

As this example illustrates, often times we supplemented the literature we read with materials such as tables and graphs, newspaper articles, biographies, videos, and information downloaded from the Internet. These were used to extend the lessons. Rhonda, Holiday and I communicated regularly which afforded consistency, continuity, and shared leadership. The feedback and encouragement we gave to one another inspired our creativity and commitment when faced with scheduling challenges, limited resources, and questions regarding direction.

Here, too, is where we found valuable support and suggestions from our involvement in LSJTRG. The combination of obtaining information regarding quality literacy instruction and resources for integrating this with racial justice/cultural literature gave us confidence in our choices. As we proceeded with the series, we documented our teaching and learning by tracking our lesson plans, instructional decisions, and students' concerns. Our documentation process was directly related to our participation in LSJTRG. Our participation in the group discussions allowed us to take our instruction to another dimension as we planned, implemented, recorded, discussed, evaluated, and adapted our process based on feedback we received from other teachers in the group.

Students responded enthusiastically to the series and clearly indicated their interest in and enjoyment of the various texts and genres we selected. After completing the African American literature series, most of the participating students were retested. We noted that those who tested at the lowest level demonstrated significant increases in their reading scores.

Mini-courses in the Critical Literacy Lab

Prompted by this success and students' expressed desire to continue with another focused series, we decided to offer a new series beginning in January 2004. We elected to shorten the series length to four weeks in order to include newly enrolling students sooner than the eight-week series would allow. Our second series focused on Africans Around the World and took on a combination literature/social studies flavor. We sought texts that highlighted the voices, experiences, and cultures of African Caribbean, African Canadian, African Native American and African American people. This literature brought out relationships and his/her stories that caused us to revise our lesson plans and collectively decide how to approach this new subject matter. This continued to be our process throughout the remainder of the program year as revised with each subsequent series including multicultural women and environment issues.

In the 2004 to 2005 year, we decided to offer mini-courses on a variety of subjects, including critical literacy. Rhonda elected to start a book club, partially based on the experience of other LSJTRG members, and Mary Ann offered Real World Reading, open to students of all levels based on Freire's (1973) concept of read the word, read the world while incorporating a feminist/critical approach.

Book Clubs

Many literacy students have not experienced reading literature for pleasure. We wanted students to learn to read better by reading and discussing quality literature. During one of our LSJTRG meetings, Carolyn Fuller (see Chapter 6) described how she used Sister Souljah's books in her classroom with her adult education students with great success. LSJTRG read and discussed the book which helped Rhonda to think about various ways to engage her students with the literature. Carolyn and our student populations were similar and Rhonda thought that the book would also be well received at our site. Rhonda started the book club with Sister Souljah's (2000) book *The Coldest Winter Ever*. Rhonda explained the purpose and structure of book clubs to her students (Raphael, Florio-Ruane, & George, 2001). The primary purpose is to encourage and provide instructional support to AEL students in meaningful activities around age-appropriate text, while also providing instruction appropriate to each student's need. Further, the goal of the book club is to provide an opportunity for all participants to practice reading, comprehending, and responding to literature that, in turn, supports their engagement with other texts and the world.

Rhonda introduced the book to her students and developed lesson plans. The class read the book over the course of two months. Her students did not like *The Coldest Winter Ever* because they found the readability too difficult and the sex and violence too explicit to talk about in the classroom. Several students dropped out of the book club. Rhonda was surprised because she had assumed that her students would find social and cultural connections with this book. Despite its urban themes and African American characters, the topic and content of the book were not engaging. This is important because sometimes we assume that if there are African American people in a book it will be culturally relevant for our African American students. However, there is a range of life experiences, geographic locations, values, politics, languages, and religions with the African American experience, as in any cultural group.

With these reflections in mind, Rhonda transitioned to the book *Because of Winn-Dixie* (DiCamillo, 2000). *Winn-Dixie* is a children's book with adult content. Opal, the young protagonist in the story, adopts a dog she names Winn-Dixie. Together, Opal and Winn-Dixie learn about issues of prejudice and individuality. Even though the main character is a young, white, rural girl the students loved reading and discussing the themes of the book. Serendipitously, the movie came out around the same time the class was reading the book and many of the students went to the movie and brought their children with them.

As the class read each book together, their understanding of literature and of each other grew. When the book clubs began, adults were unsure of the conventions of book clubs. However, as Rhonda continued to model discussions, asking questions, making connections, students began to take more of a lead in facilitating the discussions. The class also learned more about the complexity of African American culture, an important aspect of becoming critically literate.

As the class read *The Watsons go to Birmingham* (Curtis, 1963), for example, many of the older students in the class shared their experiences of living in the deeply segregated South. One man shared his experiences living as a sharecropper in Arkansas and how his boss made him change his name. We developed what is known as a critical literacy text set to accompany the teaching practices in the CLL (Leland et al., 1999; Vasquez, 2003). For instance, we started this book with a poem called "The Ballad of Birmingham." The critical literacy text set also included photos of the bombing of Birmingham and other civil rights texts.

Following the book clubs, Rhonda organized around three literacy units each lasting four to eight weeks with a size limit of 12 participants per unit. The year-long theme was "Stories and Our Lives." Unit 1 was "Family Stories." The big idea with this unit was that an individual's identity is embedded in family narrative and formed the starting point. During this unit they read the book *A Taste of Blackberries* (Buchanan-Smith, 1973). Unit 2 was "Stories of Self." In this unit, participants began by studying various ways in which authors have presented and "represented their lives." The class also read *Knots in My Yo-yo String* (Spinelli, 1998). Unit 3 was "Stories of Culture." Within this unit, students read and listened to literature of an event that changed the world and of immigrant experience. They also read *The Devil's Arithmetic* (Yolen, 1998).

When the class read *The Devil's Arithmetic*, the students knew little about the Holocaust. However, one student had lived in Germany for several years and shared his experiences, and the other adults in the class learned more about him and about the content of the literature. As they discussed the book they also discussed the cross-cultural implications of oppression, particularly for Jewish and African American people. After reading the book, the class took a field trip to the Holocaust Museum. Rhonda was pleased when we learned that the students independently brought their books with them to the museum. As they went through the exhibits, they took out their books and compared information, historical sources, an aspect of critical literacy.

The group also read *Missouri Pick* books such as *Betsey Brown* and *Memories of my Father*. LSJTRG also read and discussed *Betsey Brown* together. *Betsey Brown* focuses on three generations of St. Louis women during 1957, the year of school desegregation in St. Louis. The students really enjoyed this book because it took place just a few blocks away from the Adult Learning Center. For the critical literacy text set we also gathered newspaper articles about the author. For our special event, we went on a walking tour of the Academy-Sherman neighborhood to look at some of the places Shange mentions in the book.

Real World Reading

Although still considered under the umbrella of the CLL, Real World Reading included a few differences. First, instead of using a pre-selected focus and texts, we spent the first two sessions discussing how this series would be implemented and what we wanted to read, discuss, and learn as well as the types of reading materials we would like to use. Related to this, we discussed and determined a decision-making process for our group. We then brainstormed a long list of possible subjects and areas of interest. Since the "world" was our selection pool, suggested topics ranged widely from local to international issues. Some of these included social security, local school district concerns, police issues, health care, and neighborhood safety. Using our selected process, we finally narrowed our choices to three, collectively debated the merits of each, and voted on social security. Social security was in the national news at this time due to proposed changes by the then-current presidential administration. This afforded easy availability of relevant news articles.

Our first and subsequent sessions followed the same process we used with our CLL series with a newspaper article on this topic as our text. Each session included word work activities with an emphasis on vocabulary development as we studied the language contained in the authentic texts we read. These texts included various genres such as political cartoons, charts, graphs, editorials, and web pages. Our discussions supported comprehension as well as application of the information with the content for the next session emerging from the current one. Connecting our reading of the "word and world" moved us to action as we wrote letters regarding proposed budget cuts in adult education, participated in public literacy forums, and engaged in other related community activities. Students' active role in decisions, text selection, presentations, actions, and evaluations was critical to the success of our process.

Challenges/Lessons Learned

In the spirit of teacher inquiry, we are continually inquiring into and analyzing our teaching practices to decide where we should go next in the Critical Literacy Lab. Along the way, we have met some obstacles and learned a number of lessons that might be educative for other educators interested in experimenting with their literacy practices:

* Differentiated instruction using principles from guided reading is possible within the book club structure.
* Children's literature may be used with adult education students if the literature has adult themes.
* Critical literacy text sets may be used to supplement the literature (e.g. the Internet, newspapers, biographies, asking students to make presentations, retyping children's books to appear more adult centered).
* Often when responding to the needs of students, the instructional practices developed also met the professional development needs of the instructors.
* A lab context encourages experimentation with instructional practices.

Conclusions

Throughout our process of experimenting with teaching and learning practices in the Critical Literacy Lab, we have seen the ways in which critical literacy is promoted and sustained through authentic literature, embedded strategy instruction, and critical dialogue. Alongside our students, we have become more critically literate. It was heartening for us to see the progress our students made as readers and thinkers—certainly their reading levels steadily progressed. But there were unexpected surprises such as the time when the students brought their copy of *The Devil's Arithmetic* with them to the Holocaust Museum or when we would catch them on their breaks reading and talking about one of the books. Many of the students also reported that they shared the book with their children or with a member of their family. And they were eager to continue with the next book club.

In terms of our own continued professional development, we have presented on the CLL at adult education conferences and various teacher in-services. We also wrote a short article for the ProLiteracy newsletter. Several teachers from our in-services indicated that they wanted to start a book club at their learning site. As we continue to collaborate, observe each other, provide each other with feedback, and turn to the LSJTRG for support and ideas, we continue to stay responsive to our students and to ourselves.

Rethinking Practice

Research demonstrates that there is a direct relationship between the amount of time spent reading instructional or independent level texts and development of reading skills (e.g. Allington, 2007). Share this with your students and, together, inquire into the amount of time your students spend reading instructional level texts. Ask your students to keep track of the number of minutes they are reading connected texts during one class period. Record this in a notebook over the course of a week. Collect the notebooks and look for patterns across your students. Do your lowest level students read for as much time as your higher level students? How can you increase the amount of time spent reading?

---

10 The Center for Human Origin and Cultural Diversity

A Catalyst for Social Justice and Racial Literacy

Jacquelyn A. Lewis-Harris

In Ghana, Africa in November 2007, teachers demonstrated in solidarity with a colleague who had been demoted for speaking to the media about student enrolment at her school. The Media Foundation for West Africa (www.mediafound.org/) stood in solidarity with the teachers. Across the world, teachers are silenced and prohibited from using basic freedoms—of speech and of conscience.

Despite the cultural and ethnic diversity of the St. Louis region and the United States more generally, the teaching force is mainly composed of white, middle-class women (Garcia, 1999; King & Howard, 2000, National Center for Education Statistics, 1992; Neuharth-Pritchett, Payne, & Reiff, 2004; Sleeter, 2001) who frequently have limited knowledge about and experiences with people from cultural/ethnic backgrounds different from their own (Chapman, 1996; King & Howard, 2000; McDiarmid, 1992). In my eight years of experience teaching education classes, the majority of my students have been white females. I will have, on average, one or two minority students in a class of 25. Many of my white students were well-intentioned, dedicated teachers, but their cultural experience had been primarily monocultural with limited contact with other ethnic groups. Lawrence and Tatum (1997, p. 162) summarized the source of this type of thinking. They write:

> Due to the continuing social segregation of American society, most white teachers in the current teaching force have had limited contact with people of color. Their knowledge of communities of color is often misinformed by stereotypes or distortions communicated in the media and by family and friends. Their own educational experiences have been monocultural rather than multicultural, with major omissions concerning the contributions and achievements of people of color. This limited perspective leaves white educators ill-equipped to prepare their own students, both white and of color, to function effectively in a multicultural society.

Beyond preparing teachers in multicultural education and social studies teacher education courses, I direct experiences in a lab called the Center for Human Origin and Cultural Diversity (CHOCD) at the University of Missouri in St. Louis. Some of my students have questioned the relevance of moving through the experiences in the lab with regard to their future teaching positions. For example, after participating in several of the labs that comprise CHOCD, a young teacher wrote the following about the anti-racist curriculum: "It is great to learn about anthropology, the African culture, and evolution ... but what we experienced has not prepared me for teaching social studies."

I have experienced other types of resistance to learning about anti-racist pedagogy, too. Students often came into my classes skeptical of multicultural and anti-racist approaches because of their past experiences with multicultural education courses that were limited to specific racial issues or taught in an ineffective manner. A student reflected on her former experience: "Many students felt it only showed what 'whites' did wrong, but never answered the questions, 'Why do we need to learn this?' and 'What can we do to make it better?' The 'Why?' and 'What?' were never clear." I have found that misdirected approaches to social justice and cultural diversity can evoke a negative reaction or defensiveness.

When students come into my class with these experiences, I experience resistance. Because I am an African American professor, students often assume that I would use my power as instructor to judge them harshly if they did not embrace the material and illustrate its use in their assignments. I often remind them that the class was based on teacher inquiry and critical reflection, and that I expected them to exercise these skills at all times, to facilitate quality learning. Thus, intellectual engagement is crucial, as the misappropriation of multicultural and social justice theory in teacher education can essentially hinder the education of underrepresented children attending public schools due to the lack of proper theoretical application (Gay, 1995; Sleeter, 2001).

Still other teachers in my class resort to a "color-blind" approach where they advocate treating all children the same, which they discover is not very effective (e.g. Ladson-Billings, 1994). This approach, although well intentioned, does not take into consideration the child's culture, ethnicity, and socioeconomic background, and thus negates an important portion of the child's identity and educational experience (Cooney & Akintunde, 1999; King & Howard, 2000). Guinier and Torres (2002, p. 56) list the disabling elements of a color-blind ideology:

> First, colorblindness disables the individual from understanding or fully appreciating the structural nature of inequality. Second, it disables groups from forming to challenge that inequality through a political process. The denial of race not only reduces individuals' psychological motivation for challenging unfairness but also contributes to their internalization of it as a purely personal problem.

At first, the resistance of my students saddened me. "How could they possibly be an effective teacher with that kind of attitude?," "Do they really think that they would have a class full of young students that were a clone of themselves?" Reflecting on my own teaching and responses to my students' learning, I was able to move beyond my initial discomfort to see that, despite the usual initial resistance, there was a great deal of learning and development. As the reflective essay that began this chapter stated, many students arrive at new understandings of themselves and begin to experiment with culturally relevant and anti-racist teaching practices for the first time as they participate in experiences I have created for them.

Experiences with Pre-service Teachers at CHOCD

The Center for Human Origin and Cultural Diversity (CHOCD) is an active collaboration between the College of Education, Division of Teaching and Learning, and the Anthropology Department of the University of Missouri-St. Louis (UMSL). The Center offers learning experiences for fourth through twelfth grade students in the St. Louis area as well as for pre-service and full-time teachers and community members, through a series of experiential learning stations, located in its African Cultures and Human Origin Labs. The lab experiences embrace the fields of biology, math, geography, language, arts, and anthropology, exposing visitors to new ideas and concepts about race, human origin, and culture. Every pre-service teacher from the UMSL College of Education now participates in both of the CHOCD labs before engaging in their teaching practice and the Human Origin Lab experience is an important part of the first-year graduate program. In addition to serving pre-service teachers, annually, CHOCD serves 11 school districts and approximately 3,500 students and teachers. After-school, professional development, teacher enrichment, and science camp programs have also been developed in partnership with numerous districts. During the fall of 2007, members of LSJTRG came to the Center to experience and reflect on each of the stations.

CHOCD includes two sets of stations—the African Cultures Lab (ACL) and the Human Origin Lab (HOL) and is based on a model that encourages group participation, hands-on activities, student self-discovery, and cooperative learning. The activities in the Center model the teaching of difficult subjects like the concept of race, ethnicity, biological similarity (all of us sharing 99.7 percent of the same DNA), and cultural differences. The related curricular materials, readings, and course discussions provide a rich foundation from which the teachers gain confidence to develop an anti-racist curriculum.

Over the years, I have experimented with different pedagogical practices integrating the African Cultures Lab and the Human Origin Lab into social studies methods courses and in a social justice course required of teacher education students. I have learned how to move back and forth between anti-racist learning and multicultural experiences, critical reflection, designing curriculum materials, and continued reflection in a way that supports the teachers' anti-racist development. Through these activities, teachers also begin to develop what I refer to as *social justice literacy*, the realization that one's definition of the social components of race, class, gender, sexual orientation, and religion are vital to defining one's culture and personal interactions. Further, social justice literacy includes movement from noticing superficial differences to noticing (and acting on) structural inequities. People who are social justice literate recognize their personal and collective responsibility to shape their interactions at a micro and macro level in ways that work towards justice.

In this avocation I am always looking for allies. I have found the LSJTRG discussions and explorations around social justice helpful in exploring new ideas in my teaching and research. The mission and activities of CHOCD fit well with the goals of the LSJTRG, as they both investigate the roots of educational inequality and demonstrate ways to enrich classroom curriculum through the use of multicultural literacy resources, highlighting the relationship between literacy and social justice in classrooms, schools, and the community. I was very interested in the LSJTRG activities because here was a group of like-minds that actually researched and carried out curriculum change in the classroom.

One of the main CHOCD goals is to present an innovative approach to diversity education that is based on contemporary scientific knowledge. This is carried out through the use of two labs, the African Cultures Lab (ACL) and the Human Origin Lab (HOL). Each lab consists of four interrelated stations that present a different facet of human origin and cultural diversity as seen through the cultures of Africa. The ACL provides the opportunity for students to ascertain that the African continent is the homeland of multiple cultures and demonstrates the important African cultural aspect of ujaama, or cooperation among people with diverse skills and abilities to create successful communities (Nyrere, 1974). In addition, the ACL addresses a growing demand by the local African American population for education about the continent of Africa to counteract misinformation currently held by teachers and students. Through the ACL activities, teachers start to recognize the cultural and linguistic diversity within Africa and the systems of privilege and social grouping that operate at multiple levels. The ACL is used in the social studies methods class, while the HOL is employed in both the social justice graduate and the social studies methods classes. In the HOL, teachers interact around the ideas of the human family and race. Here, I will illustrate how teachers often interact around four stations within the HOL.

Teachers' Interactions within the Human Origins Lab

Using a learning-to-learn model (Loacker & Mentkowski, 1993; Mentkowski & Doherty, 1984), a team of faculty and students from both education and anthropology designed the HOL with integrated, hands-on learning stations. Learning stations are stand-alone, theme-based, intensive investigations through which the visitors experience a particular aspect of human origin and biological diversity.

Station 1: Human Fossil Record

In this learning station, teachers examine fossil casts of the human family and verbalize their theories and observations. They place the casts into chronological order using informational cards and a map that provide clues to the human development timeline. This station often incites deep discussion on the creationist versus evolution version of human development. Take, for example, a comment by a teacher in the class:

> I would have preferred the presenter to change her presentation slightly to accommodate for this conflict of beliefs within her field. Perhaps she could have said "some believed these artifacts to be millions of years old," rather than state the age to be fact. I know that this is a minute detail in our visit, but being that I have different views as to how old the earth is, I would have appreciated the presenter being more "honest" about the facts. I feel the same way about evolution vs. creation. Although many scientists believe in evolution, it is not fact. No one has been able to prove this theory. That is all that these are, theories. I would have appreciated them being presented as such.

My intention as a multicultural educator is to bring all perspectives and voices into the room. Through our conversations and readings, we investigate the role of religion in shaping identity and core beliefs, a particularly heated discussion in the state of Missouri. Indeed, there are many critiques of multicultural education by the Christian right around such issues as evolution, homosexuality, and world religion (Berliner, 1997; Peshkin, 1988). Our discussions take into account these

Photo 10.1 Jackie Lewis-Harris demonstrates the concept of human Universals.

issues, which allow us to engage with a larger set of arguments around the role of religion in the classroom and the separation of church and state. Students who are opposed to the fossil record dates and thus want to disregard all the station information on a religious basis are engaged in discussion and critical thinking, not to change their religious beliefs but to help them separate their religious objections from the basic scientific material being presented. We learn to find common ground between our dichotomous positions.

When controversy arises over the creationist versus evolution debate, I help students examine their interactions with children in their classrooms who might hold different religious beliefs. I ask, "Do they, as teachers, try to understand or accommodate them? Do they disregard their beliefs and customs because they are not Christian? Do they try to establish a level playing field where their students feel free to express their opinions, even though they do not reflect the religious norm?" For many of the education students this is a sobering moment.

Station 2: Archaeological Dating and Functional Morphology

In this set of activities students are asked to analyze fossils and artifacts that come from archaeology sites. They examine the relationships between teeth and diet, bones and body dimensions to understand their functional connection. This is a hard-core science and math experience, where they learn what archaeologists do once they have removed items from an archaeological dig. The idea of human universals is introduced to students at this time by performing an exercise that illustrates the ratio of their ulna to their total height (the ulna is the outer bone of what is commonly called the forearm, connecting the wrist to the elbow). The idea of human universals seems to contribute to the students' awareness of social justice and racial literacy, as it reinforces the idea that we share more commonalities than they previously believed. These activities also reveal that the perceived physical differences contributing to social injustice are arbitrary. This self-awakening often spurs students and teachers to think of ways to share this information with their students.

Station 3: Human Skin Color Variation

This station creates the most profound reaction among the students, as it contests deeply held ideas on "race" and challenges racialized thinking. Using the scientific method of testing hypotheses, students investigate how melanin (skin pigment) production is related to the geographic distribution of early modern humans. One of the major focal points of this station is skin color variation, so often used to define "race." One exercise, involving skin tone cards, uses geographical reasoning in relating degrees of latitude from the equator, to indigenous physical characteristics and skin pigmentation. This exercise seems to have the deepest impact upon the students. In describing this station, a student exclaimed:

> I appreciated learning how alike human beings are. The activities we participated in were very powerful for me. I gained a lot of insight from organizing

the color cards from darkest to lightest. It proved that there is no clear beginning and ending point of any race, and that there are actually no skin colors that are truly white or black. We are comprised of various shades of brown, yellow, peach, pink, red, and cream. I learned that sunlight affected the amount of pigment in our skin, which then in turn affected our skin color. This fact forced me to reflect upon how irrelevant our skin color actually is. I want to explain this to my students and I want them to understand this concept.

One student had a "wake-up" call moment, reflecting:

> When Griffith [a CHOCD graduate intern] asked if we saw any white or black color swatches, we all looked around and shook our heads no. My next reaction was to look around the room and see that each of the people in our class fell somewhere within the spectrum of colors we had just set out, and not one of them was white or black. I felt childish that I categorized skin color so simply—black and white.

At this station, we also explore the theoretical relationship of melanin production in relation to ultraviolet radiation and climatic change. Other activities include the testing of three hypotheses to prove human biological variation

Photo 10.2 Jackie explaining how skin pigment production is related to geographic distribution of early modern humans.

adaptation. Even students who have difficulty with accepting that whites are related to other perceived "minorities" found this station useful. In the process of exploring these stations, the students are introduced to the structure of their epidermis and the function of melanin. They are often surprised and intrigued by the model of the epidermis and the fact that the majority of the public shares the same amount of melanin cells. As one of the students reflected: "I was quite surprised to learn that there is actually only one kind of race on our Earth! I grew up with the misconception that there are millions of different races that make up our world population." The students remember this information because it piques their interest and challenges their beliefs about skin coloration.

By analyzing the geographic distribution range of skin color, participants come to realize that the concept of "race" is not supported by biology. In short, they discover that they cannot draw a physical dividing line that would define the beginning of white or black populations, as there is continuous biological variation. The concept of "race" can now be explored as a social and cultural construct. Completing these station activities is a catalyst for change, opening the door to their understanding of racial literacy and the underpinnings of social justice theory. An excerpt from a student's reflection illustrates:

> It was also refreshing to realize that there are programs that are out there that are directed at students that can help right racism. As educators we are often looking for new ways to combat these tough issues. Maybe if teachers took their students to this program then it could lead to a discussion about racism. This discussion could lead to the students taking action and trying to stop it. This program also would be good for the teachers who do not know how to deal with this issue and maybe not feel comfortable talking about discrimination.

As this quote indicates, as the teachers learn about the social construction of race and racism they can move beyond their initial reactions of "I am not racist. Racism has nothing to do with me" (Berlak & Moyenda, 2001; Tatum, 1997). I noticed at this point that they start to develop what Guinier (2004) refers to as "racial literacy." She writes, "Racial literacy requires us to rethink race as an instrument of social, geographic, and economic control of both whites and blacks. Racial literacy offers a more dynamic framework for understanding American racism" (p. 114). They learn that racism is perpetuated at individual and institutional levels and is reproduced through belief systems and practices, which they have the power to change.

Station 4: Geological Time Scale

In the fourth station students use deductive reasoning to develop a timeline related to life forms and events. The geologic timeline is a scale model of the geological and biologic history of the Earth. It encompasses a quarter of the classroom and illustrates the major geologic time periods, the introduction of the major animal groups (e.g. reptiles, mammals, humanoids).

CHOCD as Professional Development

While professional development and teacher education programs often provide courses in multicultural education, the courses tend to isolate diversity issues from the content areas. One of the major difficulties is the lack of multicultural-ism and social justice integration into general pedagogy and experiential strat-egies. Preparing teachers to internalize the role of culture and ethnicity in teaching and providing them with the skills and dispositions needed to sustain and apply this knowledge in classrooms has proven to be "easier said than done" (Pang & Sablan, 1998; Sheets & Fong, 2003; Sleeter, 2001). The education tech-niques used by CHOCD in conjunction with teacher education courses show great potential to influence teaching approaches.

After participating in the Center's stations, all teachers are engaged in discus-sions relevant to their readings or teaching experiences. I encourage all types of inquiry by telling them, "There are no unintelligent questions." When teachers enter discussions, these can either be lively or quiet depending upon the level of challenge to their core beliefs. They are asked to consider the integration of CHOCD materials into their curriculum. They either develop lesson plans that include multicultural children's books with an anti-racist focus or write essays on how this experience may have affected their pedagogical approach.

In analyzing my students' reflective essays, I have noticed patterns in their learning and development around anti-racism. Over time, I have seen many stu-dents select the CHOCD-related lesson plans to represent their best work for the standard of "individualization and diversity" in their exit portfolios. Often stu-dents request additional resources, engaging others in impromptu discussion groups based on class readings and collecting additional articles, books, and resources through which they can continue their self-education. Their responses indicate that they begin to find ways to locate themselves as "white" and to take an actively anti-racist stance.

> I will admit that at times I felt guilty being white. My race experiences privil-ege and my race has historically been cruel and violent to everyone different than us. It definitely made me uncomfortable at times. However, I began to realize that as a white person I can make a difference. I can speak up when I hear racial jokes. I can educate my family, friends, and colleagues to see dif-ferent perspectives. I realized that I cannot change the past, but that I defi-nitely have the power to change the future.

Once students understand the concept of racial literacy, they realize that they have a framework through which to address their concerns. At this time of their awareness development, I encourage them to join LSJTRG and make use of the meetings, website, and the curriculum fair, as they can now appreciate the material and support offered through this organization. Indeed, about mid-semester, they start to move from a racial literacy to a social justice literacy. They start to think about how they can become change agents in their schools and communities. For example, one student stated:

> I think the hardest thing this class has made me do was to look into the mirror. Where I once saw a woman who was confident in all she knew, I see a stranger who questions everything. It wasn't overcoming the fact that so much of the information I learned while growing up was all wrong. No, the real challenge becomes, now that I know better, how will I act upon it?

Realizations such as this can have a profound impact on racial identity development (e.g. Tatum, 1997). Some students may get angry or sad when they realize that the issue of cultural diversity moves beyond differences to structural inequalities and that, as white people, they have benefited from such inequities. I recognize the emotional reactions and point out how they can be a catalyst for changing actions. I encourage my students to move beyond anger and sadness and guilt, and to move towards social action. Another teacher reflected:

> Our readings and class discussions on social class have helped me develop a broader, more opened-minded personal view about class. I realized that not all races have equal opportunity to move upward. Not everyone can just "work hard" and experience equality and success. These readings pushed me to further become aware of my white privilege and to think about how social class plays into my professional life.

This student is beginning to disrupt the ideology of hard work and achievement, and the intersection of white privilege and class in her own opportunities. This is important because as Sleeter (2001) points out, white people are often more willing to disconnect history from the present than are people of color because for whites, racism is outside the scope of their daily experiences.

Several students commented on how the readings and class discussion sparked a domino affect in their personal sphere:

> This class has been good for encouraging open conversations both in and out of the classroom. Just think, there were around twenty-five people in the class, and if everyone had the same experience as me, you can bet there are a lot more people talking about these issues in a healthier way.

Other students move towards thinking about how they can change their schools, develop curricular sets, and take other, anti-racist actions.

Many teachers become supporters of the Center and bring their students to the HOL and ACL. For example, one student stated:

> I grew up on a farm in the 1960s and 1970s. As I look back, I can see how my standpoint has changed over the past 20 years of teaching in the St. Louis area. After reading chapters in Joel Spring's book, my current knowledge is confirmed and a question comes to mind, "How can we as educators have a greater impact upon textbook companies to publish more culturally diverse books?"

As I read the teachers' reflections I am heartened to see the ways in which their anti-racist thinking develops. I know, though, that they need to move back and forth between beliefs and practices to extend themselves as anti-racist educators. Together, we build bibliographies of anti-racist literature that is appropriate for the reading levels of the children/adolescents in their classrooms. We generate lesson plans that include anti-racist and multicultural content and perspectives. Finally, they are given bibliographies of professional materials and contact information for social justice groups to continue their learning and trans-formation as anti-racist educators.

Conclusions

Teacher inquiry and collaborative approaches modeled in CHOCD's presenta-tions present viable methods through which racial and social justice literacy can be encouraged. Through the Center's activities and assigned readings I try to encourage teachers to continue the habits of continual, critical reflection on self, their students, and curriculum. Indeed, transformative models of multicultural education involve getting to know oneself, getting to know others; and then redefining the relationship between self and others.

Attitudes and knowledge towards social justice can be changed positively during a teacher preparation program (e.g. Capella-Santana, 2003). A well-designed social justice education course in which teacher candidates from differ-ent cultural/ethnic backgrounds freely discuss multicultural and social justice issues, in addition to fieldwork experiences in culturally and ethnically diverse settings, appear to promote positive changes in teacher candidates' multicultural attitudes and knowledge (Neuharth-Pritchett, Payne, & Reiff, 2004; Sleeter, 2001; Zeichner, 1996). The CHOCD model in conjunction with open, support-ive class conversation predicated upon the understanding of racial literacy appears to be addressing most students' needs.

Introducing social justice experiences to teachers and students in an attempt to develop their social justice literacy has kept me on my intellectual toes, looking for new books and materials that address my students' needs. Finally, it has been very fulfilling seeing students become more self-aware, intelligent, critical thinking teachers through their adaptation of racial and social justice literacy.

There are ongoing challenges to my work as an anti-racist professor. First, many school systems have eliminated social studies, the most obvious place to use this set of perspectives and curricular materials, as the subject is not tested in the Missouri standardized assessment. Second, Missouri is a conservative state and issues of reli-gion and evolution and homosexuality have been brought to the ballot with con-servatism winning. Third, the historical and institutional nature of racism in St. Louis makes anti-racist work a difficult (and yet much-needed) journey.

Anti-racism is a lifelong journey and I only see the students in my class for one, sometimes, two classes. We begin the process of critical reflection on race, racism, and anti-racism in the courses but it is up to them to continue this hard work that is often not supported in classrooms and schools on their own. Thus, I encourage my students to develop alliances with social justice advocates such as the people involved with LSJTRG.

In the Center we look for opportunities to introduce teachers and college students to social justice literature as a means to broaden the Center experience and make it more relevant to classroom application. When the LSJTRG 2005 Annual "Educating for Change Curriculum Fair" call for presenters form arrived on my desk, I immediately thought of a CHOCD workshop presentation. The Center coordinator and I proposed and presented a workshop entitled "'I didn't know that!' Dispelling Myths About Race and Biological Differences." We wanted to introduce the research of CHOCD to a wider and more influential audience and to scientifically define the concept of "race," biological adaptation, and DNA commonalities in an effective and supportive dialogue. We discussed the Center's role in challenging myths and misconceptions often used to justify racial stereotypes. Our presentation was well attended and we had a lively discussion with teachers and administrators from many school districts. We also had an information table, where we met visitors and distributed information about the Center's activities.

Our ongoing goal is to support pre-service and practicing teachers in becoming "social justice literate" so that they can become agents of change in schools and society. I will end with a quote from one of my white graduate students, who candidly described her development as a culturally responsive teacher:

> In my personal culture paper I described myself and my culture as being very sheltered. Rarely have I stepped outside of my comfort zone of my own likeness and experienced others' lives and their differences. This class has changed that dramatically. At the least I have been pushed onto a platform at the edge of my own culture looking with a microscope at the others.

Through the integration of anti-racist content and principles into the curriculum, both for the teacher education students, and in turn, for their students, I hope to move towards a transformative education that challenges structural inequities, one classroom at a time.

Rethinking Practice

Maintaining social justice and racial literacy and incorporating it into your class and personal activities is an ongoing process. It is often a subtle but powerful activity when incorporated into the curriculum as part of critical thinking or an exploratory exercise. Examples of successful cross-curriculum lessons and supporting materials may be found on the CHOCD website: http://chocd.umsl.edu.

Of course there are those wonderful, spontaneous "teachable moments" in which student interaction prompts the introduction of anti-racist or anti-bias lessons. How do you address the use of the word "gay" or "china man" in your students' conversations? What do you do when your students try to exclude others because they are "mixed race"? Your degree of social justice and racial literacy will determine how well you lead your students' conversation. Visit websites such as www.teachingtolerance.org, www.addictedtorace.com, which have a series of short, witty observations on race in today's society.

11 Response Chapter—Critical Inquiry and Analysis

Making Space for Critical Literacy

Carolyn Brown, Ora Clark-Lewis, Aleshea Ingram,
Mary Ann Kramer, and Melissa Mosley

The cultural work of the teachers in this section has deep historical roots. Education has long been women's work, yet male administrators and policy-makers drive curricular reforms. Further, curriculum has been overwhelmingly static in terms of the representation of women and people of color, not to mention the style and practices of teaching. Feminist educators have called for the construction of new practices through instructional designs that make space for students' voices, strengths, and concerns (e.g. Hollingsworth, 1992). The authors in this section respond to this call.

Melissa and Margaret (Chapter 8) wrote about a summer institute for middle schoolers in which students learned about civil rights, how to think like a historian using critical literacy, and leadership drawing on cultural capital as a resource. Mary Ann and Rhonda (Chapter 9) reflected on a Critical Literacy Lab in which adult students read and responded to culturally relevant texts, drawing on their funds of knowledge. Jacquelyn (Chapter 10) wrote about another lab, a Cultural Anthropology Lab, in which pre-service and in-service teachers learn about the diversity of humans and reflect on their racial understandings as well as social justice literacies, a form of critical literacy. Through the three chapters there was a thread of critical inquiry and analysis, of action research as a feminist practice, and the construction of spaces where educational designs could meet the real needs of students to challenge oppressive traditions and build more just realities. This is a tradition that can be linked to freedom schools, literacy campaigns, citizenship schools, and other liberatory education movements (e.g. Clark, 1990; Hershon, 1984; Purcell-Gates & Waterman, 2000). Book clubs, an instructional design used throughout chapters in this book, for example, have long been drawn on as a space where women join together to construct meaning around contemporary social, economic, and cultural issues (Florio-Ruane, 2001; Kooy, 2007; Nafisi, 2003). In drawing on these instructional practices, the educators are calling forward a chorus of voices from the past, linking current struggles for freedom with historical struggles.

On a cold day in December, we met to discuss our responses to the chapters in this section. As we gathered at the Adult Learning Center there was a sense that our dialogue contributed to a larger narrative of women coming together to inquire into literacy practices that may be used to design social justice practices. Part of this rootedness comes from the place of the meeting itself—the Adult

Learning Center. For many years, this one-storey brick building has served as the site for adult literacy education for the St. Louis Public Schools (SLPS). There are many literacy-related activities at the center—literacy classes for AEL/GED students, in-services to adult education and literacy teachers and organizational meetings for conferences, educational forums, and cultural events. Indeed, the place itself is filled with the traces of experimentation around teaching practices, inquiry, dialogue, and action. And it is the place where, for over seven years, teachers involved with LSJTRG have come together from across districts and grade levels and experiences to examine our own and each other's teaching experiences—a space and community of practice not available within the traditional boundaries of any one of our schools.

We each brought different perspectives and standpoints to our discussion. Mary Ann, a European American, continued to focus the group on the intersections of gender and the cultural work of education for freedom represented in the chapters. Aleshea Ingram, an African American elementary educator in St. Louis, provided insight about how she read the chapters in light of her experiences as an elementary teacher. Carolyn Brown, a European American educator, has a background teaching writing and composition in university classrooms and is pursuing a Ph.D. in higher education. Carolyn brought a perspective on how women are constrained in institutional spaces and how the female authors of these chapters created unique spaces in which to change practices. Ora Clark-Lewis, an African American adult educator who focuses on writing in her work and current Master's student in literacy education was also present. She brought a perspective of the historical dimensions of adult literacy education in building social movements. Melissa Mosley, a European American teacher educator and former elementary teacher, brought her stance as a literacy educator to the discussion.

Photo 11.1 (from left to right) Mary Ann, Ora, Carolyn, Melissa, and Aleshea meet to discuss the chapters in this section.

What Counts as Literacy and to Whom?

Because LSJTRG is a group focused on *literacy* for social justice, over the years we have deliberately inquired into the ways in which literacy is and may be used as a tool for (personal and social) liberation and social change. We have had long-standing discussions around questions such as: What does it mean to become literate? Who defines literate? What counts as literacy? Who decides? Our discussions around literacies broaden as policies and curricular mandates narrow. Literacies—in all of their shapes and complexities—become the tools through which we inquire into social practices, interrogate discourses, challenge injustices, and build more democratic practices. In our discussion of the chapters, we split open, once again, how literacy is defined. The subject of our debate was whether (and how) social justice literacy, as defined in Jacquelyn's chapter (Chapter 10) counted as literacy. She writes:

> [Social justice literacy is] the realization that one's definition of the social components of race, class, gender, sexual orientation, and religion are vital to defining one's culture and personal interactions. Further, social justice literacy includes movement from noticing superficial differences to noticing (and acting on) structural inequities.
>
> (pp. 127–128)

As Jacquelyn presents in her chapter, in order for her students and participants in the lab to "read" social practices, they need more information on how race and other constructs are defined and operate in society.

Melissa and Margaret were interested in the literacies involved when middle school students "wrote themselves into history." They reflected on supporting students' ways to author one's own story, think like a historian, and the cultural capital and resources for leadership that one holds—types of social justice literacies needed for these students to be leaders in the St. Louis schools they attend. Mary Ann and Rhonda contemplated the types of literacies needed for students to advocate for their school building to remain open and also to advocate for themselves and their families—again, social justice literacy practices necessary in the local context of urban schooling in St. Louis. However, it was easier to see how literacy practices were designed with the middle school and adult education programs because of the types of texts and social practices that were present. In Jacquelyn's program description, the "literacy" in "social justice literacy" was less transparent. In our discussion of the chapters, we explored how each author engaged with social justice literacy *for* change.

Ora began,

> I see a difference in being literate and literacy in an area, like social justice. Because using literacy means that I can talk about social justice, but I don't necessarily know what I am talking about. Being literate means I have a better understanding of the issues around social justice.

Here, Ora made the case for literacy instruction in Jacquelyn's lab, foregrounding the process of "becoming literate" by deepening understanding of culture, race, and social justice.

Mary Ann replied, "I also see that literacy denotes reading and writing in some form." Here, Mary Ann was arguing that using the word "literacy" means that there is a text involved in the process.

Aleshea agreed. "Chapters 9 and 11 explicitly used literacy events and practices whereas Chapter 10 did not." Here, Aleshea defined literacy by the presence of written texts (e.g. books, newspapers) in the classroom.

Melissa expanded the definition of what counts as literacy practices by pointing out the different kinds of texts present in Jacquelyn's lab. She stated,

> Reading involves more than decoding print. It involves being able to understand space and location on a world map, read shades of skin color, calculate measurements of artifacts all involve "texts" and multimodal literacies.

Melissa pointed out the ways that texts were used in the lab to build background knowledge about culture and race and how that leads to a deepened form of racial literacy.

Jacquelyn defined racial literacy from Guinier (2004), who wrote: "Racial literacy requires us to rethink race as an instrument of social, geographic, and economic control of both whites and blacks. Racial literacy offers a more dynamic framework for understanding American racism" (p. 114).

At this point, Ora posed a counter-argument: "Being aware of skin pigmentation doesn't necessarily make you better at reading and writing."

We never came to a resolution to the question of "What counts as literacy?" but each member of our response group voiced an opinion, drawing on beliefs and definitions of literacy. In the process of examining a colleague's teaching practices, we could articulate more clearly our own stances and positions around literate practices. There were multiple practices within the lab that drew on students' racial literacies, evidenced in the learning that Jacquelyn cited in her chapter. Her students, for example, rethought their understandings of skin color and how skin color is linked to privilege in society, which are examples of racial literacy. At the heart of this discussion is a willingness to understand across differences, a thread in creating more socially just learning communities. Indeed, as in many of our discussions it seemed less important to come to consensus as it was to make sure our voices were heard, which points to our need as women to find spaces to work through ideas and beliefs we hold about literacy and education.

Building Space for Critical Literacy Education

Using the tools of critical inquiry and analysis such as analyzing cultural artifacts, reflecting on practices, developing case studies, and analyzing narratives, the authors in this section share the ways in which literacy practices are socially situated and historically conditioned. Because of the context of St. Louis, which Jackie points out has conserved racial segregation and racism, the authors see a need to pry open a space for critical literacy. Whether at the adult education center, at the summer program, or in the Cultural Diversity Lab, each of the educators shared how they invited their students to jointly engage in constructing learning spaces.

Designing critical literacy practices includes struggles over space—mental, social, and physical. Some teachers may bring a deliberate critical stance to every moment of their classroom—from what decorates their walls to how their curriculum is layered—to include multiple voices and perspectives from the margins to how they advocate for colleagues. Other teachers may carve out curricular time for critical literacy practices within certain topics of units—when the books the children have to read, for example, include explicit critical social issues (e.g. peace, civil rights, poverty). Teachers socially construct the space of their classroom through the talk, texts, and social practices that make up the day. Such designs are often challenged by other socially constructed norms such as schedules and time structure (50-minute class periods, a 12-week unit, a one-hour block for communication arts). Breaking learning into artificial segments of time often serves to interrupt authentic learning and teaching. When time is short, as it always is when teaching, educators struggle to find space for critical literacy practices. If knowledge is power, we need to ask questions about what knowledge is given the most time and space in classrooms and why. Sometimes, because the officially sanctioned curriculum has so much authority, teachers look for spaces outside of the traditional school structure. They design after-school programs, book clubs, teacher activist groups, cultural labs, and summer programs. In this sense, finding space for critical literacy means finding and building mental, social, and physical spaces.

Melissa and Margaret, in their use of critical literacy pedagogy with youth in a summer workshop, envisioned the students building a sense of leadership and agency that would take them beyond the summer workshop into their academic and personal lives. They noted that critical literacy included finding new contexts within which to apply one's literacies—social justice literacies, for example. They saw reading critically, debating issues, and drawing on cultural capital to build support for social movements as tools of leadership. On this project, Carolyn comments: "I saw the educational experience in Melissa and Margaret's chapter, maybe it was just a weekend, but a very important weekend in these students' lives."

Mary Ann and Rhonda also commented on the community that was built in the Critical Literacy Lab, using texts that were culturally relevant and of interest to the students. In both chapters, it was evident that these spaces for critical literacy explicitly included the students' experiences and voices. In building meaning around the texts that were read, students in the Critical Literacy Lab (CLL) drew on their experiences with segregated housing practices (red-lining), for example, and the middle school students brought their experiences with problems in their school to their discussions of cultural capital and leadership. Like the middle schoolers, the students in the CLL enacted new literacy practices in a space that was created for them and their experiences to speak louder than the hegemonic voices in the curriculum.

In Chapter 10, Jacquelyn provides a rationale for CHOCD's work with teachers and students: over time, she encountered enough resistance from pre-service teachers when she addressed concepts of race, class, sexuality, gender, and equity to know the worth of this intervention. Melissa and Margaret also envisioned their program as an alternative space for youth to explore notions of leadership and social change. Mary Ann and Rhonda also found the Critical Literacy Lab to be this kind of space, in which culturally relevant literature could take center stage rather than traditional adult literacy materials. In this chapter, as in the other two, students posed problems and addressed them, building community and understandings in the process.

Aleshea made a connection with these efforts to build a new space for educational practices by looking outside of the classroom. She began, "So often in the classroom, we only have time to get through a certain amount of material. So having the extra time and space that does not have that school-feel is so important." Aleshea's comment led us to consider again the restrictive space of the classroom, and how constrained teachers are by curricular standards and assessments in the name of reform. Our conversation took on the tone of wondering how these unique spaces might inform our classrooms, or how we might talk back to reforms that take education out of teachers' control.

Aleshea continued,

> I liked hearing about the "third space" in Margaret and Melissa's chapter. Having the extra space, you are still learning, and to get them thinking about something else. It made me think about being in summer enrichment programs. You can have different types of conversations.

Mary Ann continued,

> Talking about some other chapters, you just mentioned fear, having to sneak and do things, the reality of what is risked when you challenge … Who do need to keep your practices from? Where is the pressure coming from, why is it there? How is this a historical issue?

Carolyn made a historical connection that caused a moment of silence among the group members: "There are some historic parallels, for example, with our work as teachers and the work of educating African Americans to read in secret during slavery and Jim Crow segregation."

Melissa commented, "I mean, you see the connection, teachers having to close their classroom door to read certain books."

Aleshea added,

> People come into my classroom. You might have someone in there three days in the week. I came from another district where I felt respected as an educator. Now, I feel like, if I want to do something, I better do it from this time to this time. The pressure comes from making sure that you meet the standards. I understand it. But there is more than one way to accomplish the goal.

Mary Ann brought the conversation back to the feminist issues of authority and control:

> There was a time when teachers had complete control over their curriculum. Now women, and particularly African American women, face increased surveillance of their actions.

Aleshea, an African American teacher, explained that she worked in secret to infuse social justice teaching into her classroom. She emphasized that as an educator, she recognized the need to teach the standards, but knew from these chapters, her teaching history, and from other LSJTRG members that critical literacy instruction can be used to meet standards.

Action, Advocacy, and Social Change

Looking across the chapters in this section, we see how each of the authors/educators located historically marginalized practices and intentionally moved them from the margin to the center, using the tools of critical inquiry and analysis. At the core, these teachers' stories illustrate the work of activist women in the classroom who draw on action research to shape educational practices. Action research, as stated earlier, has a long history of use by feminist researchers to disrupt traditional power relationships between researcher and participant. Researchers accomplish this disruption by centering the problem-posing process and following research through to action. As they design educational practices, the values associated with social action and advocacy are embedded in the fabric of these authors' teaching and research.

The feminist classroom provides a safe space for people to make meaning of their experiences through new theories, rather than learn theories that are disconnected from real contexts (Maher & Tetreault, 1994). A central tenet of critical pedagogy is that it is inherently active, or ever-changing. Curriculum in public schools is predictably stable, with the same perspectives (often hegemonic) relayed through the stories of history and the literature that students read. Because critical pedagogy centers on the questions people ask, and the communities that are built based on such questions, the curriculum often changes and shifts, offering new perspectives and points of view. We saw evidence of this willingness to change in Mary Ann and Rhonda's chapter, as Rhonda chose new texts when Sister Souljah's book failed to appeal to readers. Mary Ann referred to the ability of critical literacy practices to "uproot" practices that are socially unjust.

Mary Ann pointed out that in adult education, although the teachers are under less surveillance than are K-12 teachers, having an administration that supports critical literacy practices is still key. Further, she emphasized, "Adult education has a different theoretical background. Adult educators will quote Freire. We believe that you always start with the student and use authentic materials."

Aleshea responded, "the same philosophy applies to K-12 but we're not given the opportunity." Aleshea's comment was followed by a silence, as we were struck by the position in which K-12 educators find themselves. Teachers are asked to ignore their core belief about student-centered education, and replace that belief with practices that center the acquisition of skills rather than problem-posing strategies, and the mastery of a hegemonic canon rather than an expanded notion of what counts as history.

A goal of popular education is to center the problems of students in the curriculum and to draw on students' knowledge and experience in the design of educational practices. Ora, as part of her Master's degree action research class and participation with ABC's of literacy, had involved her adult students in the exploration of Septima Clark's Citizenship Schools through field trips and writing experiences. Her project began with an exploration of Clark's work in the South during the Civil Rights Movement, and has metamorphosed into a service learning and social justice action research project. Another dimension of feminist teaching is that it is inherently relationship-based, and assumes that learning occurs when teachers and students engage in praxis-moving from understanding theories and experiences to action. The movement from theory-building to action is most evident in Mary Ann and Rhonda's chapter, as the students found ways to speak loudly against the unjust practices of the school board. However, in other chapters we get a hint of action-to-come. At the end of her chapter, Jacquelyn quotes several European American teachers who have found it easier to speak with their students, their colleagues, and their family about race and racism after taking part in the experiences of the CHOCD lab. Trung, a student in Peg and Melissa's chapter, told himself in a letter he wrote, "I will try to re-teach stuff that I have learned here to my friends and families." (This volume, p. 109.)

Lingering Questions

As a group, we were in agreement that there were "social justice" literacies present in each chapter, and that those practices were constructed because of the unique spaces educators constructed. We were less aligned in how we understood literacy in each project. We wondered if perhaps our backgrounds as educators in different grade level contexts and our standpoints as European American or African American women caused us to think differently about what counts as literacy. We were not convinced that these projects were consistently action-oriented as action research can be. We discussed at length how critical literacy instruction holds potential for action, and how in alternative spaces people build capacity for social action through examining core beliefs, learning social justice literacies, and building alliances. We hoped to have future conversations about what constitutes action in an action research project.

Part IV

An Entry Point

Building Community

Part IV comprises Chapters 12–15, which are written by teachers who are at very different places in their careers and life spans as educators. In Chapter 12, Liesl Buechler and Kate Lofton write from the perspective of brand-new teachers who are negotiating their beliefs about critical literacy with the new contexts of schools they encounter. They talk about seeking out communities that support them as learners and how their theory and practice might come together in these contexts. Janet DePasquale, in Chapter 13, shares her experiences of teaching journalism in a conservative high school in the Midwest. Janet, a teacher who has developed a strong voice as a critical literacy educator through her work with journalism and high school students again, combs the context in which she teaches for spaces for critical literacy. She writes as a person without allies in her own school who can mediate her run-in with oppressive circumstances. In Chapter 14, Sarah Beaman-Jones reflects on her experiences as a community organizer and educational activist who has a wide range of experiences within various communities of practice, particularly in the areas of adult and family literacy. Sarah's writing, like the authors who have written texts that mentor her thinking, brings us in and out of the circles of thought and influence that have shaped her thinking and understandings of oppression and justice.

We think that these chapters together help us to think about the importance of relationships, community, and solidarity. As you read each of these engaging chapters, we are certain that you will find connections with the emotional edges of designing socially just learning communities.

- Where do you see and hear moments of stability and confidence and moments of despair and frustration in each chapter? How are those linked to contexts in which voices are heard or not recognized?
- Across the chapters, what are the different ways the authors define power? How does their position as female educators and white women shape that power?
- How do relationships support each author in constructing power and voice?

12   New Teachers Developing as Educators/Activists

Liesl Buechler and Kate Lofton

Early in 2008, teachers in the United States island territory of Puerto Rico went on a ten-day strike to demand greater decision-making over the curriculum, smaller class sizes, higher wages, and repairs of neglected buildings. Education Secretary Rafael Aragunde met six of nine conditions the union set for returning to work. These included a commitment not to penalize teachers who observed the strike; an agreement not to privatize the education system (through charter schools); a $150-a-month pay hike that will raise the monthly base salary to $1,750; and an agreement to seek legislation that would gradually raise the base rate to $3,000. Negotiations are to continue on other issues, and the union reserves the option of resuming the strike. Independent Media Center (www.indymedia.org/en/index.shtml).

Introduction

One warm April day at the end of my junior year of college, I (Liesl) walked into an elementary school in a quiet suburb of St. Louis. The students were mainly European American. A few African American children attended through a desegregation-busing program. Kate, my co-author, and I were one of the many European American females working at the school. As I got close to Kate's room she popped out of the door and greeted me, smiling.

This was Kate's first year as a teacher and I, a student teacher at the time, was excited to hear about what it was like to be a *real* teacher. I wanted to know how she did everything in her classroom from constructing a balanced literacy curriculum to the class's calendar. I had come to volunteer as a part-time reading teacher in the first grade, and nothing could beat the opportunity to spend time with Kate a couple of days a week talking about her first year as a teacher. She explained to me how she came up with literacy centers that focused on all aspects of literacy from phonetics to fluency and showed me her writer's workshop materials. It was obvious that Kate spent hours putting together a classroom that supported all of her students. Each day that I went to work, I always made time to stop by Kate's room and see what new insights she had, then went back to my cohort of pre-service teachers with the strategies and lessons I had collected. As the school year came to an end, I realized that Kate was also in the LSJTRG. We talked about our shared interest in social justice education.

When the group decided that we would write a book to share our experiences individually and collectively of teaching for social change, Kate and I both attended the two-day retreat to begin the manuscript. During the retreat it became obvious that Kate and I would again be working together. Both new teachers, we were drawn to each other's eagerness and freshness, and built a relationship in which we would parse out our own stories of development as teachers working for social justice in our classrooms. We reflected on our teaching experiences, analyzing our teaching journals and reflections to chart our growth as teachers/activists. In this chapter, we share some of the "critical moments" in our development as teachers and social justice advocates. We will share with you times when we were empowered to take action and times we were silenced, experiences that shaped our development and identity as teachers working for justice.

Teachers as Activists: Kate's Journey

High Stakes Teaching

As a new teacher entering a first grade team of five veteran teachers, I (Kate) had to move carefully through a series of established teaching traditions and strained relationships. I was a 23-year-old European American woman with an undergraduate degree in elementary education and anthropology. My mentor, Maureen, a 55-year-old European American woman, was teaching her final year at Jefferson before retiring after 30 years. Maureen had children in the district, was extremely involved in district functions, and even now, as a retiree, works as a substitute teacher and volunteer at the school. Maureen cared deeply for her students and was a traditional teacher. Throughout the course of my first year, I tread carefully where Maureen was concerned, and I still managed to offend or worry her on more than one occasion; the topics of concern ranged from worksheets, to assessment notebooks, to field trips, to coloring books.

Years before, Maureen had created monthly coloring books and she encouraged the first grade teachers to use them during free time or indoor recess. I felt that there were better ways to engage our students' creativity and fine motor skills during their free time, but I used these books for the first two months of the year, nonetheless. From early in the school year, it was clear to me that my focus on social justice, balanced literacy, and critical content placed me in a vulnerable position. While most of the first grade teachers were watching me closely before they decided what to make of my classroom and me, I felt that I had to concede in many ways to their traditions. Unfortunately, concessions are rarely small and rarely last without sacrificing one's own beliefs.

When November came, and I looked through the month's coloring book, I simply could not justify giving my students the coloring pages. Each page was filled with pilgrims and American Indians, and to me, the pictures were devastating. The white pages were covered with outlines of little cartoonish Indians with round cheeks and large eyes. Even the American Indian adults were made to look adorable and childish. The pilgrims, on the other hand, were much bigger and looked more human. Compared to the cherubic Indians, the pilgrims looked authoritative and strong. As I flipped through the coloring book for December and discovered that every page included a reference to Christmas, I realized that if I was going to teach a multicultural curriculum, one that moved beyond the holiday stereotypes, the coloring books had to end in my classroom (e.g. Banks & Banks, 1995; Howard, 2006).

During this first year of teaching, I quickly found the teachers with whom I was able to build progressive alliances. Tanya, a teacher of gifted students, recommended "partial shapes" and fluency activities that would engage students' creativity. I created my own coloring books filled with squiggly lines that students turned into their own original pictures as well as fluency activities such as, "Draw as many sea creatures as you can imagine." The children loved creating their own pictures and then comparing their illustrations to others. I no longer had to worry about the social implications of coloring pages, because my students now had to think creatively even in their free time.

Photo 12.1 Kate writing a draft of her chapter for the book.

My decision to change my coloring books was only one of the things that I did differently from my mentor, in order to teach according to my training and my beliefs. Each of my choices became an act of "teaching to transgress" (hooks, 1994). Maureen gave me reams of worksheets that I placed directly into our scrap paper bins for students to complete if they were interested. Maureen approached me at least once every month to tell me how concerned she was with my teaching style; how parents had certain expectations that needed to be met by sending home worksheets; and how she did not think that I had enough evidence to defend the grades that I gave my students.

I assessed my students formally and informally on a daily basis (e.g. Hansen, 1998; Johnston, 1997; Power & Chandler, 1998). I recorded my findings in various assessment notebooks where I could include my observations, student activities, and formal assessments. Maureen simply could not grasp that there was a way to teach and to assess other than her own. I completed developmental reading assessments, observational surveys, and daily running records of my students. I knew each of my students' reading abilities, their strengths and weaknesses, and their instructional levels in the areas of comprehension, fluency, phonics, and grammatical awareness. Despite all of this, Maureen could not stand that I did not give the reading tests she had created, and one day she took action against me. Maureen went straight to the principal and assistant principal at my school. She told them that she was very concerned about my teaching, and that I was not doing any of the worksheets that she gave me. Fortunately, my administrators supported my teaching and told Maureen the same. However, this support has not always prevented me from caving in in the face of peer pressure.

Struggling Against Cultural Bias

I first became aware of how inequities and power struggles can occur in large-scale, blatant ways within a school district during my first year of teaching. One winter day, I entered my school and saw Santa and reindeer ornaments adorning most of the classrooms. Throughout the first weeks of December my shock grew. I was surrounded by Christmas ornamentations. Classrooms and the main office door were "wrapped" in Christmas paper and wreaths hung on walls and doors. Christmas music played throughout the hallways for special occasions, and as I walked through the school's lobby each day, I encountered a *faux* fireplace festooned with stockings, garlands, and gifts. There was a Christmas tree decorated with ornaments sitting adjacent to the fireplace. Against a wall and to the side of this was a small, unadorned display case in which there were canned goods on one shelf (a reminder to bring goods for our food drive) and a menorah, dreidl, and Kwanzaa book on the other. This was, perhaps, most appalling to me, because it was an acknowledgment by the teachers and parents of my school that they knew, on some level, just how inappropriate their Christmas preparations were. In fact, as one teacher hung Christmas ornaments in her classroom, she asked me to pull out a Christmas poem from her supplies. She joked about the last line of the poem which read, "Jesus Christ is born," saying that she used to hang that in her room each year, but didn't think it was appropriate any longer.

The pinnacle of my school's annual Christmas activities was called "Breakfast with Santa."

The cultural implications of these practices were appalling, and I wanted to do something. I worried that, as a new teacher, however, I did not have the status to make a change. I brought up my concerns with the members of LSJTRG at our next meeting, and was met with shock and dismay. Entering the meeting, members immediately asked how things were going. This was just the opening that I needed, and I launched into a description of Christmas at my school. I kept asking, is this normal? Was I really so naïve to think that church and state really were separate in our education system? How can we even pretend to be giving these kids equitable, just, or comprehensive educations when our actions implicitly teach otherwise? After much discussion, I felt confident in my reaction and opinion. Members of LSJTRG assured me that I not only had the power to make a change, but the duty. I left feeling both empowered and reassured.

The action that I took occurred within my classroom through lessons about holidays around the world. I taught my students about Hanukkah, Kwanzaa, and about different types of Christmas celebrations. We researched New Year celebrations and found that some cultures celebrated the New Year in completely different ways. In honor of each holiday that we studied, my class read stories, made garlands that we draped around our classroom, played games, and created hall decorations. I was vigilant about not making this a study of the "other," so my students made many connections between world holidays and themselves (Howard, 2006). For Hanukkah, my students made a giant blue menorah. On the menorah they wrote, "festival of lights," and "this holiday celebrates freedom." I received an array of reactions to our large, colorful creations. My administrators and some teachers thought that our projects were wonderful. While I appreciated the support, I was disturbed by the thought that teaching my students about beliefs and cultures around the world and within the United States was somehow groundbreaking. I wanted to engage the cultures and traditions of all of the families in my classroom (Allen, 2007; Edwards, 1999; Howard, 2006; Shockley, Michalove, & Allen, 1995).

Not a single teacher complained about my lessons but there was a continuous trickle of disapproval or discomfort. Some teachers, who considered themselves my friends, thought that I was just misguided and often told me that they were worried about me, and that I had to be careful. These teachers were effectively stimulating a culture of fear to suppress nonconformity (Giroux, 1988; Shannon, 1992).

During my first year of teaching, my district adopted a balanced literacy program. Unfortunately, we did not have enough books to support our kindergarten through second grade initiative. During one of my first meetings with LSJTRG, I brought up this dilemma and was immediately greeted with ideas and outrage. As we sat together at tables arranged in a large circle, the educators of LSJTRG began asking questions about this new program. *So this is a balanced literacy program, right? You're looking for guided reading books? Have you written a grant yet? Have you ever written a grant before? There must be some way that we can take action. How could the U.S. devote so much to our military and so little to education that our classrooms lack the books necessary to teach?! We need to have a BAKE SALE. Do you all remember the shirts and stickers that said, "It will be a great day when the U.S. military has to hold a bake sale to buy bombs?" That should be our motto.*

Ultimately, the group decided to hold a bake sale at our next meeting. Each member invited two people to come to the meeting and encouraged them to buy baked goods, or simply to make donations. From the proceeds, I was able to purchase ten six-book guided reading sets for my classroom library. This was the first time that I had seen a group of educators rally together and take action. So often I heard teachers, administrators, and parents pointing out problems. But here was a group of educators interested in making change, no matter how small. My bake sale experience was my induction to the realm of action. I learned through this experience that organizing for social action was a possible and necessary part of my life as an educator.

Teachers as Activists: Liesl's Journey

Teachers Only Teach, They Don't Think

Assessing student growth is an area where Kate's and my journeys as teachers/activists overlap. Every late October teachers begin to write their report cards. This is a time which most teachers come to loathe as they sift through mounds of student work and try to find ways to interpret test scores so that they and parents will have a fuller picture of the students' academic achievements. While I was a student teacher I did not experience the overwhelming experience of writing 22 report cards through the second-hand stress of my cooperating teacher. As Mrs. Grainger and I were gathering data for report cards, another teacher who was also writing report cards approached her. Mr. Monroe came into the room and said, "I am not writing comments on my report cards, it's a waste of my time!" With this comment began an attempt to gather support for a cause and create solidarity between teachers.

This elementary school was located in a conservative suburb of St. Louis. Though Mr. Monroe was certainly unconventional in his dress, choosing tie-dye shirts and jeans most days, he too taught in a traditional and conservative manner. The teachers at the school were not very active in teachers' unions though many were members of either MSTA or MNEA, and it was obvious that the teachers were not used to the idea of organizing together to address issues in their schools. This is not to say that these teachers were totally disenfranchised and that they did not address issues collectively, just that I believe that these teachers never saw themselves as organizers.

I considered Mr. Monroe's proposal, internally of course, as this conversation was not for my participation. It seemed reasonable to me that it took a long time to write out the very comments that would be discussed with the parents in the next few days; however, it also seemed necessary to write out certain points as written documentation on the students. As Mr. Monroe left the room, likely to rally more support, Mrs. Grainger agreed that she too would not write comments on her report cards. We discussed the situation and considered the possibilities as we went through students' portfolios of past assessments.

Later that day another teacher, Mrs. Crain, came by and Mrs. Grainger told her about the previous conversation on writing comments for report cards. Mrs. Crain had already written comments on half of her report cards. Mrs. Grainger avoided her direct questions on our progress and instead redirected the conversation back to the dilemma regarding whether to write comments on the report cards. She told Mrs. Crain that she was scared not to write comments on her report cards. As Mrs. Grainger said these words my heart dropped a little; I was stunned. Just an hour ago she had told Mr. Monroe that she would go along with his plan and now she was telling Mrs. Crain she was scared to go along with the plan. I sat there, still unsure of what to say. I knew I could not bring up that fact that she had earlier agreed with Mr. Monroe, as that would undermine Mrs. Grainger in front of another teacher. I had been told more than once that this was not appropriate.

Eventually I mustered up enough courage to enter the conversation. I blurted out, "You need to unionize!" The ladies looked at me in disbelief. Had I really just said that? I knew I needed to say something. I couldn't sit there any longer and just watch these teachers act so disempowered. I felt as though I had to say something to them, something to bring to their consciousness that they could take action within the school if they thought something wasn't right. I was new to teaching and working within the school system, and they were sure to point this out to me by scolding me for being so naïve.

"Liesl, be quiet and listen. Teachers can only teach. They can't think. They can only teach," they told me. I knew that I was not to say another word. I was completely shocked by this comment. "Teachers can only teach." I didn't agree with that at all. I have been taught to be an activist for my students and for schools, and I refused to believe that I was to teach as I was told.

I felt powerless that day. I was so uncertain as to my place, but I refused to consider my job as a teacher to end with state and district curriculum. As I reflected on this day with my colleagues I came to realize that this occasion was not one of a kind, but rather represented a whole series of conversations that have left teachers disempowered and voiceless in the educational system. It seemed to me that everyone has forgotten that teaching is an intellectual profession (Fleischer, 1998).

"Cops Need Bigger Guns!"

When I was a student teacher, I reflected on my belief that teachers can do more than teach the curriculum. I spent several weeks preparing a government unit that included an introductory lesson on writing petitions. In order to create my unit I used the district's curriculum framework, the textbook, and trade books. In poring over these materials I tried to see where I could integrate issues of justice into the curriculum. I was able to integrate a critical perspective into many of my lessons by allowing students to dialogue about their differing viewpoints to create a more democratic classroom.

I find inspiration in other educators who see their role in the classroom as promoting civil action and a democratic society (e.g. Bigelow & Peterson, 2002; Rogers & Mosley, 2004; Shor, 1997; Wink, 2000). One way that I promoted such action in my third grade classroom was by encouraging the class to write a petition to the mayor. I wanted to teach my third graders that they had the power to write their representatives and demand change in their neighborhoods. I invited the students to brainstorm things that they would like their mayor to do for the community. The students began to come up with ideas: "I think the firemen should come quicker to our houses when there is a fire."

Greg raised his hand and said, "I think that cops need bigger guns." I was a little taken aback by this suggestion but I nevertheless added it to our growing list of ideas. A few other students agreed with Greg when he initially made his suggestion. Many of the boys were fascinated by the military, wearing camouflage and soldier Halloween costumes. They drew M-16s and tanks on much of their work. Despite all of this, I was a little shocked that some of the students wanted the local police to have larger guns. To my chagrin, the suggestion won the initial vote. I did not really like this suggestion but I was sure that I could not disaffirm their feelings. I needed to be persuaded as to why it was appropriate to write the mayor about this subject. So began a debate among students who thought cops needed bigger guns and those who felt it was unnecessary. I wanted the students to choose another topic, but I did not want to seem as though I was making the decision. I taped this lesson, and when I analyzed the tape I can see the tensions in the lesson. I see that the reason it was so stressful was because the students were in charge. They were leading the discussions and making the decisions.

Following this lesson I spoke with a few teachers in the school about my lesson. Some were quite shocked that I even allowed the students to talk about guns at all in the classroom. Others were surprised that I allowed the students to consider the gun proposal during the voting stage of writing our petition. However, it seems that allowing the students the time in class to consider alternative viewpoints had caused them to consider if their original perspective was the best choice. The students were encouraged to question themselves and others in a respectful way. For this reason, if for no other, I believe that allowing students to lead discussions and debates, though intimidating for the teacher, is an excellent way to bring students into the reflection process.

Designing Culturally Relevant Instruction

During college I learned a less intimidating practice that I find to be just as powerful for student learning. As part of my teacher education program, I took a literacy methods block that was taught at an elementary school. In the courses we spent 40 minutes of each class teaching students one-on-one using an accelerative and balanced literacy program. The reading program began from a strengths-based perspective that sought to capitalize on students' interests as an entry to appropriate leveled books. I had the privilege of working with Marcus, a second grade student who attended the urban elementary school where the tutoring program was held. Through our conversations I came to find out that Marcus enjoyed reading about animals and basketball.

Although Marcus seemed to enjoy the books I brought on these subjects, I began to wonder if they were culturally relevant. In class we had been learning about how reading culturally relevant books positively impacts interest in reading (e.g. Ladson-Billings, 1994). After realizing that the books I chose were not focused on people and social interactions, I looked for books that realistically represented Marcus' cultural experiences. It felt awkward choosing books with the premise that Marcus was African American. This idea seems naïve to me now. I also realize now that just because a book has African American characters does not mean it is any more culturally relevant than a book featuring white characters if the storyline portrays an irrelevant experience of which Marcus had no prior knowledge. The next semester, I was ready to bring culturally relevant texts to our tutoring sessions. The reaction was exhilarating; Marcus read with more fluency and his reactions to the books were more developed. He picked up on the rhythmic pattern of the books I chose and began to write songs with recurring characters after he read each day. It was affirming to see the vast improvement as a result of book choice. It was through constant reflection on Marcus' progress, my teaching style, and comfort level that I was able to change my practices. In order for Marcus to continue to develop into an independent reader I needed to challenge Marcus as well as myself. When Marcus read with few errors I felt more confident.

Photo 12.2 Liesl and Melissa attend a peace vigil to end the U.S. occupation in Iraq.

Educating for Change Curriculum Fair and Community Actions

When I joined the Literacy for Social Justice Teacher Research Group they were in the middle of planning the first annual Educating for Change Curriculum Fair. Though I was hesitant at first, I eventually jumped right in and headed up the food donations committee. As the fair drew closer I worked to post flyers, recruit teachers, and prepared the schedule. I planned a workshop of my own based on my work with Marcus.

My workshop was during the first session of workshops. I wondered whether people would be interested in my ideas. Would Marcus be able to make it to the presentation? The title of my workshop was "Reading and Writing with Purpose: Introducing Culturally Relevant Texts into an Accelerative Literacy Program." Marcus did show up, and together we shared stories of our lessons. He read some of the songs that he wrote and I was able to show the audience, including Marcus' mother and brother, how he had grown as a reader and writer as a result of our work together. During my session and afterwards, I talked with educators from all across the city about their classrooms and how they were integrating justice into their schools. I was empowered to see that I was not alone, that others in my community were working for justice and were being successful in a time when schools are being held more and more accountable and are losing funding to private companies. The Curriculum Fair is just one way that we bring the community together to educate for change.

As a student and teacher activist I stay active in my community. I have done this by joining community groups and by showing solidarity to peace movements. It is important to be an active participant in the current democracy, as I teach my students. During my final semester at college I attended organizing meetings to counteract NCLB, attended candidate forums for the local school board, canvassed and supported campaigns for the local school board, attended peace rallies, and joined a group called Mother's Day for Peace along with moving into a leadership role in LSJTRG. Each of these experiences showed me the power of community organizing and has empowered me to think more critically about my world.

I continued to develop these skills through my involvement with the LSJTRG, my community involvement, and through my coursework. In the winter of 2006 I became involved with the St. Louis City School Board election, first by attending a candidate's forum held at a local college. The following week one of the candidates attended a LSJTRG meeting and discussed his candidacy as well as his future plans for the school board. I was very impressed by the candidates who were parents in the district and who genuinely wanted to hear from teachers, parents, and community members. This was the first campaign I had ever worked on, but I quickly learned how to canvass, participate in a letter-writing campaign, and work at the polls and phone bank, learning the democratic process. During this election period, I spent time connecting with other teachers who were also interested in social change. These teachers were just as committed to their students as they were committed to justice. All of this action was taking place within the climate of silence that has surrounded the school district. The tally of votes came in at around two o'clock in the morning with the grassroots campaign winning over two big business candidates.

My commitment to political involvement culminated during my senior year when I took a class called Literacy Education in the Context of Human Rights and Global Justice with Dr. Rogers. The class consisted of several projects that connected our class to the real world. One of the projects that I completed for this class was a book on teachers' rights. Each student was supposed to create an activism project that dealt with an educational issue. As a new teacher, I decided to learn more about teachers' civil rights in schools and in public. I searched the Internet and the library for information about school law and found that there was a lot to be said about students' civil rights in schools. For teachers, the information was either out of date or difficult to find. After finding some solid resources to use for background research I decided that I wanted to talk with teachers about their rights. I wondered, were teachers' civil rights being protected to the fullest extent possible? Were there unwritten rules about freedom of speech and association that were being used in schools? Were these limitations constitutional? As I spoke with teachers, I noticed that few knew the laws about what teachers can and cannot say in schools or about schools. I created a small book of laws and stories that would contain information about some of the most prominent cases in teacher law. I could not learn everything there was to know about teacher law but I wanted to be a catalyst for myself and for other teachers. One way I did this was by facilitating a workshop for LSJTRG on what I had learned.

Conclusion

Often when teachers think of social action, we consider great acts that garner media attention and publicity. These moments are important. They bring social action and its significance to the public eye. But these giant, publicly scrutinized moments are not the beginning and end of social action (e.g. Fleischer, 2000). The idea of social action demands that the actions themselves be implicit in all that we do as educators. One great culminating activity with a class or with a group of educators has little meaning if the act is not the end result of a thousand smaller moments in education. Our actions emerge daily as we interact with our students and peers. As teachers, we are learning to make conscious choices regarding which books we read to our class, how we facilitate discussions, and when and in what ways we challenge and critique long-held institutional practices.

As we inquire into the critical moments that have shaped our development as literacy teachers and activities, we are struck by our realization that personal agency forms or dies in a series of venues. Teacher education at the university and school-based professional development are traditional types of professional development opportunities. However, the professional development that is traditionally recommended or encouraged would not have met our interests, questions, or needs as beginning teachers. We had real struggles and concerns about how to design an academically rigorous classroom and also promote democracy and social justice. LSJTRG provided an authentic learning community where we could express our uncertainties, our fears, and concerns and where, together, we could solve problems that arose in the classroom.

Rethinking Practice

Analyze your curriculum to look for ways to integrate justice into your day. Start small with a discussion, a read-aloud, or ask children critical questions. Keep a journal with you throughout the day. Record the moments you feel uncomfortable in your teaching. When do these moments arise?

Often, we hear other teachers say that they will "get in trouble" if they talk about social justice issues in their classrooms. One of the most powerful tools we can have as teachers is knowledge of our rights. Know the rights that protect you: freedom of speech, freedom of association, and political activity. Some of the laws have changed over time, specific to districts and states, but here are some resources to have on hand:

Donehower, R. W. (2003). "Boring lessons: Defining the limits of a teacher's first amendment right to speak through the curriculum." *Michigan Law Review, 102,* 517–541.
Essex, N. (2002). *School Law and the Public Schools: A practical guide for educational leaders.* Boston, MA: Allyn and Bacon.

Surround yourself with a community of activists—join a teacher network, become familiar with alternative media outlets and educational journals such as *Rethinking Schools, Edutopia, The Radical Teacher,* or *The Progressive,* talk with politicians and local leaders, and know your union leaders.

---

13 Working Within and Against Heterosexist and Homophobic Schools
Social Justice and High School Journalism

Janet DePasquale

What began as a teachers' strike in Oaxaca, Mexico, in May 2006, evolved into a massive movement for social change on June 14 when police attacked demonstrators using bullets and tear gas, which transformed the teachers' strike into a democratic social movement demanding the resignation of the governor and the creation of a new state constitution. The teachers' strike raised issues over resources for students, teachers' wages, and the threat of privatized education. These demands resonated with many other social groups including hundreds of labor unions, women's groups, indigenous federations, left-wing political formations, student groups—all who joined the movement. The movement became known as APPO (The Popular Assembly of the Peoples of Oaxaca). APPO coordinated a massive campaign of civil disobedience that brought the state government to a standstill. Alternative media, such as *Radio Plantón*, the radio station of the teachers' union, played a central role throughout the movement. The police destroyed the equipment at the radio station, making it impossible to broadcast news about the movement. Again in an act of solidarity between university students and workers, the University of Oaxaca radio station was taken over and became the voice of the movement. They became known as *Radio de la Verdad* (Truth Radio) (Gold, 2008). View Jill Freidberg's films about the teachers' movement in Mexico. You can find the films at http://corrugate.org/.

Introduction

"Why are we doing this, anyway?"

Every high school teacher has heard this question at least once. I encourage students to question any assignment, as it helps them take ownership of their own education. But this time was different.

This time, the question derived from a conversation about the latest center spread for our student newspaper. In journalism, the term "center spread" describes the two pages in the exact center of the newspaper, often used to show-case a current hot-button issue, noteworthy aspect of the community, or a photo-driven story, to catch the reader's eye. This time was different for our center spread because the students had decided to tackle gay and lesbian issues in the high school.

Finding a Center Spread Topic

At the beginning of the school year, the center spread editor led the charge. A highly opinionated, politically conservative female with true steadfast dedication to the newspaper, she promptly told the class, "We need to start tackling more serious social issues on our center spread than 'My 50 favorite things to do over the winter break.'"

So the class began brainstorming possible topics for all seven issues of the year. One student mentioned that the anniversary of Matthew Shepard's death was approaching. She discussed how this teen's brutal death in Laramie, Wyoming, brought hate crimes against homosexuals to the American forefront. Another student mentioned that many schools in St. Louis have student-led gay–straight alliances and asked, "Why doesn't our school have one?"

Someone else said, "We should do a center spread about homosexuality."

Others tossed additional social justice ideas into the ring: the ongoing increase in teen obesity, teen substance abuse, teen pregnancy and birth control, or

Photo 13.1 Janet provides a student with feedback on the layout of the newspaper.

diversity within the school. Some students suggested lighter topics like Halloween or student artwork and poetry. The center spread editor wrote all the possibilities on flip chart paper, and told everyone that they would vote in the next class.

However, in journalism, *rushed* is the keyword. Deadlines. Deadlines. Deadlines. There never seems to be enough time in a class period to cover all the necessary items: assigning stories, conducting interviews, editing/revising drafts, reporter/editor conferencing, discussing journalism ethics, and the list goes on. So in the midst of our ten "to-do" tasks for the next period, they voted. The homosexuality center spread earned the most votes, and so we began.

They generated solid story ideas: the advent of gay–straight alliances in St. Louis high schools, the national debate over gay marriage and adoption, and the continuing danger of soaring suicide rates for homosexual teens. However, after the brainstorming session, the center spread editor asked for volunteers, and no one raised their hands. It took some coaxing on her part, but slowly, people began to volunteer until all the stories were assigned. Two students, Amy and Holly, decided to work together on the gay–straight alliance story. But they seemed like the only two who were genuinely excited about their assignments. They decided to call as many area schools as possible to determine which ones had gay–straight alliances.

School Reactions to the Process

Schools, in general, are typically heterosexist and homophobic institutions (Owens, 1998). Heterosexism manifests in many ways throughout the school day—from the absence of gay and lesbian people in the texts and curriculum materials that students read to policies about activities and lifestyles (Donelson & Rogers, 2004; Hermann-Wilmarth, 2007). As the students began work on this particular issue, I knew we would break new ground at the school. This particular district, with multiple high schools in suburban St. Louis, served predominantly European American, religious, blue-collar workers with conservative views. The faculty mirrored that conservatism, with only one African American teacher at our high school, a couple of openly homophobic teachers, others who joked in the faculty lounge about the African American students' dialect, and a member of the administrative staff with a penchant for sending forwarded emails to everyone in the building about the need for prayer in schools. With all of this in mind, I did not fully understand how faculty and students would receive gay and lesbian issues in the school newspaper. But if my journalism students wanted to tackle the tough issue, I was proud of them, and I would help them any way I could.

A few days later, Amy and Holly approached me during our first-period class.

"Ms. D, I've tried to call a bunch of schools to see if they have gay–straight alliances, but no one will return my calls," said Amy.

"I've tried, too. I just keep getting sent to someone's voicemail," said Holly.

"Yeah, I called one school and they were really rude to me. The athletic director told me 'No, we don't have a group like that,' and then he hung up on me," said Amy.

I told them that I belonged to a local journalism advisor group, Sponsors for School Publications, and I would ask the other advisors to see if anyone could give them some leads. Both girls said they appreciated it and would keep trying.

Not more than an hour after this conversation, in the middle of teaching my next class, my telephone rang. It was one of the school administrators.

"Ms. DePasquale, are we writing about gays in our newspaper?"

I confirmed that yes, indeed, among other topics, my journalism students were writing some stories that dealt with homosexuality.

"Well, I wanted to know because I got a call from a friend of mine over at— [one school Amy had called]—who said that one of your students called there yesterday and started asking a bunch of questions about their school policies and gays. He said the reporter asked him if the school had a policy against gay–straight alliances."

I laughed at that statement and said, "Well, that sounds like an odd question for my reporter to ask because the existence of such a policy would seem to be unconstitutional." I assured him that I would speak to my student about the interview she had conducted.

When I saw Amy later that day, I asked her about the interview. She told me that she had *not* asked him about a policy against gay–straight alliances, but had instead asked about any policy that might relate to gays and lesbian students. He had answered, "We have a basic policy that does not allow any public displays of affection, for any students."

I found his response a bit strange. Amy had asked about *any* policies that might relate to gay or lesbian students. He hadn't discussed any policies that protected students from discrimination of any kind. Instead, he spoke about public displays of affection. Why did he react that way?

Later that day, I saw the administrator who had phoned me. When he noticed me, he smiled broadly and said, "So, Ms. DePasquale, what exactly *are* we putting in our newspaper?"

I explained that we were addressing the gay and lesbian issues in schools, as it was a topic the students had decided was important to address.

"Oh really? The *students*?" he speculated.

I told him that my editor-in-chief had come up with the idea after attending a summer journalism camp, where she had learned about the growing trend of high schools across the country developing gay–straight alliances. However, I did not like the implication behind his question. I felt myself growing defensive. In my three years at the school, I had always had an amicable, professional rapport with this man. I knew he felt comfortable talking to me, but I also knew that he was implying the idea had been mine.

"Ms. DePasquale, this is Missouri, not Boston. People have very different views about gays around here, and some people won't be too happy to read about it in the paper," he said, referring to my roots in New England.

I had taught in Boston for three years before moving to Missouri. The glaring irony of it all was that I had moved from Massachusetts, the only state in America to legalize gay marriage in May 2004, to Missouri, whose residents voted (just three months later) by an overwhelming 71 percent in favor of a constitutional amendment to ban gay marriage. In other parts of the country, progressive strides were made for gay and lesbian people. In 2000, Vermont became the first state in the country to legally recognize gay/lesbian civil unions; in November 2003, the Massachusetts Supreme Judicial Court ruled that prohibiting gay marriage would violate the state's constitution; and in October 2005, Connecticut legalized civil unions. However, in other states, the lives of gay and lesbian peoples were on the ballot and in 2004, 11 states passed a ban on gay marriage. The legislative weight of these decisions may readily be used as support for heterosexism and homophobia in classrooms and schools (Hermann-Wilmarth, 2007).

Teaching Journalism in the Wake of Hazelwood School District v. Kuhlmeier

At my first school, in suburban Boston, the principal told me that he did not expect to review the newspaper before it was published. He told me, "We pay you a stipend to make those decisions about what goes in the paper." Since that was my first teaching job, I had little concerns whether the First Amendment freedom I had enjoyed as a reporter would extend to my student journalists. I did not realize at the time that I had the benefit of teaching in one of only six states in the country with state laws that guaranteed specific freedoms of the high school press.

When I began teaching journalism, I learned about Hazelwood School District v. Kuhlmeier, the 1988 Supreme Court decision that granted public high school officials authority to censor school-sponsored student publications. Also as a result of the Hazelwood case, school officials were granted the right to review a publication before it went to press. So I taught my students in Boston about this case so they could understand that, ultimately, student journalists had limits on their First Amendment freedoms, limits that *New York Times* reporters didn't have. But this posed no immediate problems with a *laissez-faire* principal and Massachusetts' position as one of the "Sweet Six" (along with Arkansas, Iowa, Kansas, California, and Colorado), the only states with specific laws to protect students' right to free expression, in the wake of Hazelwood. However, when I moved to St. Louis, the Hazelwood case and its local history proved important in my next journalism job. Ironically, Hazelwood School District may be found in none other than St. Louis County, Missouri.

When I moved to St. Louis, my new principal knew all about the Hazelwood case and demonstrated a very different philosophy about his role in the newspaper. He wholeheartedly believed in prior review, stating that *he* would be the one taking the heat if something "bad" appeared in the newspaper. It was this mindset that prompted him to declare to my horrified journalism class one day that they shouldn't be confused about whose paper it was—"It's my paper," he said.

The principal's censorship of the paper functioned to officially sanction some topics as important and worthwhile and others as unsafe and unimportant. Censorship around literature that contains gay and lesbian characters is not new, and functions to silence the voices of diverse peoples and maintain the status quo (Day, 2000; Stewig, 1994). As a journalism teacher I found myself working within and against the official and unofficial censorship of the lives and issues of gay and lesbian people in the school curriculum.

Transitioning the Journalism Program

I spent the first year simply teaching the students what it meant to write a news story, the importance of knowing Associated Press style, and how to interview. The second year, they honed their skills, but by the end of that year they had begun to ask questions. When I set up a newspaper exchange through the local journalism advisor group, they would look at newspapers from other area schools and say, "Why can they write about this, but we can't?" By the third year, I had a great crew of leaders who were not only ready but anxious to tackle those issues. Enter the ambitious center spread editor and the gay and lesbian issues center spread. I knew I'd need to sit down with my principal and explain what they were doing and why.

He was a reasonable man, and I think that in his heart he believed he was doing a good thing for the newspaper, providing a safeguard of sorts. So I spoke with him from that angle, that we both wanted what was good for the news-paper. I also told him I understood why he wanted to review the paper before-hand, and I was not coming to try to argue that philosophy. However, when he called the paper "his paper," it flew in the face of the sense of ownership I wanted to instill in the students. In the end, he said that as long as the subject of homo-sexuality was handled responsibly and objectively, he would support it.

As I stood up to leave his office, he smiled at me and said, "Thank you for causing me to lose yet another hair on my head."

I replied, "And thank you for upholding the First Amendment." When I left his office I felt a huge relief. This was one potentially major obstacle that we had hurdled. I was reminded that I needed to work with and against heterosexist schools and policies.

In the midst of these discussions, though, I also felt somewhat conflicted about being the one to address these issues with the principal. By my third year, I sent the students (usually my editor-in-chief) more often with a question or concern. I also knew that the principal preferred to talk to me, so I had to build his trust.

Once the principal offered his support of this center spread, I did not worry when the other administrator questioned our topic. But when he implied that I was pushing my own agenda, my frustration grew. He was implying that exam-ining gay and lesbian issues was serving the students' narrow interests rather than part of the responsibilities of public education to serve all students.

We stood in the hallway talking about gay–straight alliances and the history of discrimination in this part of the country. Then he remarked, with a hearty laugh, that it was quite obvious to him that there wouldn't be a gay–straight alliance at this school because "there aren't any gays here." In spite of his laugh-ter I could not tell if he was joking or being serious. Then he said that another high school in the district had a diversity club, but he didn't see that flying here, either.

"If you had a club to highlight differences, everyone at this school would be in it because we have that much diversity," he said.

He told me about a student years ago who was openly gay and he used to wear buttons to voice his homosexuality. The administration made him take the buttons off because, in this administrator's words, "We were following the codes of decency for all students." He described how, in the past, some school districts did not allow prom dates to be of the same sex, but added that this school never had any policy prohibiting it. He remarked that I needed to understand the conservative climate of the community.

I told him that gay and lesbian people and the challenges that confronted them were present in our society regardless of whether people liked it or not, and we would make sure to cover the issues responsibly. He then backed off and said that he was not saying he had a problem with it, but for me to understand the nature of the community.

His responses, I have come to understand, are examples of "heterosexist/ homophobic talk" that privilege the rights of heterosexual students at the expense of gay and lesbian students. Teachers often provide excuses for not integrating gay and lesbian issues into their curriculum by arguing that students are "not ready" (Schall & Kauffmann, 2003), there is a lot of diversity in the school, and we do not want to single out any one group of students (Marinoble, 1998), there are no gay students here (Hermann-Wilmarth, 2007), and gay and lesbian issues are about sex and politics and neither should be discussed in school (Swartz, 2003). All these types of responses imply that gay and lesbian people are unimportant and perpetuate anti-gay resolutions that are explicitly or implicitly condoned by schools.

What did I need to *understand*? I understood what was right. I understood that discrimination isn't OK just because a majority of the community believes it is. I understood that I was teaching in a new community, but that didn't mean that I would abandon my values and not take a stand in the name of social justice.

Many times since moving to St. Louis, in situations like this, I felt isolated by my beliefs. At the time of the move, I had known that the South and the Midwest were typically conservative regions, but I felt alienated and craved my old, familiar surroundings. Of course, a few other teachers shared my commitments to social justice, but on a daily basis I often found it hard to find common ground with my colleagues. So, when I joined the Literacy for Social Justice Teacher Research Group in the first months after my move, I found a haven for open-minded thinking, discussion of sensitive issues, and the camaraderie of many dedicated individuals at all levels of education. Through this sense of unity in the LSJTRG, I gained strength to continue the social justice fight in my school community.

Meeting the Issue Head-on

Back in the journalism classroom, the students continued to work on their stories. However, within a week, I sensed a lack of overall excitement about the center spread. I began to hear rumblings of "Why are we doing this?" from more than one person.

I could sense something different in the air about this issue. I was not sure if it was tension, confusion, or lack of interest. Personally, I knew the topic had merit and was an example of courageous journalism. I also knew that a few of the current events-savvy students recognized gay and lesbian issues as a hot-button topic, including the editor-in-chief as well as the center spread editor. But the majority of the class was not really invested. I spoke to my editor-in-chief about it, and she said that Amy and Holly seemed to be the only two really dedicated ones. So, in spite of that constant rushing in the world of journalism, I decided that we needed to address the issue head-on. It is part of a teacher's responsibility to help keep the motivation high, but I sensed something more than teenage slacking. Who really wanted to tackle this issue? Did the decision to tackle the issue have to be unanimous? How could I gauge the interest level? How would I get everyone back on board and excited again? Should we save it for another issue when we would have more time to sift through the complicated parts of the issue?

When I had asked for advice from LSJTRG, they encouraged me to create an atmosphere of open communication. As I sat at home planning the lesson, I knew that I needed to stimulate dialogue about the complexity of issues that surrounded gay and lesbian rights—issues that divided the region, and quite possibly the class, but there were so many unknowns about the next day's class.

Also, there was another voice in my head that night. It was the voice of that assistant principal, questioning whether this center spread had been my students' idea. Had I somehow pressed them to write about this topic because of my own biased view? Had I in some way "pushed my own agenda," something I always told them never to do in their stories? Personally, as someone who has numerous gay friends and who participated in a gay friend's wedding ceremony in Massachusetts the previous summer, this was a topic close to my heart. But I hoped I had not, even subconsciously, tried to persuade my students to write about something they didn't believe in.

That thought bothered me months later, after the issue had been published. Why was I so concerned about pushing something I believed in? Why didn't I question myself in my English classes when I told everyone that Shakespeare was one of the most brilliant writers in history? When I taught *To Kill a Mockingbird* in my freshmen English classes, we discussed the horrors of racism and how it destroyed lives. Themes in that book lent themselves to discussions about how racism continues today in many forms. I never felt that I was pushing my beliefs at my students, but I never made any apologies for my outspokenness about the impact of racism. So what was the difference when it came to integrating lesbian and gay issues into the newspaper?

I think it has something to do with using society as a measure. Fifty years ago, it would not have been acceptable for me to teach *To Kill a Mockingbird* the way

I teach it today. The majority of society viewed African Americans as lesser individuals, worthy of segregating. The activism during the Civil Rghts Movement used to be viewed as radical thinking, but has now become accepted belief. But does that mean that teachers must wait until the majority of society catches up to the social justice movement? If I asked myself, "When am I allowed to impose my beliefs of social morality with my students?" I would answer, "Never." Teachers should not *impose* their convictions and expect their students to follow· the teacher's belief system nor second-guess themselves when they fall upon a community that practices social injustice on a regular basis. It also speaks to the ways in which we as teachers self-censor ourselves out of fear—fear of working against the institutional norms, losing our jobs, offending parents, of not knowing enough about the issue.

Breaking the Silence: The Class Forum

On the drive to school that morning, I worried, What if they won't be honest? What if I try to engage them but I can't do it successfully? How far should we take the discussion? What if this plan fails? Well, I had to try.

When the bell rang, I told everyone to take out a piece of paper. I wrote the following sentence on the board: "Why are we doing this center spread?" I told the students to answer this question as truthfully as possible, that I wasn't grading it, but we really needed to find the truest answer by the end of class. I scanned the room, watching the 15 girls and three boys write dutifully. This class, all European American except for one Asian student, ranged in age from 15–17 and provided a varied mix of interests. They all came together to write an answer to this one question.

After five minutes of writing, I read the question aloud. Everyone sat for a minute, and then one male student raised his hand.

"OK, I'll start, and I'll be totally honest. I really don't know why we're doing it," he said.

Someone else said, "I'm not comfortable writing about it, but others were, so that's how it was suggested."

"Some feel it's a good cause, but others want it for shock value."

"We're doing it to inform and open people's eyes about what being gay means."

"We want to raise awareness and also help people (even ourselves) to see beyond their own opinions."

"It's our job, even if it's uncomfortable, to report about this. It's an issue that's out there in the world."

"It's an uncomfortable topic, but we could use it to educate others."

As they spoke, I wrote their responses on the board without names. I did not call anyone out to share their ideas if they had not raised their hands, but I encouraged the quiet ones by saying that I believed it was important to hear everyone's ideas in order to try to reach common ground.

The more they talked, the more obvious it became that, in their own minds, they were divided about the topic. Some students admitted that homosexuality was against their religion, and it made them uncomfortable. But no one said, "This is a stupid idea. We shouldn't be writing about it." The division in the class came from deciding *how* we should write about it.

Linda, the cheerleader, asked how this center spread might impact our newspaper's reputation. She wondered about the close-minded people who would read it and throw it away as soon as they saw the topic.

"What if people open our paper and say, 'Why are they writing about fags?'" she asked.

I capitalized on this response to address the use of this "group-biased name calling" (Gordon, 2003). I told the class that 40 years ago people were openly and violently racist, using the n-word without thinking and committing terrible acts against African Americans. It took thousands of people during the Civil Rights Movement to stand up and say, "Wait a minute." But someone always has to be first. By connecting the oppression of gay and lesbian people with the oppression of other marginalized groups in class, I hoped that my students would begin to see the fabric of oppression and the ways in which issues of race, class, gender, sexuality, and religion are woven together.

Someone asked, "How can we possibly reach consensus? How can we write this in a way that everyone on staff will agree? Is that possible?"

John, our opinions editor (and future editor-in-chief), said, "We are like a microcosm of society—the division of opinions in this class mirrors the division in our society today. That's why there's no common ground for people on this issue."

Then I interjected. Was there *some* way to reach consensus? I went back to Linda's comments about student reaction. What were we hoping to achieve through this publication?

I asked the class, "Can everyone agree that, regardless of what you believe religiously, scientifically, or morally, it's wrong to discriminate against someone who is gay?" Everyone agreed. "OK. Then, that's our starting point. That's our consensus. We can write this to inform others about rights and justice. Is that something we can agree on?"

John raised his hand. "That's why we have to stick to the facts and let our audience form their own opinions," he said.

And that's what they did. They conducted a student poll of approximately 240 students and analyzed the results. Students answered questions concerning the use of derogatory jokes about gays and lesbians, personal feelings about homosexuality, and comfort levels around someone who is gay or lesbian. They wrote four other stories with headlines including "Gay–straight alliances impact metro area," "Making school a safer place," "Nation debates same-sex marriage and adoption," and "R.I.P. Matthew Shepard." The main headline read "Breaking the Silence: Raising awareness about tolerance."

The main story, "A Petition against Violence," came from a contributing writer. The senior in an English honors class wrote a personal narrative about hateful remarks he overheard during the senior class panoramic photo-taking. It was a story that described the pain of guilt he felt when he did not stand up and speak out for his own beliefs.

Acting as Change Agents: Reflecting on the School Year

After the school year had ended, I had dinner with a friend who is gay and also a teacher, and told him the story of this experience. He listened, and said he would love to see a copy of that newspaper issue.

Then he said, "I'm sure you already know this, but the kind of impact that you must have had on those students is nothing short of amazing. You might not think it's much, but just describing that scene in the classroom, allowing that conversation to take place. Do you realize how starkly different or how quickly a conversation could have been shut down by a different teacher, with different values, with a different mindset?"

Until he said it that way, I had not really processed it. As teachers, we always look at the end product—the lesson objectives, the goals and outcomes for our units. As a journalism teacher, the emphasis lies on that final product—the newspaper. I was proud of that conversation my students were able to have in class, as a truly "teachable moment," but I had not thought about the lasting implications that a conversation like that could have for them. My focus had been on the reaction of the student body. But in the course of this conversation I realized that I had been too busy looking at the big picture. We published a center spread about gay and lesbian issues, and we went on to cover future center spreads about teen substance abuse and diversity in the school.

Beyond the publication, I had helped educate a class of 18 about critical analysis and group discussion of these sensitive issues for a handful of times in one year. Maybe when they are far beyond the walls of high school, or college, if they can draw on this discussion, this sharing of ideas in a constructive way, exploring topics that might make them uncomfortable but ones they know should be discussed, that would cause them to enlighten others and the chain could continue. And it is through discussion in an open forum, with constructive conversation, that a teacher can encourage students to break down society's barriers. Sometimes students do not realize that those barriers even exist, or sometimes they are perfectly content to perpetuate them. But if a teacher can help challenge students to think about these things, even if it takes years for that light bulb to shine in their minds, it's worth it. And that is why I teach.

Reflecting on this project, there are changes I would have made. I would have liked to have more resources (including literature) with gay and lesbian people and issues available for my students to use as background material. I might have tried to find more allies in the school who were willing to explore gay and lesbian issues with their students in and out of the curriculum. But the conversations I had with my students and with LSJTRG started new explorations. The following year, Leo Miller, a middle school teacher, facilitated a workshop for LSJTRG on integrating gay and lesbian issues into the curriculum. Together, we analyzed children's books such as *And Tango Makes Three* (Richardson & Parnell, 2005), *Heather Has Two Mommies* (Newman, 1989) and *King and King* (de Haan & Nijland, 2002). We discussed questions such as: How are gay and lesbian people presented in literature? What is the range of ways teachers can integrate GLBT issues into their curriculum? Should we integrate GLBT issues proactively or as a response to an "issue" that arises? I know that challenges still exist but I am hopeful that we are on our way to building more inclusive schools for all students.

Rethinking Practice

View the movie *It's Elementary: Talking about Gay Issues in Schools* (Chasnoff & Cohen, 1996) with colleagues in your school. Following the screening facilitate a discussion. You might ask: What surprised you about this movie? In what ways do you already integrate gay and lesbian issues into your curriculum? What are barriers to teaching about gay and lesbian issues in your school? What support networks are present in your school?

Become familiar with literature that includes the stories, lives, perspectives, and issues of gay and lesbian people. Day's (2000) book called *Lesbian and Gay Voices: An Annotated Bibliography and Guide to Literature for Children and Young Adults* is a good resource for literature. As you read various books ask yourself: How can I integrate the lives and histories of gay and lesbian people into my classroom? Visit the website Gay Lesbian and Straight Education Network (GLSEN) to learn more about resources that are available for creating safe and diverse schools at www.glsen.org/cgibin/iowa/all/home/index.html.

---

14 Following the Circles

Organizing for Justice through Literacy Education

Sarah Beaman-Jones

In Venezuela, an adult literacy campaign was initiated under the leadership of democratically elected president Hugo Chávez. Educational programs have been established to educate the millions of people who did not have access to education under former regimes. Over 1,400,000 formerly illiterate Venezuelan adults have learned to read. The government paid for this educational campaign through a massive redistribution of budgets away from foreign debt and corporations and into education, health care, and social welfare. Venezuela spends 20 percent of its national budget on education.

More recently, in November 2007, more than 50,000 students marched in favor of Venezuelan President Hugo Chávez's recently proposed constitutional reforms. The student population included university and high school students. The rally also commemorated the student uprising of 50 years ago that culminated in the downfall of dictator Marcos Pérez Jimenez. The reforms were defeated at the polls. To read more about the peaceful revolutionary process in Venezuela, go to www.venezuelanalysis.com.

Introduction

Organizing for Learning

At one of the Acting for a Better Community (ABC's) student leadership forums, I stood before the group as a moderator and offered a metaphor for our organizing around literacy education. ABC is a student-centered movement for equity through adult literacy education. I compared our grassroots organizing to a starfish. Like the starfish, our groups have multiple arms that constitute the whole. Each arm is responsible for an important part of the whole. Sometimes, all of the arms work together. Other times, certain arms take over more of the work while other arms rest. Together, we apply constant, steady pressure to injustice and inequity. Such pressure, over time, forces change in people, in processes, and in institutions. This chapter is an illustration of my journey as a community organizer and how the overlapping themes of relationships, organizing, and social change have played out in my work and life.

In considering one of our forums, the ABC's planning committee, of which I am a member, decided there was a need to focus on advocacy. Students were asking for others to develop advocacy plans. We wanted the students to understand the process of how movements evolve. In order to activate prior knowledge we gave participants a note card and asked them to write about a time that they had seen a need to speak out about something and whether they had taken action or not. We were practicing the popular education model brought back to us from Highlander by a fellow LSJTRG member, Melissa (Horton, Kohl, & Kohl, 1997; Mosley, 2007).

Marcia, another member of the planning committee, facilitated the discussion. She opened the meeting by describing personal experiences. Once when she was a child she was going with her family to the Chicago Zoo. As they drove through an upscale neighborhood, a group of demonstrators were throwing rocks at any car occupied by African Americans. This was soon after Martin Luther King had been assassinated. Her dad told them all to get down. After they had made their way to safety, he talked to them about times to take a stand versus times when there was no way to change events.

Later in 1975 Marcia was in her college dorm washing her hair and a dorm mate was staring and staring at her hair. Finally Marcia was so uncomfortable about the attention that she asked the girl if there was something wrong. The girl said she had never seen an African American's hair all frizzy before. She was from a "sundown town." This meant that while African Americans were allowed to come into the town to work, they had to be gone by sundown. They continued talking and both learned a lot about each other. This was a time when speaking up led to new learning.

We then had two leaders give a presentation on movements. We showed some video clips about the Civil Rights Movement and talked about Septima Clark and the Highlander School. Jason Murphy, a professor at St. Louis University, described some activist experiences he knew about. Our goal was for the students to begin to understand that a grassroots movement takes planning and commitment. As we became fond of saying, "Rosa Parks did not just sit down because she had had a hard day." Students then shared some of what they had written on their cards and signed their names to various possible actions.

This was one of 17 or so events we held over four years that generated a student leadership movement.

As the ABC's committee planned the first conference in 2003 to 2004, we all felt strongly that we wanted to use the event to build a community of those concerned about social issues that impact adult literacy students. We decided to end the conference with small lunch box discussions led by a facilitator who asked a series of questions: What are the most important things learned at the conference? How will what you have learned change what you do at work? What support do you need to make these changes? What are the next steps? We then asked people to sign a list if they wanted to be contacted about the next event. We reviewed all the comments and looked for themes and patterns. We wanted to understand the social problems that people were concerned about so we could use those as a point of departure in our organizing. Like Myles Horton, we see literacy as a way to solve social problems, not an end in itself. Horton said,

> We weren't thinking of it primarily as a literacy program because teaching people to read and write was only one step toward their becoming citizens and social activists. The immediate goal was getting the right to vote. Becoming literate was only a part of a larger process.
>
> (Horton, Kohl, & Kohl, p. 100)

Many people were interested in strategies to advocate for social change. Our forum in November 2004 was focused on collaboration, political action, and student voice. I was the facilitator for the group focused on student voice. Our goals were to develop an action plan based on the group's sense of urgency and need. The intensity of feelings generated by this discussion was powerful; so much so I had a hard time standing in front of the group and taking comments. Sometimes I wanted to hide behind the flip chart. The group saw themselves as the role models for others who needed to get their GED. Students who were parents also wanted to work with the schools to make them more welcoming to all parents. In this and many other ways the forums developed into Freire's cultural circles.

Freire (1970b) reminds us,

> to be an act of knowing, then, the adult literacy process must engage the learners in the constant problematizing of their existential situations ... their act of knowing is elaborated in the *círculo de cultura* [cultural discussion group] that functions as the theoretical context.
>
> (p. 27)

Our student leadership forums are similar to Freire's cultural circles.

With a growing awareness of the potential of involving adult students in the organizing process, we planned the second ABC's conference with the students at the center. They helped plan the conference, worked on the conference as volunteers, and presented at the conference. Following this very successful conference, we again regrouped, analyzed patterns, and moved forward with student leadership. We continued looking for experiences that the students could take part in and develop their leadership skills.

At the 2006 Educating for Change Curriculum Fair run by LSJTRG, there was a student leadership strand where students presented table displays and talked about their experiences. Students involved in the process received awards for their presentations. The focus of the Educating for Change Fair was Immigrant and Refugee Rights in the Context of Racial Justice. We were interested in breaking down the racial and immigrant boundaries that often divide our adult literacy students from our English as a second language students (Cho, Paz, Yoon Louie, & Khokha, 2004). Our group also worked on producing a variety of events that eventually led to the creation of three student leader intern positions.

I have described how our focus evolved toward empowerment. I also want to

Photo 14.1 Sarah introducing the winner of the Courageous Educator Award at the Educating for Change Curriculum Fair.

describe my personal journey as my knowledge and awareness changed and grew. Mary Ann (Chapter 9) has helped me most of all to see events in a larger context. When I want to rant and rave, she presents another viewpoint. Sometimes I feel small in comparison, but mostly I have been so grateful that she is willing to keep the conversation going and share her viewpoint. Once we were driving to the lake for a meeting. It is a three-hour drive and we were talking about the changes we wanted to see happen in our society. Mary Ann said, "We are the people, we are the ones who need to ask for what we want." After talking about the possible state takeover of the public schools, she said, "We keep talking about the state as if it is a separate entity. We are the state." What this does for me is remove the "us versus them" mentality. We are the people and so we do have the power to make changes. We need to own our power. This is what I learned long ago from the women's movement. Women often give away their power without even knowing what they had in the first place. Like the adult education students, I had strong ideas about what should be happening but I was not speaking in a way that acknowledged I had any power to make changes.

My husband taught me the power of taking action rather than looking for someone to tell me it was OK. He gave me the saying, "It's better to ask for forgiveness than permission." When he first said that, I was a little shocked, but that is indeed how he operated. It was said in good humor, but also in the belief that often when one acts, no one objects. I had always looked for permission to act, which gave others the power to say no. When I learned to give myself permission, I gained strength and clarity. Adult students are conditioned by the authoritarian public school system. Even when students take action, it is assumed that adults are involved. So if they act, they must have permission. On the other hand, students recently occupied the mayor's office in protest at the state takeover of the city schools. They acted without permission and eventually had their meeting with the mayor. They never had to ask for forgiveness, but the media suggested that adults were using them for political reasons. The question is how to transform ourselves for action. Literacy is part of the answer.

Speaking and Being Heard

Change is tough. This whole process of working towards increasing student leadership has been one of learning to take small steps. Revolutions come from needing to create big changes quickly. I want change, but I don't want to have to foment a physical revolt in order to achieve an attitude change. This is what Freire's work does for me—it allows a powerful growth and "takeover" of the world without a drop of blood shed.

The word is more powerful than the gun. As Mary Ann says, it is not literacy for its own sake, but literacy in the financial world, the health world, and the education world ... as a means toward something. Literacy is knowing how to speak in a way that you are heard.

Labels others put on us are limiting. My own experience of this sensitized me to the struggle of others. When I was young, while reading a magazine, I reversed the numbers of the page where the story continued. My sister was with me and, with all her newly gotten knowledge with a Master's in social work, she casually dismissed the error with, "Oh that just means you are brain damaged." Whoa! I had a serious problem and I had no idea how to fix it. The problem was in my mind, where I thought and figured out how to fix things. I was caught between the devil and the deep blue sea. Just last year a GED graduate, Phyllis, told me about dropping out of eleventh grade. She had a baby and her mother didn't want her to stay in school. She kept telling Phyllis that she was no good and then would go to the principal and cause trouble. Finally, Phyllis dropped out and kept herself down. It's amazing what we do to ourselves that we would never let others do to us.

Just nine years ago, I kept my voice still. I did not have Mary Ann's strength to speak our needs. Now I speak. I ask. I listen to others to help them speak and ask.

Purcell-Gates, in her book *Other People's Words*, describes an Appalachian woman (Jenny) who was unable to read (Purcell-Gates, 1995). Jenny tells Purcell-Gates that when she first went to school, a teacher said that she spoke with such a dialect she would never be able to learn to read. Many of us have been given messages that imply an inability to be successful, though few of us hear it expressed so succinctly. Teachers react to students who come to school without lunch, clean clothes, parental support, and appropriate manners. Their reactions may include an unwillingness to give adequate attention to reading skills so that a student who may be dyslexic and poor simply never learns to read. As a parent educator, I used to visit a mother who did not read well. She had six children and they all went to school every day. She cooked for them. This was in stark contrast to some of the mothers I saw who were in community college, but who fed their children pop and potato chips. This mother knew she was "street smart," but felt inadequate when with someone like myself who was a reader (Luttrell, 1997). I appreciated her survival skills—providing for six children with very few resources. She even figured out how to get two turkeys one Thanksgiving when she'd been told there was only one per family.

Another attitude that limits many people who are successful is that they are scared that someone will discover them and expose them for a charlatan. I also had heard of, but never felt so fully, the "fear of success." When I was preparing my portfolio to be certified as a state Equipped For the Future (EFF) trainer, I went into the full throes of fear of success. I was undermining my own efforts and at times felt that I was truly in a state of confusion in an epic manner. Suddenly phrases like "I can hardly think straight" became meaningful to me in a gut-wrenching way. I did not create a wonderful portfolio and the remarks given back to me indicated that many items I thought I had presented were not apparent to the review board. Questions were asked that I knew I had covered. It was as if someone had slipped into my files and pulled out little bits and pieces. Eventually I was certified and never revisited the boxes of documentation that are now stored away. What is not stored away is my gut knowledge and visceral understanding. When faced with a test, a very public test, I had to struggle with those feelings of wild panic and foggy thinking. I am sure that many students who do not want to take their GED test are feeling the same way. Septima Clark, a civil rights leader and founder of the Citizenship Schools, said,

> As we go along, it will take that hundred years for attitudes to change. They will change … I think there will always be something that you're going to have to work on, always. That's why, when we have chaos and people say, "I'm scared. I'm scared," I say, "Out of that will come something good." It will, too. They can be afraid if they want to, afraid of what is going to happen. Things will happen and things will change. The only thing that's really worthwhile is change. It's coming.
>
> (Clark, 1999, p. 126)

Transforming Identity through Literacy

One of the most powerful approaches I have learned was the iterative process used by EFF. When people speak and organize around their needs, change happens. EFF really did rise from people speaking their needs. Granted it was done through a systematized approach and federally funded, but the goal was to develop a standards-based system that would reform the adult education system (www.eff.cls.utk.edu). The question was asked of adult students: Why are you in adult education? One clear answer arrived at through the iterative process: To give voice to ideas and opinions with the confidence that they will be heard and taken into account. Another clear answer was to solve problems and make decisions on our own acting independently, as parents, citizens, and workers, for the good of our families, our communities, and our nation. These were two of the four purposes. Also included was, to gain access to information and resources so we can orient ourselves in the world and to continue learning in order to keep up with a rapidly changing world. EFF taught me the word *iterative*. Because that was the process. Ask questions, combine answers, generalize from these to larger concepts; go back to the people and ask, "Is this what you said?" Do it again. It seems repetitive, but if you don't probe and explore, students say they are in adult education to get a GED or to become a lawyer, or to read the Bible. By asking again and again, the answers become truer and more universal.

Part of our effort is to continue to probe why someone wants to get a GED. Asking a series of why questions will usually get to an answer that relates back to those four purposes.

What do I mean by "our effort" for myself and for the students and for those with whom I work? For all of these groups, I wish to join an effort to create for everyone the possibility of a richly textured, informed, and joyful life. That is a core value for me. I believe that education—true education—is liberating and leads to the possibility of a life that is fulfilled (Freire, 1970b).

In family literacy, I have seen lives become more developed and enriched, filled with possibilities. Most of those families I worked with primarily comprised young, single women with small children and abuse issues. The connection many of these women had to their communities was limited to a small circle and many felt like outcasts from the larger community. For some with a dominating man as the significant other, the relationship with the community was always filtered through his control. When a person's life goes against the larger community's mores, a self-imposed exile begins (Horsman, 2000). Few of these women felt empowered to have any effect on that community, although often these young women were the fulcrum point of an extended family that relied on their youth, energy, and knowledge to survive. In my current job I visit family literacy programs operating throughout Missouri in urban, rural, and small towns. Prior to this, I had been a parent educator for Parents as Teachers in St. Louis and had visited the homes of many families, most designated "high risk" owing to poverty, single parenting, and low education. I had seen many amazing examples of families' literacy and cultural practices (Auerbach, 1989; Gadsden, 1994; Taylor, 1997).

As I visited programs, coordinators would tell me the stories of both the successful students and those who returned to addiction or abusive mates. Some cycled back into the class as they escaped from partners who were trying to prevent them from owning the power of an educated adult. It gave me such insight into the struggles common to these young women. Whether in the country or in the city, black, white, or brown, if you were a young student who needed to finish an education path, the barriers to success seemed the same. If you were a young mother with a boyfriend who wielded power over you, the barriers were compounded: transportation, babysitting, fear of beatings, temptations. Meth took one of these women. She was clean, had a position as a VISTA volunteer, and I heard her give a class on drug abuse. She talked about the power a drug has on you once you've tried it. "It's like a wolf, lurking in your brain. Waiting to pounce if you let your guard down." She did and it did, and I haven't seen her for five years.

Learning Power

bell hooks (1994) talks about coming out from behind the desk as a college professor and how that changed the power relationship between her and the students. I remember observing a kindergarten teacher who stayed behind her desk. She would tell the kids, "Get off of my floor" as a discipline technique. I thought she was one of the worst teachers I had ever seen. The kids were frightened of her. If they learned, it was in spite of her. One doesn't learn from fear.

So I never hid behind a desk and I never felt threatened by sharing power in a learning situation (Shor, 1996). Somehow I have always felt that learning was a social activity. Adult education students are also sometimes dismayed when teaching styles that they were used to in high school are not reflected in their adult education classes. In some ways, working as an equal is more disconcerting than looking to the teacher for all the answers. It's an odd feeling to discover that there really isn't "an answer" that other people have and if you could just discover it, you would be on a smooth sailing track. Once you as a student or teacher are able to understand that we are all on this journey together *and* we can both make contributions, the learning experience can soar. I met women in EFF who were well respected in their fields and who had years of experience. Without exception, those who were the most qualified respected my learning, my presentation style, and my knowledge. The only times I stumbled—felt dismissed—was from someone who I later learned was uncertain of her own position.

One of the first actions I took when I joined LSJTRG was to read Becky's book, *A Critical Discourse Analysis of Family Literacy Practices* (Rogers, 2003). The book linked into LSJTRG's focus on language and power and gave me a clear understanding of how powerfully and subtly language can be used to manipulate. The LSJTRG, like the teacher activist groups discussed in *Learning Power: Organizing for education and justice* by Oakes, Rogers, and Lipton (2006), is engaged in a three-part process of learning about power, learning to be powerful, and experiencing the power of learning. In many ways, organizing for literacy education in St. Louis is a process of following overlapping circles. There are many intersections between my involvement with ABC's and LSJTRG. LSJTRG and ABC dovetail around women organizing for more equitable and just educational experiences.

I think it is a disservice to us that we think of social power as an overt force. The manipulations can be so delicate that we think we are making a choice of our own free will without being influenced. My husband has the gift of a silver tongue. He used to fire people and then have them thank him for freeing up their lives to explore other avenues. I, on the other hand, have always struggled to keep my communications clear and precise. The struggle comes from not fully comprehending the nuances for others of some of the language I use. I learned more about this through LSJTRG. When our focus as a group was on African American language and linguistic diversity, we watched a video about the grammatical structures of the African American oral language, which was fascinating. Another time a young man who grew up in the projects came to talk, and we discussed Sister Souljah's book *No Disrespect*, the book that Carolyn used in her classroom (Chapter 6). He spoke of growing up in the community as if it were a village and talked about how those who did not live in the projects projected fears and imagined violence that simply were not there. I knew about this project from a different point of view. While he was growing up, my husband, an African American police officer, patrolled that area. He was on constant guard both from snipers on rooftops to "accidental" shootings from the white police officers with whom he patrolled. As I sat and listened to this young man, I was unable to speak. In this group I was white, even though in this city I passed for black many times. Here, in this group, the authentic voice was this young black man. There were too many levels of understanding, too many cultures to pass through for me to believe I would be heard. I was silent, silenced.

Many times I have thought of that experience, knowing that others for other reasons go through the same silencing.

A great gift that came from LSJTRG was Melissa's presentation of the popular education model she learned about during her trip to the Highlander Research and Education Center in Tennessee. In the 1930s and 1940s, Highlander's main focus was labor education. In the 1950s, the center turned its energy to the issue of desegregation. In the 1960s and 1970s, Highlander began to focus on worker health and safety in the coalfields of Appalachia, and played a role in the emergence of the region's environmental justice movement (Glen, 1996). In the 1990s, a group went to Highlander and formed the national coalition for adult students, VALUE. This was the group that came to St. Louis and trained 30 of us on student leadership and deeply informed our work in ABC's. Melissa demonstrated the circle of popular education. Not only have we followed the model for the past four years in our actions as the ABC planning committee, I began to follow that pattern in workshops and presentations. It is remarkably effective as a process that attends to concerns and yet keeps moving forward.

Sometimes I find myself looking for models of successful organizing in adult literacy education but then reflect on our process, of following intersecting circles. I am reminded that the process emerges from our practices. It is as Horton says, "the thing to do was just find a place, move in and start, and let it grow" (1998, p. 53). We are helping the process to grow.

Rethinking Practice

Put yourself in a situation outside of your comfort zone and become a personal advocate for adult education. Have you spoken with your state representative or senator that influences the money spent for your salary? Do you have paid planning time like other teachers—even preschool teachers? As a professional, you need to take responsibility for establishing your professionalism with funders, be they governmental or corporate. If you've never written a letter, do so. If you've never visited an elected official, do so. Guidelines for these activities abound. Keep close to key points, be polite, but make your case.

Have you supported your students' development of voice? You may be surprised to hear the passion when students talk about their early educational experiences and how they want their younger brothers and sisters to have a different experience. They might want to understand the changes in the positioning of public education in the policies of the corporate government. Encourage them to explore these ideas and discuss possible actions.

With colleagues, view and discuss our locally produced documentary called "Organizing for Change" which documents the ABC's process. You can find more information about this video by going to http://abcsofliteracy.blogspot.com/.

15 Response Chapter—Building Relationships of Struggle and Solidarity

Angela Folkes, Cristina Mann, Melissa Mosley, Rebecca Rogers, and Alina Slapac

Teachers who work to challenge the oppressive impacts of education exhibit agency with instructional choices and search out relationships based on struggle and solidarity. In the chapters of this section, educators explain how the authentic problems in their classrooms led to action, focusing on the social and political contexts of such actions including the relationships that were formed through the process. Each of these educators tells her story of working to disrupt traditional educational boundaries. Finally, their stories move beyond the classroom to connect with the experiences and actions of other social justice educators and community activists.

In Kate and Liesl's chapter (Chapter 12), we heard the voices of new teachers constructing identities as activist educators. Their identities as educators were constructed through the small actions each took, actions that together formed part of a larger process of becoming critical literacy teachers. Many of the actions that these new teachers took included asking questions and making curricular decisions for themselves. Janet's chapter (Chapter 13) illuminates the social and political nature of action, as she made decisions to pursue homophobia through the newspaper with high schoolers in a conservative political school climate. In Sarah's account of her work as an adult educator and organizer (Chapter 14), we can see how the work of an educator activist involves moving through many spaces, building relationships that lead to positive social change. Sarah describes the process of changing practices as following the circles—cycles of speaking, questioning, collaborating, and acting—both in concert with other educators and with the lessons of earlier teaching moments. Across all of the chapters we hear echoes of the importance of community.

As fellow social justice educators and LSJTRG participants, Cris Mann, Alina Slapac, Angela (Angy) Folkes, Becky Rogers, and Melissa Mosley came together on a November morning to reflect on and discuss the chapters. We gathered around a table at Angy's house with tea, Romanian bread and cookies, and the spirit of camaraderie fostered through our multiple opportunities to work together. Just as the chapters in this section represent different points in the teaching and learning lifespan (elementary school, high school, and adult education), so too did our discussion of the chapters. Cris is a European American woman and special education teacher at an elementary school in the public school system. She brings years of activism and community organizing—particularly around workers' rights and anti-war activism—to the table. Angy Folkes is a

Photo 15.1 (from left to right) Becky, Cris, Melissa, Angy, and Alina discussing a draft of
this chapter.

European American woman and an ESOL teacher for adult students at the International Institute. She is actively involved in workers' rights and civil rights
struggles. Alina Slapac's native home is Romania where she taught K-12 education. She is a teacher educator whose area is multicultural education. Melissa and
Becky, who have been introduced already, are former elementary teachers and
currently teach teachers at the university. While there are differences across our
experiences, we share a commitment to social justice education.

As we discussed the chapters in this section we moved in and out of sharing
stories about our own teaching and activism. Together, we found that these
chapters brought up issues about curriculum, organizing, balancing time, locating resources, and building communities and networks of support. These chapters were about building relationships to support social justice-focused literacy
practices in educational spaces. We call on the ways teachers develop critical
stances which we have discussed earlier, and then reflect on the importance of
relationships and community in the process.

The Importance of Building Relationships

Reading the chapters in this section provides us with a window to the internal
and external struggles of Kate, Liesl, Janet, and Sarah as they sought to design

critical literacy practices. As fellow educators we know these struggles all too well but reading them somehow made them more real, more public. We felt less alone as we read about their struggles. Struggles that showed up in the types of questions they asked themselves, the injustices they took on, and how they worked with others to design more just practices.

Kate, for instance, inquired about the discrepancy between curricular goals and access to materials when a balanced literacy program was adopted in her district. Janet wondered if the injustices she faced in her journalism class were her own rather than the interests of her students. They also reflected on the resistance they confronted as teachers working for social change. For instance, when Janet's principal questioned why she and her students were writing about "gay issues" and when Liesl's co-teacher told her that "teachers don't think, they teach." We discussed how teachers are often silenced through the culture of fear.

Cris said, "In education there are a million ways to scare people out of working for social change."

Angy reflected, "I was surprised to see that many of the same roadblocks that are in adult education are also in K-12 education. For some reason, I thought it would be easier to make change in K-12."

"And I think adult education has managed to resist the standardization movement and remain more flexible and responsive to learners' needs than K-12 education," Becky responded.

Angy noted, "I am working on a state-level curriculum committee that decides what is taught in adult English as a second language class. In the discussions, I did not hear critical social issues being taken up in instruction or assessment. I added a culturally responsive, multicultural, social justice strand to the curriculum but I do not know if the curriculum will make it through each level of the review with my ideas intact."

Alina raised an important point around educating teachers for a diverse society: "I am also surprised that there is not more of an emphasis on culturally responsive teaching in higher education. Many of my students (who are teachers or who are practicing to be teachers) often think of diversity only in terms of race and ethnicity and not in terms of a diversity of learners. They wonder why diversity education is important for them if they teach a homogenous population. These are the teachers who will teach tomorrow's children."

We discussed the standardization and assessment movement in K-12 education and how difficult and slow-moving resistance to these movements has been. Liesl, in her chapter, was dismayed at how quickly her co-teachers abandoned quality reports of student achievement for a more standardized version of report cards. She made a plea to her co-workers to "unionize." We thought the spirit of unionizing was about more than joining a union. Rather, it seemed Liesl was making a plea for collective thinking and action that comes from teachers working together. Cris commented on the power of camaraderie: "My colleagues have saved my teaching life on more than one occasion." Angy pointed out that for some teachers, though, that camaraderie does not exist: "Many teachers leave jobs because they feel isolated and powerless in the current state of education."

Often, we hear our colleagues lament that our "district" won't let us [fill in the blank]. In an era of standardization, taking responsibility for teaching is especially hard work. The boxed curricula make it easy for teachers to abdicate responsibility and to respond that they are simply doing what they are told, what the book (or the district) tells them. In not veering from the mandated curriculum, teachers are rewarded for their compliance and disciplined for their nonconformity. The system works so well that some teachers begin to question the books they read with their children every day. In a LSJTRG workshop on GLBT issues in children's literature, one teacher commented that she would love to use these books in her classroom but the "district won't let me. They aren't on the approved list of books." Here, the "district" has become an extension of the "state" policing the choices made around curriculum, testing, discipline, and even book choices. Fear operates in another insidious manner: it functions to separate us from our students. When we operate from fear we no longer make instructional and professional decisions based on what we know will work for our students but, rather, from what we are told to do. What conditions are present that makes an otherwise capable teacher deny the possibility of choosing to make her classroom library as inclusive as possible?

Part of our work as social justice educators is locating the specific barriers and points of resistance to our work. This entails critical inquiry and analysis of educational policies at local, state, and national levels. This includes personalizing the policies so that the all-encompassing metaphor of the "state" or the "district" or "X or Y" policy is not a faceless entity but is socially constructed by individuals like you and me. We also need to build relationships based on struggle and solidarity with our colleagues and also with our students. In our discussion, we reflected about how in each of the chapters in this section, the educators' greatest allies were their students. Janet, for example, explored with her students a marginalized set of voices from the curriculum—the presence of people who are gay, lesbian, bisexual, and transgender. In the process, students began to discover the ways in which the officially sanctioned curriculum has hidden some voices and privileged others. As they carried out the research for the newspaper and dialogued with each other they began to see how in the act of representing a marginalized issue or set of voices they are changing the official script. They learned that they can act and be in the world in ways that make a difference and, in doing so, develop a sense of agency. Janet worked with her students to split open the biased curriculum—a curriculum of heterosexism that had been kept in place by administrators who make statements like "we don't have any gays here." The newspaper did come out, and for the first time in the history of the district there was an open discussion about the rights of people who are gay and lesbian. This experience is added to Janet's repertoire of strategies that accumulates, over time, into her agentic role as a social justice educator. As important, she opens up a space for her students to expect a certain type of educational practice—and to question when it is absent. Finally, in Janet's story, we see an additional example of social justice teaching which, in turn, builds our agency.

The Courage to Act

Across these three cases, we see that alongside of designing critical literacy practices are the stories of becoming critical and courageous educators. The reflections that each educator made about her teaching illuminated both the steps that happened within classrooms as well as the learning that came from reflections on those steps. These reflections capture what Freire refers to as the process of "conscienization" where our colleagues were at the edge of recognizing themselves as part of the fabric of schools and movements for literacy, and perhaps identifying their power and complacency in the systems. We saw the courage to act as a result of the relationships that each educator built both inside and outside of classroom walls.

Drawing on Students' and Colleagues' Voices

Students have voice in the literacy practices of the classrooms that we have read about. The authors have made choices to illuminate the voices of students in their decision-making and action processes. Sarah illustrated in her chapter that social justice teaching occurs when students' voices become the center of the problem-posing as well as the problem-solving of social justice education. In fact, in each of the chapters, the students' voices, to various degrees, shaped the inquiry of the teacher. Cris, in our discussion of the three chapters, made the point that social justice teaching must bring in the values and positions of students, especially when students are from low-income and racial minority backgrounds like Sarah's students in the Acting for a Better Community (ABC) Forums. Cris stated, "[a]cting with and for our students provides teachers with the first-hand experiences that ultimately bring them closer to the struggle."

Listening to student voices is part of the idea that different groups of people hold different types of knowledge and is crucial to our work as feminist educators. The views and perspectives of the oppressed provide a view of reality that is different from that offered by those in conditions of privilege. Recognizing the standpoints of the oppressed provides a deeper understanding of injustice and is helpful in the development of constructing the conditions of justice.

We can also see places where the teachers used their stories to demonstrate the development of a public voice—a voice that reached beyond the walls of the classroom because it was a chorus of voices. Liesl discussed how she and her students presented the writing project they had worked on together at LSJTRG's Educating for Change Curriculum Fair. She also recalled canvassing for a school board candidate and creating a booklet about teachers' political rights. It was a need for a public voice that led Sarah to be a part of a student leadership movement, because she knew that the public voice on adult literacy could and ought to be represented by the students themselves. A clear example from Janet's chapter illustrated her shift in perspective—from considering the "action" of creating a center spread in the newspaper to raise awareness of homophobia to considering the "action" of teaching critical analysis through group discussion.

Text Box 15.1 Teachers as Activists

In the fall of 2007, a group of teachers from LSJTRG traveled to Chicago's Teachers for Social Justice Curriculum Fair. We presented a table display, conducted a workshop, and also spoke on a panel focused on "Teachers as Activists." Our workshop was called "Connecting our Educator/Activist Selves" and we shared our experiences navigating the ground between our roles as educators and activists, and to have participants share their own experiences. As participants came into the room, we handed them mini-protest signs and asked them to write something they "stand for" on their sign. We used the signs to introduce ourselves. The issues ranged from health care, public education, ending the war, equitable assessments, and fair wages. This was a way of demonstrating how designing picket signs includes using language and literacy practices.

Next, we facilitated a "story circle." Story circles are a formalized way of telling about one's experiences. For each session there is a topic, and everyone tells a story, based on his or her personal experience, that relates to the topic. The idea is that by telling our stories around teaching and activism, we will hear the common threads and patterns that inform our experiences. Simply put, the story circle is a small group activity designed to engage people in sharing their life stories (in this case around being a teacher/activist) with others. It is predominantly a group listening activity. Listening creates a time for group members to be profoundly present for each other. This process can be useful for moving discussions to a deeper level within community groups.

Story Circle Guidelines
- No more than five participants in a group.
- There is a two-minute time limit for each speaker.
- You may choose not to speak or to speak for less than two minutes if you so desire.
- A timer is used as a general guide to help the group share their time equally.
- Only one participant may speak at a time, and please, no interruptions, questions, comments, or advice-giving.
- The point of a story circle is for each person to tell his or her story, not to comment on what the other person has said.

Role of the Facilitator
- Start the introduction process. Each person can introduce herself and display the picket sign she had made.
- Facilitators will provide the participants in their group with the questions (below) to activate the telling of a story that is relevant to the theme of our workshop. (teacher/activist).
- Ask for a volunteer to begin. Each person is allocated two minutes of time to tell his or her story. They are told when the two minutes is over. The person to his or her left continues the story circle chain. Each person tells his or her story without interruption or feedback. The process is repeated until all participants in the circle have told their story.

Questions to Prompt your Story
- Why/how did you become a teacher/activist?
- What struggles do you face as a teacher/activist?
- What was the best/worst event that has happened?

The types of actions that each educator took, inside and outside of the classroom, reflect an understanding of the problems of practice in social and political contexts. In each chapter in this book, teachers have discussed how they bring their problems navigating boundaries to outside colleagues, such as members of LSJTRG, but rarely collaborate within their own schools. Cris mentioned in our discussions that many of her colleagues are activists in different parts of their lives but coalitions are rarely built within school buildings. This situation is all too common owing to the isolating and frenzied organization of teachers' workdays. Darder (2002) writes: "the antidialogical arrangements of labor prevents teachers from establishing deeper trust and knowledge about one another's practice, in terms of both strengths and limitations" (p. 69).

Angy reflected on a conversation she had with a fellow ESOL teacher at the International Institute about affirmative action. The state of Missouri, along with other states around the nation (Washington, Michigan, and California), was the front line of the battleground over affirmative action. Conservative groups pushed a ballot initiative that was ultimately defeated. Angy's colleague was against affirmative action but did not know much about the ballot initiative. Angy wanted to talk with her more about the impacts of affirmative action for new citizens, women, and people of color. The conversation was cut short, Angy said, because they were on a break and needed to get back to their classrooms. She stated, "It was easier to have a conversation about issues when I worked on the shop floor as a welder than it is to have a conversation with my co-teachers at a school."

Action, Advocacy, and Social Change

We were personally and collectively empowered by reading these chapters because we recognized both the process and struggles our colleagues faced as they designed critical literacy practices. We were also moved to consider our own process of becoming critical educators and the constraints we face.

In each chapter, language and literacy practices are used to challenge and disrupt hegemonic discourses. Indeed, we see how literacy is a vital part in the process of people claiming, using, and building their voice and moving beyond silence. In Chapters 7 and 11, we reported on discussions of what counts as social justice instruction, what counts as literacy instruction, and how the various writers of these chapters drew on local, critical issues in the literacy classroom. We noted the ways in which teachers accomplished critical literacy teaching was closely related to a feminist standpoint: by being observers, questioners, and interrogating multiple positions. In this chapter, we add that the authors did not act alone. They worked across boundaries and formed alliances with their students and with other teachers. Each was a member of the LSJTRG and discussed how the group provided models and discussion formats that helped them do their work. Liesl and Kate, as new teachers, came across literacy practices in their classrooms that did not feel right to them based on their knowledge of socially just teaching. They brought their concerns to the group. Kate reflected that her colleagues held different viewpoints and beliefs, and reflected on how her own perspectives developed in relation to what she saw as the status quo. Both Liesl and Kate worried about the impact of their voice on their relationships with colleagues, bringing problems from their local contexts to a group that was not connected to the districts in which they teach. Janet also asked LSJTRG members for advice when she came across barriers to addressing a critical social issue with her students. The popular education model and the readings that Sarah shared with LSJTRG members were part of her model of educational organizing and change, as she discussed throughout her chapter. In each of these chapters, our colleagues turned to a community of progressive educators who, in the words of Darder (2002), "is a vital support and eases the path toward a more conscientious revolutionary practice" (p. 69).

As a discussion group, we were surprised at how our conversations kept coming back to the types of actions that we each take as teacher/activists. In our initial writing workshop for this book, we each filled out a graphic organizer to reflect on the different ways we enact teacher/activist roles and how those roles are supported. These organizers visually represented the multiple positions we bring to our work as critical educators. We each brainstormed the dimensions of our teaching lives that included "Social Justice Education," "Activism," and "Literacy Education."

We recognize that we can continue to work through struggles not only because we have the support and relationships of our colleagues, but also because we feel a collective sense of what it means to be an educator/activist. As we shared our graphic organizers, we noticed the connections between each of us along the lines of projects and movements that we share. Teacher/activists have

Figure 15.1 Graphic organizer.

too much at stake—jobs, families, colleagues, students, a more just world—to act alone.

Lingering Questions

We were inspired by the variety of perspectives that each educator shared and, looking across all of the narratives of practice in this book, we wondered how we would continue to work with one another. Our discussion ended with a plan for participating in a conference call with other teacher/activist groups to discuss and take action against the privatization of public education. What are some of the roadblocks that keep us from collectively organizing with our colleagues? How can we navigate through the boundaries—such as those that Liesl met when asking her colleagues to unionize around assessment policies and practices—and continue to have conversations about our beliefs and practices? These are the questions that lingered for us as a group.

Part V

What Is and What Might Be

Part V includes Chapter 16 and Appendices. Chapter 16 is called "Designing Socially Just Learning Communities Across the Lifespan: What Is and What Might Be." Here, we reflect, as a group, on the connections that can be made across the lifespan as we teach and learn for more socially just classrooms, schools, and communities. We lay out an argument for a model of critical literacy education across the lifespan that situates learning as a product of working the hyphen, the in-between space between what is (reality) and what might be (possibility) (Anzaldúa, 1987; Collins, 1998; Palmer, 2007). We conceptualize the space between what is and what might be as the place where learning occurs, as we move back and forth between two contexts of learning. The first context, the schooling spaces in which we work, often do not look, sound, or feel just to us, nor result in socially just outcomes for students. On the other hand, the contexts of the learning and actions that we engage in through LSJTRG feel like spaces of possibility, the places where our own critical literacy learning thrives. We know, however, that engagement between these two spaces is a borderland where we can try on different practices and identities, with the constant reflection and dialogue that is at the center of democratic processes.

16 Designing Socially Just Learning Communities Across the Lifespan
What Is and What Might Be

As the school year comes to an end, so, too, do our bi-weekly LSJTRG workshops. We begin planning our annual Educating for Change Curriculum Fair held in September. This year, our focus is "Defining Democracy," a deliberate engagement with the principles that we see gradually being eroded in our increasingly privatized world. We chose this theme to "talk back to" the lack of democracy that has underlined many of the decisions around public education in St. Louis, Missouri. This pattern of privatization, occurring in St. Louis, is being carried out all over the country and the world. It is within this context that many of our teaching colleagues experience despair, apathy, and silencing. It is for and with these teachers that we organize the Educating for Change Fair every year.

The fair is a teacher-led public space where teachers share how they are teaching for social justice. During our planning meeting we debate what we mean by democracy and how best to capture this message for the fair. We agree that democracy carries diverse and conflicting meanings and concepts, not all of which are liberating. We talk about the protected rights in a democracy—political, civil, cultural, and educational—and also the tensions between individual and collective rights. We agree that education is the cornerstone of our democracy and we decide our goal for the fair is a public deliberation about what democracy means. As a group we have learned to hold tensions such as this one in a generative way. Together, we agree to stand in what Parker Palmer (2007) refers to as the "tragic gap," the metaphorical space between reality, "what is," and possibility, "what might be." Palmer argues that neither standing in reality, with its cynicism, nor standing in possibility, or irrelevant idealism will move us forward. Instead, learning to live in the gap rather than resolve it prematurely is a healthy and productive way to live and work for new possibilities.

After this discussion, we begin to imagine the details of the fair. Together, we brainstorm the image for a fair flyer, moving from abstractions to a concrete visualization of our theme, democracy. We take stock of what needs to be done and divvy up the work. Together, we write our call for proposals, design a poster for the fair, and invite colleagues to present a table exhibit displaying their teaching and students' learning as it relates to democracy. We reflect on what units of study went well in our own classrooms and choose the teaching practices we want to share at the fair. Ben Yavitz has been working throughout the year with his fifth grade students exploring global warming. Cris Mann continues working on counter-recruitment in high schools. Meredith Labadie and Aleshea Ingram both designed a social justice-focused writers' workshop. Becky Rogers continues to work with literacy specialists at the university to integrate critical literacy into their practices. Carolyn Brown is working on a handbook for teaching assistants at university level that includes social justice principals. We continue the popular education cycle, drawing on the strengths and resources of individuals and groups in our own practice while continuing to pose problems for the group to collectively address. We organize the fair because we believe our democratic practices can set a model for others to follow.

What Is and What Might Be

In this book we have shared a framework for critical literacy education that emerged out of our collective and individual work as educators. This framework merges popular education with critical literacy education and is made up of four dimensions (critical inquiry and analysis, developing critical stances, building community, and action, advocacy, and social change) and their associated tools. It uses the process of popular education to generate deep and meaningful learning. Popular education considers many of the challenges we face as world citizens (e.g. environment and health, development and sustainability) as questions that can be solved when people work together and imagine new solutions, drawing on tools and resources in a generative manner. This type of educative experience leans on process as much as content because part of the solution requires that we learn new ways to work together. We know learning involves the process of acquiring practices, dispositions, and relationships through observation, guided practice, and independent practice. We not only become teachers. We become certain types of teachers who care (or do not care) about the environment and peace, for example. In turn, these identities transform the community of practice within which we work, in our case LSJTRG. Thus, we might think about learning within a joint popular education/critical literacy framework as a trajectory of development and change in practices and associated identities that unfold across time and contexts. We recognize that this framework is neither exhaustive nor original but we believe it emerges from our practice and holds potential for the design of new practices in the democratic experiment of education.

A philosophy of critical literacy education across the lifespan holds the potential for transformation—of individuals, groups, communities, and societies. The process of becoming critically literate is, indeed, a lifelong process. The cases in this book have demonstrated how young people, adolescents, and adults all wrestle with some of the most challenging issues in society, including sexism, homophobia, school privatization, war, and racism. We also see how teachers at different stages in their careers enter into the process of becoming critically literate alongside their students and colleagues. We may also think about the different sorts of lifespans that exist—the lifespan of a group, the lifespan of our participation in a group, the lifespan of our participation as a novice before we move into expertise. Thus, there is no one lifespan—rather, multiple life paths that intersect at the nexus of contexts, cultures, and activities. More so than life-long learning, a lifespan perspective of critical literacy education considers what is and what might be in our lives, our classrooms, and the groups in which we participate. It requires that we use our social imagination to imagine new possibilities and courses of action.

A lifespan perspective of critical literacy education invites us to center the irreconcilable tension of "what is" and "what might be" that is at the core of our praxis. This perspective challenges us to disrupt notions of "what is"—traditional grade-level boundaries, boundaries between schools and communities, boundaries between teachers and activists, linear notions of learning and development. Thus, learning becomes situated as a product and process of working the hyphen, the in-between space between what is (reality) and what might be (possibility) (Collins, 1998; Palmer, 2007). We conceptualize the space between what is and what might be as the place where learning occurs, as we move back and forth between two contexts of learning. The first context, the schooling spaces in which we work, often does not look, sound, or feel just to us, nor result in socially just outcomes for students. On the other hand, the contexts of the learning and actions that we engage in through LSJTRG feel like spaces of possibility, the places where our own critical literacy learning flourishes. We know, however, that engagement between these two spaces is a borderland where we can try on different practices and identities, with the constant reflection and dialogue that is at the center of democratic processes (Anzaldúa, 1987). Indeed, we would argue that it is the disruption of familiar patterns in thinking that creates new insights. It is in these moments that we are often forced to stop and rethink our practices. Similarly, we hear and see these moments of transition for our colleagues in this book as they move out of one context and into another; for example, Liesl Buechler moving from her university program to work in an elementary school, then into the LSJTRG to write about her experiences as a new teacher. These transitions provide relief for the teachers to see their contexts with new eyes. Within these borderlands, educators engage in ongoing imagining of what might be in my classroom, group, or community. It is the habit of entering into critique with hope.

Thus, we believe designing socially just learning communities involves leaving room for multiple entry points and points of departure. This is necessary to account for the process of becoming critically literate. Returning to the framework we introduced in Chapter 1 (Figure 1.1), we visualize the dimensions of critical literacy education as an open circle, providing many different entry points. We also recognize that teachers are at different points in their critical stances. Some have participated in social justice movements; others have recently begun to question their own practices. There needs to be room for both at the table. A way of seeing education that leans on "what is" and "what might be"— on the twin pillars of critique and hope—asks us to notice and name what exists and to use our collective imaginations to visualize new futures. We might ask of each of the chapters in the book—what is and what might be? We might ask the same of our own teaching lives. We might ask the same of our group.

Photo 16.1 Protest sign at the Defend Public Education rally.

Principles of Critical Literacy Education across the Lifespan

Through our analysis of the cases across the book, we have developed principles of critical literacy education that we believe ring true across the lifespan. The following section brings together the images and narratives of the teachers throughout the book to illustrate these principles.

Curricular Conversations

Across the chapters, we hear the ways in which literacy practices are put to use to solve important social issues. In the process of becoming socially just, students (and teachers) are developing their literacy skills. These practices, activities, and associated identities are not isolated conversations or practices. Rather, in case after case we hear the ways in which teachers set up curricular conversations that involve matters of equity and justice. Such conversations span the course of the year and weave in and out of literature sets, writing projects, and classroom discussions.

The teachers immerse themselves in professional development experiences where they can try out the practices and associated identities of social justice teachers. We hear this in their ongoing commitment to inquiring and reflecting on their own classroom practices. We hear this in their participation in LSJTRG. Further, they are active in their own lives (recall Text Box 2.3 in Chapter 2). Thus, they immerse themselves in social justice, advocacy, and activism inside and outside of the classroom, building their repertoires and skills in this area.

Teaching/Leading by Example

Critical literacy teaching demands that teachers, too, become critically literate. Teachers construct identities as critically literate people by participating in the practices associated with critical inquiry and analysis as well as action and advocacy. Then, teachers engage their students in those very practices. Thus, critical literacy begins to permeate the very fabric of the classroom—the dialogue of the learning space—through class discussions.

The teachers in this collection demonstrate for their students through the formal and hidden curriculum what social justice looks like, sounds like, and feels like. Indeed, while, at times, there is a conscious focus on matters of equity—whether it is exploring gay and lesbian issues in a high school classroom, social security in an adult education classroom, or culture in a fifth grade classroom. But there is another layer, too. We hear how the teachers show the students they value their voices and concerns by taking a problem-posing, problem-solving approach to education (Freire, 1970b; Horton, Kohl, & Kohl, 1997).

Melissa Mosley, with her students, brainstormed issues they were concerned about that ultimately led into discussions about work, littering, and civil rights. Similarly, Rebecca Light delved with her students into their funds of knowledge. Liesl Buechler and her students brainstormed all of the different issues that they could write to the mayor about. Janet DePasquale and her high school students brainstormed issues to write about in the school newspaper. In each case, the teachers apprentice their students to see the wisdom and knowledge they already possess and in the process of solving new problems, they expand what they know. As they go about modeling how literacy practices can be put to use, they set up the types of communities that support students in developing the tools of critical inquiry and analysis—such as caring, empathy, cooperation, conflict resolution, using multiple perspectives, and valuing surprise and conflict.

Similarly, LSJTRG models a type of professional development that follows the needs, interests, and questions of teachers, rather than setting an agenda a priori. As teachers participate in LSJTRG they observe how teacher learning can be set up in a way that values teacher insight and provides teachers with the opportunity to see, hear, and witness the teaching practices of other teachers through videos, sharing of classroom examples, writings, ongoing inquiry into practices, and speaking at conferences about their teaching.

Balancing Resistance and Engagement

As we listened to the students in Rebecca Light's fifth grade classroom design timelines that reflected their development as readers and writers or tell stories about their family traditions, we see their engagement with the activity. Engagement is a necessary precursor for learning because it indicates when the learner has vested interest in the activity. Engagement is not always a simple matter, though, when the issues concern matters of equity and justice. The literature that students may find engaging may reproduce sexist or classist arrangements. On the other hand, literature that might be considered culturally relevant may not be engaging, as we saw in Rhonda Jones' classroom. Those (teachers and students) who benefit from systems of privilege are not likely to find critiquing such privileges engaging.

Similarly, students who have historically been shut out of schools may paradoxically expect a certain type of instruction—one that is not learner-centered, relevant, and engaging. Carolyn Fuller and Rebecca Light demonstrate the complexity of histories of participation in schools in their respective adult education and fifth grade classrooms. Their stories demonstrate how students who have not experienced success in school carry with them cultural models of what school practices and activities should be like—models that do not necessarily support them as learners. Sometimes, adult education students (or elementary students) resist democratic and critical instruction because it does not feel like school. As a way around this, Carolyn Fuller reminds her students, "the GED is a reading test and there are lots of current event materials on the test" (this volume, p. 84). Carolyn moves back and forth between the test and the curriculum of the classroom, reassuring the students that they can become critically engaged people *and* pass their GED, the heart of teaching for acceleration within a critical framework.

Similarly, Sarah Beaman-Jones writes, "Adult students are conditioned by the authoritarian public school system. Even when students take action, it is asumed that adults are involved. So if they act, they must have permission" (this volume, p. 175). People need to be re-socialized to think about their participation in the educational process in different ways. Sarah writes,

> Adult education students are also sometimes dismayed when teaching styles that they were used to in high school are not reflected in their adult education classes. In some ways, working as an equal is more disconcerting than looking to the teacher for all the answers.
>
> (This volume, p. 178)

Thus, critical literacy teachers find ways to encourage critical inquiry and analysis without evoking resistance. We hear the teachers in Jacquelyn Lewis-Harris' classes, for example, start to move through the stages of racial identity development as they see themselves as white and begin to understand that whiteness is a social construct which carries with it unearned privileges.

Teachers, too, need to be engaged in professional development and learning activities that are relevant and meaningful to them. After years of participating in professional development that is top-down and irrelevant to classroom practices, teachers expect that they will not be engaged in their own learning and development. Professional development that is inquiry based assumes that teachers take responsibility for their learning.

Assuming Agency and Power Exist

One of the markers of culturally relevant and exemplary teachers is high expectations for students (e.g. Ladson-Billings, 1999, 2001). Expectations can be set in a host of subtle and not so subtle ways. When teachers provide students who are struggling with reading, less, rather than more time reading manageable connected texts, they are communicating their low expectations to these students. When teachers silence or do not participate in a conversation around racism or sexism, they are communicating subtly to students that they do not expect them to take on such big issues. Many teachers follow an approach to teaching and learning which assumes that development leads learning, rather than learning leading development. Set in the context of learning about matters of social justice, this means that the teacher waits until a child or adolescent is ready to learn about matters of racism, classism, or pro-justice content. From years of research and teaching in this area, we know that children in preschool classrooms, for example, are already making sexist, ageist, classist, and racist comments (Berlak & Moyenda, 2001; Van Ausdale & Feagin, 2001). Thus, if children are not too young to enact prejudice and stereotypes they are not too young to engage in a justice-oriented curriculum. Teachers committed to social justice expect that all people can participate in building more just communities of learners.

Rhonda Jones and Mary Ann Kramer use children's books and adolescent literature in their adult education classroom. Melissa Mosley engages her second graders in a conversation about the war. In both scenarios, people would ask: is that "appropriate"? These chapters offer insights into why it is not only appropriate but also necessary and what can be learned when we envision education as a connected set of experiences and trajectories rather than isolated into grade levels and ages. Take, for example, Melissa's expectations for her second graders. She expects that they are capable of discussing critical social issues and solving problems in their communities, and they are. Similarly, the adult education students in Mary Ann and Rhonda's classroom—the same adults that society has passed over—are expected to be active contributors to a better world. Indeed, they resisted the privatization of their school when they took on the Board of Education and made sure that their school building was not sold.

Sometimes, our society's expectations for teachers seem unreachable, but at other times we underestimate a teacher's power. Sarah Hobson comments on this irony in expectations: "Why are we tying the hands of our teachers with crippling policies for high test scores at all costs? If we do not leave room for teachers and schools to address the real world issues their students are already struggling with and will continue to struggle with for life, then what good are we to students?" (this volume, p. 74.) Professional development and learning for teachers should recognize the pivotal role teachers might hold in reforming schools and society. At the same time, the needs and resources that educators need to carry out these jobs have to be understood.

Collective Responsibility

More often than not, responsibilities are framed as individual practices, rather than as social and collective practices. In the social justice classroom, both are necessary. Indeed, a common refrain in education is that it is important for learners to "take responsibility" for their learning. And yet, learning is a social construct, dependent on contexts, texts, and interactions between students and teachers. Further, many of the dispositions of social justice include emotional aspects such as caring and empathy that are learned and acquired by individuals within communities of practice (e.g. Claxton & Carr, 2004). Thus, the responsibility for cultivating such dispositions falls to individuals as well as communities.

Throughout the book, our colleagues have worked from the assumption that communities have collective responsibility for social problems such as hunger, poverty, discrimination, war, violence against women, gender inequity, and human rights. They encourage their students to inquire into these issues and move to action through their reading and writing.

Jacquelyn Lewis-Harris introduces us to the term "social justice literacy" which involves a move from individual to social responsibility; "the realization that one's definition of the social components of race, class, gender, sexual orientation, and religion are vital to defining one's culture and personal interactions" (this volume, p. 127). Social justice literacy includes movement from noticing superficial differences to noticing (and acting on) structural inequities. People who are social justice literate recognize their personal and collective responsibility to shape their interactions at a micro and macro level that works towards justice (pp. 127–128). Challenging white privilege and a color-blind mentality (Ladson-Billings, 1999) is both an individual and a collective responsibility in the struggle toward an equitable society.

Matching Texts, Readers/Writers' and Contexts

Critical literacy educators also need to attend to the details of literacy education. As we look across the chapters, we see teachers who are confident with their expertise as literacy teachers. They feel comfortable negotiating the demands of assessing students' reading, writing, and spelling, establishing flexible groups and creating mini-lessons to support students' reading or writing. In addition, they are familiar with the reading materials that support students at their instructional and independent reading levels. The teachers in this book have found that when they are teaching literacy for a purpose that is student driven and is connected to asking and answering real questions, students become better readers and writers. For some, it is this firm foundation with the details of literacy education that supports their pedagogical leap to critical literacy and social justice.

When the teachers make this pedagogical leap, they do so in a way that respects the integrity of critical teaching and literacy teaching. Indeed, we see exemplary literacy practices including: writing and reading in a range of genres for real social purposes; a range of instructional and independent-level texts that support the exploration of critical social issues; and talking, reading, and writing in ways that support literacy acceleration. We see snapshots of Socratic Seminars, reading and discussing literature, writing letters to the mayor, talking about the war, reading bodies and symbolic images, and designing newspapers to report on important issues.

The strategies and dispositions for designing critical literacy text sets transcend grade level boundaries. A second grade teacher needs to think about texts—and all of their complexities—with the same level of detail and sophistication as a high school English teacher or a college professor. Similarly, there are markers of literacy instruction that are important, regardless of grade or age: the sheer amount of time spent reading, instructional-level texts, setting purposes and goals for reading, reading strategically, and debugging texts.

What is fairly routine practice in a second grade classroom, a book introduction, or a word wall is novel and innovative in an adult education classroom. In Carolyn Fuller's chapter we hear her use some of the best practices for teaching literacy that are used by elementary teachers—book introductions, read-alouds, interactive readings, and book clubs. In Mary Ann Kramer and Rhonda Jones' chapter we see how a word wall and book clubs are put into practice in the Critical Literacy Lab. Conversely, the critical literacy education that is often in place in adult education classrooms appears innovative in K-12 classrooms. On this synergistic learning, Carolyn Fuller wrote,

> I can think of many times during a LSJTRG meeting when an adult education teacher learned about a literacy strategy from a K-12 teacher and when an adult education teacher educated K-12 teachers about the complexity of learning for adults.
>
> (This volume, p. 86)

Examining language is a thread through all of the chapters. Janet DePasquale points out what she refers to as "heterosexist talk," which "privileges the rights of heterosexual students at the expense of gay and lesbian students" (this volume, p. 165). Similarly, Sarah Hobson writes, "I wanted them to know that their language shaped how they saw who they were and could be in the world" (this volume, p. 67). Carolyn Fuller brings many voices together around literature in her classroom—the voices of historical mentors (e.g. Frederick Douglass), the voices of current mentors (e.g. students who earned their GED), the students in her classroom alongside the voices of the authors of the books they are reading. This implicitly teaches her students that they can talk back to texts. Each of the teachers recognize that learners, regardless of age or level, can have critical discussions around almost any topic when they are using the practices of critical literacy.

Expecting (and Valuing) Risk-taking

The scariest part about engaging with critical literacy practices is that we do not have all of the answers and we are never sure where the learning will go. Teaching experiments often lead to new insights. Discoveries made, though, are not always liberatory. Often, when given the opportunity, students (and teachers) will reproduce unjust social relations. We saw examples of this in classrooms throughout this volume—Sarah Hobson's students who reproduced sexist relations while in the Socratic Seminar, Melissa Mosley's students who reified the use of guns and violence in internment camps; Liesl Buechler's students who wanted the police to have bigger guns to protect the city; Rhonda Jones' students who rejected literature she thought would be culturally relevant; Jacquelyn Lewis-Harris's teacher education students who resisted white privilege. We hear how Jacquelyn addresses the resistance her white college students experience when they are invited to learn about anti-racism. She shares with us how she began to look for growth and development in small ways, accepting her students' resistance and approximations as part of their racial identity development. The model she sets forth through CHOCD—experiential learning, reflection, and integration into practice—is a model that can be used at any grade level.

This condition also includes the related issue of risk-taking, for students and for teachers. Melissa Mosley, for example, made the courageous choice to veer from the traditional curricular focus of "non-Western" countries (usually enacted through celebrating the culture and celebrations of Japan) to a more serious engagement between the literature and the current war. Kate Lofton, too, chose the path of most resistance when she challenged the holiday traditions in place at her school. Jacquelyn Lewis-Harris writes, "When controversy arises over the creationist versus evolution debate, I help students examine their interactions with children in their classrooms who might hold different religious beliefs" (this volume, p. 130). Further, there needs to be room for growth and development with adults, in the same way that there is for children. As they participate in the CHOCD stations and associated discussions and readings, they learn that race, class, and other markers are social constructions. Once these markers are unveiled not as universals or natural properties, teachers can begin to see the ways in which they are constructed and the ways in which they participate in that construction.

Teachers, too, are expected to approximate as they are trying out social justice practices. Writing about her early experiments with culturally relevant pedagogy, Liesl came to realizations about what kinds of books were culturally relevant for Martin. Similarly, Rebecca Light took risks with culturally relevant pedagogy and discovered,

> The key to culturally responsive teaching is recognizing and being critical of your own values, understanding where they came from, and revising them to include understanding your students' values. Only within the framework of this constant synthesis can true critical literacy and social justice teaching become the discourse of the classroom.
>
> (This volume, p. 64)

Learning to Work Together

We cannot design socially just learning spaces by ourselves. We need to learn how to build allies, cultivate networks, and work with people to accomplish social change. We need experiences working together if we are expected to build a similar community in our classrooms. As Johnston (2004) reminds us, often when teachers work in a group they are rarely working *as* a group, sharing ideas and strategies towards a common goal.

We have reflected on this process of learning to work together, which relates to the dimension of our critical literacy learning framework, "building a community." We believe that our socialization as women impacts the ways that we interact with one another and the value we place on relationships in our critical literacy learning. This value of relationships sometimes puts us outside of the norms and routines of the schooling system, in which educators often work in isolation. As teachers and women, we rely on one another to help us develop a sense of individual and collective voice, especially when we find ourselves in a position to question practices that exist at the institutional level. We are reminded of Liesl's response when she saw the disempowerment of her fellow teachers and told them, "You need to unionize!" She writes, "I felt as though I had to say something to them, something to bring to their consciousness that they could take action within the school when they thought something wasn't right." She was told, "Liesl, be quiet and listen. Teachers can only teach. They can't think. They can only teach" (this volume, p. 153). Working within such learning systems can be isolating.

Sarah Hobson's story gives us a rare insight into the psychological dilemma of committed teachers. She writes, "I had become so immersed in their lives, so ready to respond to everyone else's needs, that I ceased to fully exist." At the point of mental and physical exhaustion, she found the answer was "to step back and let them do the bulk of the work." As she did this, "I could hear their questions, recognize their journeys, and hear where they needed encouragement or inspiration" (this volume, pp. 72–73). Each teacher and classroom is a situated context but it is also part of a larger community of practice. Think, for example, if Sarah Hobson had the opportunity to connect with Sarah Beaman-Jones when she was struggling with the silencing of women in her high school English classroom. What if Sarah Beaman-Jones had said the words to Sarah Hobson that she writes in her chapter: "We need to own our power. This is what I learned long ago from the women's movement. Women often give away their power without even knowing they had it in the first place" (this volume, p. 174). I think of how liberating this movement from the individual to the collective might have been for Sarah Hobson. Janet realized, "Through this sense of unity in the LSJTRG, I gained strength to continue the social justice fight in my school community" (this volume, p. 165).

We also see the different incentives and constraints placed on critical literacy teaching at different schools, grades, and cultures. What became very clear in Liesl Buechler and Kate Lofton's chapter, for example, was how a culture of fear was cultivated and sustained which maintained the status quo. Similarly, we heard the difficulties that Janet DePasquale experienced at her high school when she and her journalism students tried to integrate gay and lesbian issues into the school newspaper. At the Adult Learning Center, by way of contrast, the culture supported critical teaching and innovative approaches to education. The juxtaposition of these stories helps us to see the ways in which teachers can work within and against such conservative and oppressive cultures to build a curriculum that is more inclusive and just.

Janet DePasquale wrote about the conservative, homophobic context of her school and how she worked within and against the heterosexist norms and values of the school. Just a year before her students took on this issue, the state of Missouri had passed a legislative ban on gay marriage. Janet witnessed how the weight of this decision could spark students' interest but could also be used as support for heterosexism and homophobia in the school and community. Further, the Hazelwood School District v. Kuhlmeier case in 1988 ruled against the First Amendment rights of student journalists, granting public high school officials authority to censor school-sponsored student publications.

Whether censorship occurs in officially sanctioned ways such as the censoring of the school newspaper, or in micro ways such as peer pressure from teachers or self-censorship, the message is clear: that schools are a place to reproduce tradition, routine, and the status quo. There are alternatives. Sarah Hobson wrote, "Thanks to the collective wisdom of LSJTRG, I now have multiple models for how women can be in the world and what people who come together can do" (this volume, p. 74). More and more teacher networks, inquiry groups, and advocacy groups are emerging. This is important, because as Johnston writes:

> [People] learn better in a supportive environment in which they can risk trying out new strategies and concepts and stretching themselves intellectually. This is not just because a supportive community enables individuals to extend their minds beyond themselves without risk, but also because the relationship associated with the learning is an inextricable part of what is learned.
> (Johnston, 2004, p. 65)

Imagining Next Steps

A simple yet profound truth radiates from each of these chapters. Teachers must experience the types of learning, practices, and reflections that we hope they will create for the students in their classrooms. This book project, from start to finish, has been an example of teachers using their voices, sharing their courageous teaching, inquiring into their practices, and committing themselves to becoming more socially just. Indeed, writing each of the chapters has been part of this process. The dialectic of voice and silence is always present, though. Even in the writing of the chapters, authors asked: "Will I get into trouble if I write what really happened? What happens if someone at the school reads this? I don't have tenure yet, can I get into trouble? What if my colleagues get mad? Should I really be teaching about sexism in my English class?" Liesl wondered if her student teaching placement was the best place to experiment with a non-violent curriculum. Melissa wondered about the appropriateness of teaching about war in a second grade classroom. As they shared their concerns with other writers in LSJTRG, colleagues recognized the risks (perceived and real) inherent in their stances but also encouraged them to take a courageous approach to their teaching. They received responses such as: "If I am controversial as a teacher, so be it, I will seek the truth."

Educators interested in the fight for public education must continue to fight against the numbing and silencing power of public education. For, as Boler (1999) writes, "beneath the numbness, which often signified powerlessness, lies a force that can be transformed into an immediate source of power." We continue to try to understand how democratic processes such as popular education, critical literacy, and our relationships with one another contribute to building more just learning spaces for our students.

When we posed the idea of writing a book together, many of the contributors responded with trepidation. Several people wondered, "What do I have to write about?" Others knew that they had something to say. Writing this book has been part of our work in the space between reality and possibility, Palmer's (2007) "tragic gap." In the months and years that we have worked with each of the authors, we have seen transformations. Our role throughout this process was to support each of the writers as they discovered their own story and came to believe that they, indeed, had something worthwhile to say. As Kate Lofton and Liesl Buechler remind us,

> Often when teachers think of social action, we consider great acts that garner media attention and publicity. These moments are important. They bring social action and its significance to the public eye. But these giant, publicly scrutinized moments are not the beginning and end of social action.... Our actions emerge daily as we interact with our students and peers.
>
> (This volume, p. 157)

A lifespan perspective on critical literacy education, such as has been offered in this book, can enable us to ask deeper and different questions about the roles of literacy education and democracy in the lives of our students. As Sarah Hobson writes, "the battle ahead is risky, but not as risky as losing our children to teaching that does not do justice to their lives" (this volume, p. 75).

Too often, our commitment to matters of equity is contained either in our classroom or in the community. Yet, our advocacy efforts need to connect what happens in the classroom with what happens in the community (Cherland & Harper, 2007). We are always juggling our roles within multiple institutions: the family, community, institution of schooling, and our many affiliations and community projects. Often, these roles are in tension, because we are participants in the very structures we seek to change. LSJTRG has been one such experiment in reconciling the tensions inherent in being a teacher/activist/scholar.

In imagining future directions for critical literacy education, we call for scholarship that celebrates the connections between social activism, research, and teaching. We have shared the parallel tools of the critical literacy education framework put to use by both individuals and the group using a process that parallels our framework of learning. We have shown how the processes and products of our teaching and research were intentionally organized to design socially just communities. We would argue that engaged scholarship is inherently reflexive because in our work as teachers, researchers, and activists we are inquiring into and acting on issues we care about; which in turn changes us and the world we live in. The trustworthiness of the investigation is not based solely on whether the knowledge created in each context rings true in another setting, but whether the project has made a difference in the lives of those involved and whether it inspires additional change. It is this engagement with the social world that is at the core of our methodology as researchers, teachers, activists, and human beings.

Appendix I
Declaration Statement

Public education builds democracy and changes society. Public education is under siege by corporations, politicians, and legislation seeking to privatize it for a profit. We stand together with educators—including pre-school through twelfth grade, adult, university, and community educators—and alongside community members, parents, and activists who believe now is the time to support and defend public education.

We, as educators and community members, in order to create a more equitable system of public education for all and ensure literacy as a basic civil right, call for:

- An immediate halt to the privatization of public schools for profit via charter schools, vouchers, tax credits, and outsourcing of curriculum.
- An increase in funding appropriations to effectively support education across the lifespan: preschool, elementary, secondary, adult, college, continuing, community education.
- Recognition of educators as the experts in their profession as the source for decisions affecting classroom practices and systemic change.
- An end to testing as the primary goal of education and means of determining student achievement and teacher proficiency.
- Immediate action by the Department of Education to provide funding, personnel, and training to seriously address the growing achievement gaps due to inequities based on race, class, and gender.
- Transparency from politicians of their beliefs about public education.
- Unity of all educators to come together and join the fight to strengthen our democracy through public education.

SIGNATURE _____ CITY/STATE _____

_____

_____

_____

_____

_____

_____

_____

_____

_____

_____

_____

This declaration grew out of a series of forums and actions around literacy and social justice among teachers and students, of all ages and levels in St. Louis, MO, and in relationship to advocacy efforts of adult education on a national level. In the face of unjust educational "reforms," this declaration is one attempt to collectively express our concern and the need for a united action among advocates for public education. All of the signed declarations will be copied and sent to local, state, and national elected officials.

Appendix II

Frameworks of the Critical Literacy Lab: Engaged Instruction, St. Louis Public Schools Adult Education and Literacy

Student–Teacher Relationships Reflect Genuine Mutuality and Respect

1. Teacher is connected to students' community.
2. Instruction is not a teacher-to-student "depositing" experience.
3. Both teacher and student learn from each other and respective experiences.

Based in Students' Language

1. Students provide examples of their own words in teaching phonics.
2. Help students see the ways in which their own spoken language can be helpful to them in developing their literacy skills.
3. Help students see the ways in which their oral language differs from the printed language they are reading and help bridge the gap.
4. Word wall of familiar, student-used but problem, irregular words.
5. Move from students' words to others' words (language experience ... other texts).

Uses Authentic Texts for Real Life Purposes

1. Balanced literacy instruction—process driven and skills based.
2. Use a student interest survey to identify topics.
3. Reading and writing are learned best when used to accomplish real life tasks.

Content and Activities are Centered Around Themes Critical to Students' Lives

1. Start the class introducing a critical theme or relevant word to initiate discussion on content meaningful to students, connecting to social/cultural/gender issues.
2. Student(s) provides a summary sentence or key statement (in student's own words) to be written on board.
3. Teacher reads statement; teacher and students read together several times.
4. Students copy statement into their notebooks and read aloud. *(Tutor option)*

5. Students write additional thoughts and opinions on this theme.
6. Students read their writing and use similar to language experience.

Includes Explicit Explanations of Reading and Writing Process in the Context of Critical, Meaningful Content

1. Structured, strategic, consistent instruction.
2. Reading components (alphabetics, vocabulary, fluency, comprehension) integrated in a Guided Reading Process.
3. Assessment used to develop individual student profiles to determine instructional strategies and sequence to promote literacy acceleration.

Teacher/Tutor Assumes Students are Able, not Disabled or Unable

1. Use and build on students' strengths in planning and implementing instruction.
2. Pair/group students according to need and strengths.

Encourages and Facilitates Relevant Action Related to Content and Community Needs

1. Activities/learning continue in community; community engaged in class room.
2. Connection drawn between text and community issues and values.
3. Use problem-solving process to identify issues and relevant next steps.
4. Small group direct action consistent with content and students' interests.
5. Goals achieved through action planning.
6. Leadership development and values clarification.

Contributors

Rebecca Rogers is an Associate Professor of Literacy Education at the University of Missouri-St. Louis.

Melissa Mosley is an Assistant Professor of Language and Literacy at the University of Texas at Austin.

Mary Ann Kramer is Coordinator for Adult Education and Literacy in the St. Louis Public Schools.

Sarah Beaman-Jones serves as a literacy program developer for LIFT-Missouri, a statewide literacy resource center.

Carolyn Brown is a doctoral student in the College of Education at the University of Missouri-St. Louis.

Liesl Buechler is a an elementary teacher in Danbury, Connecticut.

Ora Clark-Lewis is the Beginning Babies with Books coordinator with the YMCA Literacy programs.

Janet DePasquale is currently a high school English teacher at Kirkwood High School in St. Louis.

Margaret Finders is the Director of the School of Education at the University of Wisconsin La Crosse.

Angela Folkes, formerly an active member of the International Association of Machinists and Aerospace Workers Union, has taught English to Speakers of Other Languages (ESOL) for eight years and is currently a senior master teacher at the International Institute, an adult education site for St. Louis Public Schools.

Carolyn Fuller is a writing instructor in the St. Louis Community College system.

Sarah Hobson is a doctoral student in Education at the University of Pennsylvania.

Aleshea Ingram lives in St. Louis, Missouri where she teaches second grade.

Bridgette Jenkins works at the University of Missouri-St. Louis in the Office of Multicultural Relations.

Rhonda Jones has over 30 years' experience in K-12 and Adult Education and Literacy.

Meredith Labadie is currently an elementary literacy coach and teacher in St. Louis.

Jacquelyn A. Lewis-Harris is the Director of the Center for Human Origin and Cultural Diversity and is an Assistant Professor in Anthropology and Education.

Rebecca Light is currently a doctoral candidate at the Steinhardt School of Culture, Education, and Human Development at New York University.

Kate Lofton currently writes books for early readers and young adults in Minneapolis, Minnesota.

Cristina Mann is currently a Special Education teacher for children with Autism in the St. Louis Public Schools.

Kathryn Pole is an Assistant Professor in the Department of Educational Studies at Saint Louis University, in St. Louis, Missouri.

Alina Slapac is an Assistant Professor in the College of Education at the University of Missouri-St. Louis.

Ben Yavitz is a sixth grade teacher in St. Louis, Missouri.

Films and Children's Books

Films

Chasnoff, D. & Cohen, H. S. (writer) (1996). *It's Elementary: Talking about Gay Issues in Schools*. New Day Films.

Cohen, R. (writer) (2001). *Going to School*. Newsreel Cinema.

Freidberg, J. (writer) (2005). *Granito de Arena: Grain of Sand*. Corregated Films.

Richter, R. (writer) (1984). *The Business of Hunger*. Maryknoll World Productions.

Tulento, J. D. (writer) (2003). *Public Schools, Inc., Frontline*. PBS.

Children's Books

Buchanan-Smith, D. (1973). *A Taste of Blackberries*. New York: HarperCollins.

Coerr, E. (1997). *Sadako*. New York: Putnam.

Curtis, C. P. (1963). *The Watsons go to Birmingham*. New York: Bantam Doubleday.

de Haan, L. & Nijland, S. (2002). *King and King*. Berkeley, CA: First Tricycle.

dePaola, T. (1996). *Tony's Bread*. New York: Putnam.

DiCamillo, K. (2000). *Because of Winn-Dixie*. New York: Candlewick Press.

Dipucchio, K. & Pham, L. (2008). *Grace for President*. New York: Hyperion.

Greenfield, E. (1973). *Rosa Parks*. New York: Harper Trophy.

Himmelman, J. (1990). *Ibis: A True Whale Story*. New York: Scholastic.

Hughes, L. (1994). *The Dream Keeper and Other Poems*. New York: Scholastic.

Kelso, R. (1993). *Walking for Freedom: The Montgomery Bus Boycott*. New York: Steck-Vaughn Company.

King, C. & Osborne, L. B. (1997). *Oh, Freedom!* New York: Alfred A. Knopf.

Lucas, E. (1997). *Cracking the Wall: The struggles of the Little Rock Nine*. Minneapolis, MN: Carolrhoda Books.

Martin, L. A. (1999). *A March for Freedom*. Bothell, WA: Wright Group Publishing.

Miller, W. (1998). *The Bus Ride*. New York: Lee & Low Books.

Mitchell, M. K. (1993). *Uncle Jed's Barbershop*. New York: Simon & Schuster.

Mochizuki, K. (1995). *Baseball Saved Us*. New York: Lee and Low Books.

Morrison, T. (2004). *Remember: The journey to school integration*. Boston, MA: Houghton Mifflin Company.

Nevinski, M. (2001). *Ruby Bridges*. Bothell, WA: Wright Group Publishing.

Newman, L. (1989). *Heather Has Two Mommies*. Los Angeles, CA: Alyson.

Polacco, P. (2002). *Mr. Lincoln's Way*. New York: Philomel Books.

Rappaport, D. (2001). *Martin's Big Words: The life of Dr. Martin Luther King, Jr*. New York: Scholastic.

Richardson, J. & Parnell, P. (2005). *And Tango Makes Three*. New York: Simon & Schuster.

Ringgold, F. (1995). *My Dream of Martin Luther King*. New York: Dragonfly Books.

Rochelle, B. (1993). *Witnesses to Freedom: Young people who fought for civil rights*. New York: Puffin Books.

Spinelli, J. (1998). *Knots in My Yo-yo String*. New York: Alfred A. Knopf.

Thomas, J. C. (2003). *Linda Brown, You Are Not Alone. The Brown v. Board of Education Decision: A collection*. New York: Jump at the Sun/Hyperion Books for Children.

Tsuchiya, Y. (1951). *Faithful Elephants: A true story of animals, people and war*. Boston, MA: Houghton Mifflin Company.

Uchida, Y. (1993). *The Bracelet*. New York: Philomel.

UNICEF (2001). *For Every Child*. New York: Dial Books for Young Readers.

Williams, V. B. (1984). *A Chair for My Mother*. New York: HarperTrophy.

Woodson, J. (1990). *Martin Luther King, Jr. and His Birthday*. Englewood Cliffs, NJ: Silver Press.

References

Abu El-Haj, T. (2003). Constructing ideas about equity from the standpoint of the particular: Exploring the work of one urban teacher network. *Teachers College Record*, 105(5), 817–845.

Acting for a Better Community Organizing Team (2008). Educating for change in St. Louis. *The Change Agent*, 26, 26–27.

Allen, J. (2007). *Creating Welcoming Schools: A practical guide to home–school partnerships with diverse families*. New York: Teachers College Press.

Allen Gunn, P. (1986). *The Sacred Hoop: Recovering the feminine in American Indian traditions*. Boston, MA: Beacon Press.

Allington, R. (2007). Interventions all day long. Hope for struggling readers. *Voices from the Middle*, 14(1), 1–14.

Alvermann, D. (2001). *Effective Literacy Instruction for Adolescents*. Executive Summary and Paper Commissioned by the National Reading Conference. Chicago, IL: National Reading Conference. www.coe.uga.edu/reading/faculty/alvermann/effective.pdf (retrieved September 19, 2006).

Alvermann, D., Hinchman, K., Moore, D., Phelps, S., & Waff, D. (eds.) (1998). *Reconceptualizing the Literacies in Adolescents' Lives*. Mahwah, NJ: Lawrence Erlbaum Associates.

Anzaldúa, G. (1987). *Borderlands/La Frontera: The New Mestiza*. San Francisco, CA: Aunt Lute Books, 3rd edn.

Ares, N. (2006). *Political Aims and Classroom Dynamics: Generative processes in classroom communities*. Produced by ICAAP: Radical Pedagogy. http://radicalpedagogy.icaap.org/content/issue8_2/ares.html (retrieved August 10, 2006).

Ashmore, P., Brown, K., Akura, O., & Murphy, C. (2005). Teaching and diversity: Collaborative lessons learned. In M. Ouellett (ed.), *Teaching Inclusively* (pp. 117–124). Stillwater, OK: New Forums Press.

Atwell, N. (1998). *In the Middle: New understandings about writing, reading and learning*. New York: Boynton Cook.

Au, W., Bigelow, B., Burant, T., & Salas, K. D. (2005/2006). Action education: Teacher organizers take quality into their own hands. *Rethinking Schools*, 20(2). www.rethinkingschools.org/archive/20_02/orga202.shtml (retrieved May 25, 2008).

Auerbach, E. R. (1989). Toward a socio-contextual approach to family literacy. *Harvard Educational Review*, 59, 165–181.

Ayers-Salamon, M. (2005). *A Recipe for Failure: A year of reform and chaos in the St. Louis Public Schools*. Victoria, BC: Trafford Publishing.

Bakhtin, M. M. & Holquist, M. (1981). *The Dialogic Imagination: Four essays*. Austin: University of Texas Press.

Baltzer, A. (2007). *Witness in Palestine: A Jewish American woman in the occupied territories*. Boulder, CO: Paradigm Publishers.

Banks, C. & Banks, J. (1995). Equity pedagogy: An essential component of multicultural education. *Theory into Practice*, 34(3), 152–158.

Banks, J. A. (1999). *An Introduction to Multicultural Education*. Boston: Allyn & Bacon, 2nd edn.

Bell, B., Gaventa, J., & Peters, J. (eds.) (1995). *We Make the Road by Walking: Conversations on education and social change*. Philadelphia, PA: Temple University Press.

Berlak, A. & Moyenda, S. (2001). *Taking it Personally: Racism in the classroom from kindergarten to college*. Philadelphia, PA: Temple University Press.

Berliner, D. (1997). *Educational Psychology Meets the Christian Right: Differing views of children, school, teaching and learning*. New York: Teachers College Press.

Berman, P. (1992). *Meeting the Challenge of Language Diversity: An evaluation of California programs for pupils with limited proficiency in English*. Paper presented at the annual meeting of the American Educational Research Association, San Francisco.

Bhahba, H. (1994). *The Location of Culture*. New York: Routledge.

Bigelow, R. & Peterson, R. (2002). *Rethinking Globalization: Teaching for justice in an unjust world*. Milwaukee, WI: Rethinking Schools.

Blackburn, M. (2002). Disrupting the (hetero)normative: Exploring literacy performances and identity work with queer youth. *Journal of Adolescent and Adult Literacy*, 46(4), 312–324.

Blackburn, M. (2004). Understanding agency beyond school sanctioned activities. *Theory into Practice*, 43(2), 102–110.

Bloom, B. (1984). *Taxonomy of Educational Objectives* [electronic version]. Adapted by permission of the publisher, Pearson Education. www.coun.uvic.ca/learn/ program/ hndouts/bloom.html (retrieved August 10, 2006).

Bloome, D. (1985). Writing as a social process. *Language Arts*, 62, 134–145.

Boal, A. (1985). *Theatre of the Oppressed*. New York: Theatre Communications Group.

Boler, M. (1999). *Feeling Power: Emotions and education*. New York: Routledge.

Bomer, R. & Bomer, K. (2003). *For a Better World: Reading and writing for social action*. New Haven, CT: Heinemann.

Boyle Baise, M. & Grant, C. A. (1992). Multicultural teacher education: A proposal for change. In H. C. Waxman, J. Walker de Felix, & H. Prentice Baptiste (eds.), *Students At Risk in At Risk Schools* (pp. 174–193). California: Crown Press.

Brantlinger, E. A. (1999). Inward gaze and activism as moral next steps in inquiry. *Anthropology & Education Quarterly*, 30(4), 413–429.

Brookfield, S. (2005). *The Power of Critical Theory: Liberating adult learning and teaching*. San Francisco, CA: Jossey Bass.

Capella-Santana, N. (2003). Voices of teacher candidates: Positive changes in multicultural attitudes and knowledge. *The Journal of Educational Research*, 96(3), 182–190.

Chandler-Olcott, K. (2001). Teacher research as a self-extending system for practitioners. *Teacher Education Quarterly*, 29(1), 23–38.

Chandler-Olcott, K. & The Mapleton Teacher Research Group (1999). *Spelling Inquiry: How one elementary school caught the mnemonic plague*. Portsmouth, NH: Stenhouse.

Chapman, S. M. (1996). *Using effective teaching strategies to improve the academic performance of culturally diverse students in a public elementary school*. ERIC Document Reproduction Service No. ED401012.

Cherland, M. & Harper, H. (2007). *Advocacy Research in Literacy Education: Seeking higher ground*. Mahwah, NJ: Lawrence Erlbaum Associates.

Cho, E., Paz, F., Yoon Louie, P., & Khokha, S. (eds.) (2004). *BRIDGE: Building a race and immigration dialogue in the global economy.* Oakland, CA: National Network for Immigrant and Refugee Rights.

Clark, S. (1990). *Ready from Within: Septima Clark and the Civil Rights Movement.* Trenton, NJ: African World Press.

Claxton, G. & Carr, M. (2004). A framework for teaching learning: The dynamics of disposition. *Early Years: Journal of International Research & Development,* 24(1), 87–97.

Clay, M. (2003). *Observation Survey of Early Literacy Achievement.* Portsmouth, NH: Heinemann.

Cochran-Smith, M. (1995). Uncertain allies: Understanding the boundaries of race and teaching. *Harvard Educational Review,* 65(4), 541–570.

Cochran-Smith, M. (1999). Learning to teach for social justice. In G. Griffin (ed.), *98th Yearbook of NSSE: Teacher education for a new century: Emerging perspectives, promising practices, and future possibilities* (pp. 114–144). Chicago, IL: University of Chicago Press.

Cochran-Smith, M. (2000). Blind vision: Unlearning racism in teacher education. *Harvard Educational Review,* 70(2), 157–190.

Cochran-Smith, M. & Lytle, S. L. (2001). Beyond certainty: Taking an inquiry stance on practice. In A. Lieberman & L. Miller (eds.), *Teachers Caught in the Action: Professional development that matters* (pp. 45–57). New York: Teachers College Press.

Collins, J. & Blot, R. (2003). *Literacy and Literacies: Texts, power and identity.* Cambridge: Cambridge University Press.

Collins, P. (1998). *Fighting Words: Black women and the search for justice.* Minneapolis, MN: University of Minnesota Press.

Comber, B. (2006). Pedagogy as work: Educating the next generation of literacy teachers. *Pedagogies: An International Journal,* 1(1), 59–67.

Comber, B., Nixon, H., & Reid, J. (eds.) (2007). *Literacies in Place: Teaching environmental communication.* Newtown: Primary English Teaching Association.

Comber, B., Thomson, P., & Wells, M. (2001). Critical literacy finds a "place": Writing and social action in a low-income Australian Grade 2/3 classroom. *Elementary School Journal,* 101(4), 451–464.

Cook-Sather, A. (2002). Re(in)forming the conversations: Student position, power and voice in teacher education. *Radical Teacher,* 64, 21–28.

Cooney, M. & Akintunde, O. (1999). Confronting white privilege and the "color blind" paradigm in a teacher education program. *Multicultural Education,* 7(2), 9–14.

Cooper, M. W. (2006). Refining social justice commitments through collaborative inquiry: Key rewards and challenges for teacher educators. *Teacher Education Quarterly,* 33(3), 115–132.

Cope, B. & Kalantzis, M. (1993). *The Power of Literacy: A genre approach to teaching writing.* London: Falmer Press.

Cope, B. & Kalantzis, M. (eds.) (2000). *Multiliteracies: Literacy and learning and the design of social futures.* New York: Routledge.

Cowhey, M. (2006). *Black Ants and Buddhists: Teaching critically and teaching differently in the primary grades.* Portland, ME: Stenhouse.

Croteau, D., Hoynes, W., & Ryan, C. (eds.) (2005). *Rhyming Hope and History: Activists, academics, and social movement scholarship.* Minneapolis: University of Minnesota Press.

Darder, A. (1993). How does the culture of the teacher shape the classroom experiences of Latino students? In S. W. Rothstein (ed.), *Handbook of Schooling in Urban America* (pp. 195–223). Westport, CT: Greenwood Press.

Darder, A. (2002). *Reinventing Paulo Freire: A pedagogy of love.* Cambridge, MA: Westview Press.

Darling-Hammond, L. (1997). *The Right to Learn*. San Francisco, CA: Jossey-Bass.

Day, F. (2000). *Lesbian and Gay Voices: An annotated bibliography and guide to literature for children and young adults*. Westport, CT: Greenwood Press.

Deelan, G. (1980–1981). The church on its way to the people: Basic Christian communities. *Cross Currents*, 30(4), 385–408.

Degener, S. C. (2001). Making sense of critical pedagogy in adult literacy education. In J. Comings, B. Garner, & C. Smith (eds.), *Annual Review of Adult Learning and Literacy* (pp. 26–62). San Francisco, CA: Jossey-Bass.

Delpit, L. (1995). *Other People's Children: Cultural conflict in the classroom*. New York: The New Press.

Delpit, L. D. & Dowdy, J. K. (2002). *The Skin That we Speak: Thoughts on language and culture in the classroom*. New York: New Press.

Dewey, J. (1966). *Democracy and education: An introduction to the philosophy of education* (1st Free Press paperback edn). New York: The Free Press.

Donehower, R. W. (2003). Boring lessons: Defining the limits of a teacher's first amendment right to speak through the curriculum. *Michigan Law* Review,102, 517–541.

Donelson, R. & Rogers, R. (2004). Negotiating a research protocol for studying school-based gay and lesbian issues. *Theory into Practice*, 43(2), 128–135.

Dowdy, J. (2001). Carmen Montana: The general education diploma and her social network. *Journal of Literacy Research*, 33(1), 71–98.

Dozier, C., Johnston, P., & Rogers, R. (2005). *Critical Literacy/Critical Teaching: Tools for preparing responsive teachers*. New York: Teachers College Press.

Duncan-Andrade, J. (2004). Toward teacher development for the urban in urban teaching. *Teaching Education*, 15(4), 339–350.

Duncan-Andrade, J. (2005). Developing social justice educators. *Educational Leadership*, 62(6), 70–73.

Edelsky, C. (ed.) (1999). Making Justice Our Project: Teachers working toward critical whole language practice. Urbana, IL: National Council of Teachers of English.

Edwards, P. (1999). *A Path to Follow: Learning to listen to parents*. Portsmouth, NH: Heinemann.

Ellsworth, E. (2005). *Places of Learning. Media, architecture, pedagogy*. New York: Routledge Falmer.

Essex, N. (2002). *School Law and the Public Schools: A practical guide for educational leaders*. Boston, MA: Allyn and Bacon.

Fecho, B. (2000). Developing critical mass: Teacher education and critical inquiry pedagogy. *Journal of Teacher Education*, 51(3), 194–199.

Fecho, B. & Allen, J. (2003). Teacher inquiry into literacy, social justice, and power. In J. Flood, D. Lapp, J. Jensen, & J. Squire (eds.), *The Handbook of Research on Teaching English Language Arts* (pp. 232–246). Mahwah, NJ: Lawrence Erlbaum Associates (2nd edn).

Finders, M. & Hynds, S. (2007). *Language Arts and Literacy in the Middle Grades: Planning, teaching, and assessing learning*. Columbus, OH: Merrill, Prentice Hall.

Finders, M. & Tatum, A. (2005). Hybridization of literacy practices: A review of what they don't learn in school: Literacy in the lives of urban youth. *Reading Research Quarterly*, 40, 388–397.

Fleischer, C. (2000). *Teachers Organizing for Change: Making literacy learning everybody's business*. Urbana, IL: NCTE Press.

Florio-Ruane, S. (2001). *Teacher Education and the Cultural Imagination: Autobiography, conversation, and narrative*. Englewood Cliffs, NJ: Lawrence Erlbaum Associates.

Fountas, I. C. & Pinnell, G. S. (1996). *Guided Reading: Good first teaching for all children*. Portsmouth, NH: Heinemann.

Fountas, I. & Pinnell, G. (2001). *Guiding Readers and Writers (Grades 3–6): Teaching comprehension, genre, and content literacy.* Portsmouth, NH: Heinemann.

Frank, C. (1999). *Ethnographic Eyes.* Portsmouth, NH: Heinemann.

Freire, P. (1970a). The adult literacy process as cultural action for freedom. *Harvard Educational Review*, 40, 205–225.

Freire, P. (1970b). *Pedagogy of the Oppressed.* New York: Continuum Press.

Freire, P. (1973). *Education for Critical Consciousness.* New York: Seabury Press.

Freire, P. (2004). *Pedagogy of Hope.* New York: Continuum Press. First published 1992.

Freire, P. (2001). *Pedagogy of Freedom: Ethics, democracy and civic courage.* New York: Rowman & Littlefield.

Freire, P. & Macedo, D. (1987). *Literacy: Reading the word and the world.* Westport, CT: Bergin & Garvey.

French, J., Garcia-Lopez, S., & Darling-Hammond, L. (2002). *Learning to Teach for Social Justice.* Australia: Scribbly Gum Books.

Gadsden, V. (1994). Understanding family literacy. *Teachers College Record*, 96, 58–96.

Garcia, E. (1999). *Student Cultural Diversity: Understanding and meeting the challenge.* New York: Houghton Mifflin (2nd edn).

Gay, G. (1995). Bridging multicultural theory and practice. *Multicultural Education*, 3(1), 4–9.

Gee, J. (1992). Literacy, discourse, and linguistics: Introduction and what is literacy. *Journal of Education*, 171, 5–17.

Gee, J. (1996). *Social Linguistics and Literacies: Ideology in discourses.* London: Taylor & Francis (2nd edn).

Gee, J. P. (2000). *The New Literacy Studies: From 'socially situated' to the work of the social.* In D. Barton, M. Hamilton, & R. Ivanic (eds.), *Situated Literacies* (pp. 180–194). London: Routledge.

Gee, J. P. (2005). *An Introduction to Discourse Analysis Theory and Method.* Abingdon, Oxon: Routledge.

Gee, J. P., Hull, G., & Lankshear, C. (1996). *The New Work Order.* Sydney: Allen & Unwin.

Gibson, P. (1989). Gay male and lesbian youth suicide. In M. R. Feinleib (ed.), *Prevention and Intervention in Youth Suicide* (Report of the Secretary's Task Force on Youth Suicide, Vol. 3, DHHS Publication No. ADM 89–1623, pp. 110–142). Washington, DC: U.S. Department of Health and Human Services.

Giroux, H. (1999). *The Mouse that Roared: Disney and the end of innocence.* Lanham, MD: Rowman & Littlefield.

Giroux, H. A. (1988). *Teachers as Intellectuals: Toward a critical pedagogy of learning critical studies in education series.* Granby, MA: Bergin & Garvey.

Glen, J. (1996). *Highlander, No Ordinary School.* Knoxville, TN: University of Tennessee Press.

Gold, T. (2008). A rainbow in the midst of a hurricane: Alternative media and the popular struggle in Oaxaca, Mexico. *The Radical Teacher*, 81, 8–13.

Gonzalez, N., Moll, L. C., & Amanti, C. (eds.) (2005). *Funds of Knowledge: Theorizing practices in households and classrooms.* Mahwah, NJ: Lawrence Erlbaum Associates.

Gordon, L. (2003). What do we say when we hear "faggot"? In B. Peterson & B. Bigelow (eds.), *Rethinking our Classrooms* (pp. 86–87). Milwaukee, WI: Rethinking Schools.

Greene, M. (1988). *The Dialectic of Freedom.* New York: Teachers College Press.

Guajardo, M., Guajardo, F., & del Carmen Casaperalta, E. (2008). Transformative education: Chronicling a pedagogy for social change. *Anthropology & Education Quarterly*, 39(1), 3–22.

Guinier, L. (2004). From racial liberalism to racial literacy: Brown v. Board of Education and the interest–divergence dilemma. *Journal of American History*, 91(1), 92–118.

Guinier, L. & Torres, G. (2002). *The Miner's Canary: Enlisting race, resisting power and transforming democracy*. Cambridge, MA: Harvard University Press.

Gutiérrez, K., Baquedano-Lopez, P., & Tejeda, C. (1999). Rethinking diversity: Hybridity and hybrid language practices in the third space. *Mind, Culture, & Activity: An International Journal*, 6, 286–303.

Guy, T. (1999). Culture as context for adult education: The need for culturally relevant adult education. *New Direction for Adult and Continuing Education*, 82, 5–198.

Hackman, H. (2005). Five essential components for social justice education. *Equity & Excellence in Education*, 38, 103–109.

Hansen, J. (1998). *When Learners Evaluate*. York, ME: Stenhouse.

Harste, J. & Vasquez, V. (1998). The work we do: Journal as audit trail. *Language Arts*, 75(4), 266–276.

Heffernan, L. & Lewison, M. (2005). What's lunch got to do with it? Critical literacy and the discourse of the lunchroom. *Language Arts*, 83(2), 107–117.

Henkin, R. (1998). *Who's Invited to Share? Using literacy to teach for equity and social justice*. Portsmouth, NH: Heinemann.

Hermann-Wilmarth, J. (2007). Full inclusion: Understanding the role of gay and lesbian texts and films in teacher education classrooms. *Language Arts*, 84(4), 347–356.

Hershon, S. (1984). *And Also Teach Them to Read*. Westport, CT: Lawrence Hill.

Hicks, D. (2002). *Reading Lives: Working-class children and literacy learning*. New York: Teachers College Press.

Hinchman, K. & Moje, E. (1998). Locating the social and political in secondary school literacy. *Reading Research Quarterly*, 33(1), 117–128.

Hollingsworth, S. (1992). Learning to teach through collaborative conversation: A feminist approach. *American Educational Research Journal*, 29, 373–404.

hooks, b. (1994). *Teaching to Transgress: Education as the practice of freedom*. London: Routledge.

Horsman, J. (2000). *Too Scared to Learn: Women, violence and education*. Mahwah, NJ: Lawrence Erlbaum Associates.

Horton, M., with Kohl, J. & Kohl, H. (1997). *The Long Haul: Autobiography of Myles Horton*. New York: Doubleday Books.

Horton, M., Freire, P., Bell, B., Gaventa, J., & Peters, J. M. (1990). *We Make the Road by Walking: Conversations on education and social change*. Philadelphia, PA: Temple University Press.

Howard, G. (2006). *We Can't Teach What We Don't Know: White teachers, multiracial schools*. New York: Teachers College Press. Originally published 1999.

Howard, T. (2003). Culturally relevant pedagogy: Ingredients for critical teacher reflection. *Theory into Practice*, 42(3), 195–202.

Hubbard, R. S. & Miller, B. M. (1999). *Living the Questions: A guide for teacher researchers*. York, ME: Stenhouse.

Hull, G. & Schultz, K. (2002). *School's Out: Bridging out-of-school literacies with classroom practice*. New York: Teachers College Press.

Hyland, N. & Noffke, S. (2005). Understanding diversity through social and community inquiry: An action research study. *Journal of Teacher Education*, 56(4), 367–381.

Janks, H. (2000). Domination, access, diversity and design: A synthesis for critical literacy education. *Educational Review*, 52(2), 175–186.

Jenson, R. (1998). *White Privilege Shapes the U.S.* First appeared in *Baltimore Sun*, July 19.

http://uts.cc.utexas.edu/~rjensen/freelance/whiteprivilege.htm (retrieved August 10, 2006).

Joftus, S. (2002). *Every Child a Graduate: A framework for an excellent education for all middle and high school students.* Washington, DC: Alliance for Excellent Education. www.all4ed.org/publications/EveryChildAGraduate/index.html (retrieved June 14, 2007).

Johnston, P. (1997). *Knowing Literacy: Constructive literacy assessment.* Maine: Stenhouse.

Johnston, P. (2004). *Choice Words: How our language affects children's learning.* Portland, Maine: Stenhouse Publishers.

Jones, M. A. (1992). *American immigration.* Chicago, IL: The University of Chicago Press (2nd edn).

Jordan, N. L. (2005). Basal readers and reading as socialization: What are children learning? *Language Arts,* 82(3), 204–213.

Kellner, D. (2007). Critical media literacy is not an option. *Learning Inquiry,* 1(1), 59–69.

Kemmis, S. & Wilkinson, M. (1998). Participatory action research and the study of practice. In B. Atweh, S. Kemmis, & P. Weeks (eds.), *Action Research in Practice: Partnerships for social justice education* (pp. 21–36). New York: Routledge.

Keresty, B., O'Leary, S., & Wortley, D. (1998). *You Can Make a Difference: A teacher's guide to political action.* Portsmouth, NH: Heinemann.

Kim, S., Clarke-Ekong, S., & Ashmore, P. (1999). Effects of a hands-on multicultural education program: A model for student learning. *The Social Studies,* 90(5), 225–229.

King, J. & Howard, G. (2000). White teachers at the crossroads. *Teaching Tolerance,* 18, Fall.

Koh, J. (1994) *My Brown Eyes* (film). Cincinnati, OH: Master Communications, Inc.

Kooy, M. (2007). *Telling Stories in Book Clubs: Women teachers and professional development.* New York: Springer.

Kramer, M. A. (2005). Literacy for Social Justice Action Research Group. In J. Lewis, K. Stumpf-Jongsma, & A. Berger (eds.), *Educators on the Frontline: Advocacy strategies for your classroom, your school and your profession* (pp. 48–49). Newark, DE: International Reading Association.

Kress, G. & Van Leeuwen, T. (2001). *Multimodal Discourse, the Modes and Media of Contemporary Communication.* London: Oxford University Press.

Kress, G. R. (2003). *Literacy in the New Media Age.* London; New York: Routledge.

Kruidenier, J. (2002). *Research Based Principles for Adult Basic Education Reading Instruction.* Washington, DC: National Institute for Literacy (Partnership for Reading).

Ladson-Billings, G. (1994). *Dreamkeepers: Successful teachers of African American children.* New York: Jossey Bass.

Ladson-Billings, G. (1999). Preparing teachers for diverse student populations: Critical race theory perspective. *Review of Research in Education,* 24, 211–247.

Ladson-Billings, G. (2001). *Crossing Over to Canaan: The journey of new teachers in diverse classrooms.* San Francisco, CA: Jossey-Bass.

Lather, P. (1991). *Getting Smart: Feminist research and pedagogy with/in the postmodern.* New York: Routledge.

Lawrence, S. & Tatum, B. (1997). Teachers in transition: The impact of antiracist professional development on classroom practice. *Teachers College Record,* 99(1), 162–178.

Leland, C., Harste, J., Ociepka, A., Lewison, M., & Vasquez, V. (1999). Exploring critical literacy: You can hear a pin drop. *Language Arts,* 77(1), 70–77.

Lensmire, T. J. (2000). *Powerful Writing. Responsible teaching.* New York: Teachers College Press.

Lewis, C. & Ketter, J. (2004). Learning in social interaction: Interdiscursivity in a teacher and researcher study group. In R. Rogers (ed.), *An Introduction to Critical Discourse Analysis in Education* (pp. 117–146). Mahwah, NJ: Lawrence Erlbaum Associates.

Lewison, M., Flint, A. S., & Van Sluys, K. (2002). Taking on critical literacy: The journey of newcomers and novices. *Language Arts*, 79(5), 382–392.

Lewison, M., Leland, C., & Harste, J. C. (2008). *Creating Critical Classrooms: K-8 reading and writing with an edge.* New York: Lawrence Erlbaum Associates.

Lipman, P. (2003). *High Stakes Education: Inequality, globalization and urban school reform.* New York: RoutledgeFalmer.

Lipman, P. & Haines, N. (2007). From Accountability to Privatization and African American Exclusion: Chicago's "Renaissance 2010." *Educational Policy*, 21(3), 471–502.

Lipson, M. & Wixson, K. (2003). *Assessment and Instruction of Reading and Writing Difficulty: An interactive approach.* Boston: Allyn & Bacon, 3rd edn.

Loacker, G. & Mentkowski, M. (1993). Creating a culture where assessment improves learning. In T. W. Banta (ed.), *Making a Difference: Outcomes of a decade of assessment in higher education* (pp. 5–24). San Francisco, CA: Jossey-Bass.

Luke, A. (1995). Texts and discourse in education: An introduction to critical discourse analysis. *Review of Research in Education*, 21, 3–48.

Luke, A. (2000). Critical literacy in Australia: A matter of context and standpoint. *Journal of Adolescent & Adult Literacy*, 43(5), 448–461.

Luke, A. (2004). Teaching after the market: From commodity to cosmopolitanism. *Teachers College Record*, 106(7), 1422–1443.

Luna, C., Botelho, M., Fontaine, D., French, K., Iverson, K., & Matos, N. (2004). Making the road by walking and talking: Critical literacy and/as professional development in a teacher inquiry group. *Teacher Education Quarterly*, 31(1), 67–80.

Luttrell, W. (1997). *School-smart and Mother-wise: Working-class women's identity and schooling.* New York: Routledge.

Maher, F. & Tetreault, M. (1994). *The Feminist Classroom.* New York: Basic Books.

Mahiri, J. (1998). *Shooting for Excellence: African American & youth culture in new century schools.* New York: Teachers College Press.

Marautona, T. (2002). A critical analysis of literacy practices in Botswana. *Adult Basic Education*, 12(2), 82–99.

Marinoble, R. (1998). Homosexuality: A blind spot in the school mirror. *Professional School Counseling*, 60(1), 4–7.

Massengill, D. (2004). The impact of using guided reading to teach low-literate adults. *Journal of Adolescent & Adult Literacy*, 47(7), 588–602.

McDaniels, C. (2006). *Critical Literacy: A way of thinking, a way of life.* New York: Peter Lang.

McDiarmid, G. W. (1992). What to do about differences? A study of multicultural education for teacher trainees in the Los Angeles Unified School District. *Journal of Teacher Education*, 43(2), 83–93.

McLaughlin, M. & DeVoogd, G. (2004). Critical literacy as comprehension: Expanding reader response. *Journal of Adolescent & Adult Literacy*, 48(1), 52–62.

McIntosh, P. (1988). *White Privilege: Unpacking the invisible knapsack.* Working Paper 189. "White Privilege and Male Privilege: A personal account of coming to see correspondences through work in women's studies." Winter 1990 issue of Independent School. www.case.edu/president/aaction/UnpackingTheKnapsack.pdf (retrieved August 10, 2006).

McIntyre, A. (2003). Participatory action research and urban education: Reshaping the teacher preparation process. *Equity and Excellence in Education*, 36(1), 28–39.

McMahon, S. I. & Raphael, T. E. (1997). *The Book Club Connection.* New York: Teachers College Press.

Mentkowski, M. & Doherty, A. (1984). Abilities that last a lifetime: Outcomes of the Alverno experience. *AAHE Bulletin*, 36(6), 5–6, 11–14.

Mercado, C. (1998). When young people from marginalized communities enter the world of ethnographic research: Scribing, planning, reflecting, and sharing. In A. Egan-Robertson & D. Bloome (eds.), *Students as Researchers of Culture and Language in Their Own Communities* (pp. 69–92). Cresskill, NJ: Hampton Press.

Miner, B. (2005/2006). Action education: Teacher organizers take quality into their own hands. *Rethinking Schools*, 20(2), 15–16.

Moje, E., Ciechanowski, K. M., Kramer, K., Ellis, L., Carrillo, R., & Collazo, T. (2004). Working toward third space in content area literacy: An examination of everyday funds of knowledge and discourse. *Reading Research Quarterly*, 39, 38–70.

Moje, E. B., Young, J. P., Readence, J. E., & Moore, D. W. (2000). Reinventing adolescent literacy for new times: Perennial and millennial issues. *Journal of Adolescent & Adult Literacy*, 43(5), 400–410.

Moll, L. & Gonzalez, N. (1994). Lessons from research with language minority children. *JRB: A Journal of Literacy*, 26, 439–456.

Moll, L., Amanti, C., Neff, D., & Gonzalez, N. (1992). Funds of knowledge for teaching: Using a qualitative approach to connect homes and classrooms. *Theory into Practice*, 31, 132–141.

Monaghan, E. (1991). Family literacy in early 18th century Boston: Cotton Mather and his children. *Reading Research Quarterly*, 26, 342–370.

Moore, D., Monaghan, E., & Hartman, D. (1997). Values of literacy history. *Reading Research Quarterly*, 32, 90–102.

Morrell, E. (2006). Critical participatory action research and the literacy achievement of ethnic minority groups. *55th Yearbook of the National Reading Conference*, 60–77.

Morrell, E. (2008). *Critical Literacy and Urban Youth: Pedagogies of access, dissent, and liberation*. New York: Routledge.

Morrell, E., & Duncan-Andrade, J. M. R. (2002). Promoting academic literacy with urban youth through engaging hip-hop culture. *English Journal*, 91(6), 88–92.

Morgan, M. (2002). *Language, Discourse and Power in African American Culture*. Cambridge, MA: Cambridge University Press.

Morrison, T. (2004). *Remember: The journey to school integration*. Boston, IL: Houghton Mifflin.

Mosley, M. (2007). Highlander Center. In G. L. Anderson & K. G. Herr (eds.), *The Encyclopedia of Activism and Social Justice*. Thousand Oaks, CA: Sage Publications.

Moyer, B. (2001). *Doing Democracy: The Map Model for organizing social movements*. Gabriola Island, Canada: New Society Publishers.

Muspratt, S., Luke, A., & Freebody, P. (1997). *Constructing Critical Literacies*. Cresskills, NJ: Hampton.

Myers, J. & Beach, R. (2004). Constructing critical literacy practices through technology tools and inquiry. *Contemporary Issues in Technology and Teacher Education* [Online serial], 4(3).

Nafisi, A. (2003). *Reading Lolita in Tehran: A memoir in books*. New York: Random House.

Naples, N. (2003). *Feminism and Method: Ethnography, discourse analysis, and activist research*. New York: Routledge.

National Center for Education Statistics (1992). Digest of education statistics (NCES 98–015). Washington, DC: U.S. Government Printing Office.

Neuharth-Pritchett, S., Payne, B., & Reiff, J. (2004). *Perspectives on Elementary Education*. Boston, MA: Pearson Education.

New London Group, The (1996). A pedagogy of multiliteracies: Designing social futures. *Harvard Educational Review*, 66(1).

Nieto, S. (2003). *What Keeps Teachers Going?* New York: Teachers College Press.

Nyerere, J. (1974). *Freedom & Development, uhuru na maendeleo, dar es Salaam.* Oxford: Oxford University Press.

Oakes, J., Rogers, J., & Lipton, M. (2006). *Learning power: Organizing for education and justice.* New York: Teachers College Press.

Owens, R. (1998). *Queer Kids: The challenges and promises for lesbian, gay and bisexual youth.* New York: Harrington Park Press.

Palmer, P. (2007). America's democratic experiment: Holding the tension between reality and possibility. www.commonwealthclub.org/archive/ (retrieved March 8, 2008).

Pang, V. O. & Slaban, V. A. (1998). Teacher efficacy. In M. E. Dilworth (ed.), *Being Responsive to Cultural Differences* (pp. 39–58). Thousand Oaks, CA: Corwin.

Perry, T., Steele, C., & Hilliard, A. G. (2003). *Young, Gifted, and Black: Promoting high achievement among African-American students.* Boston, MA: Beacon Press.

Peshkin, A. (1988). *God's Choice.* Chicago, IL: University of Chicago Press.

Picower, B. (2007). Supporting new educators to teach for social justice: The critical inquiry project model. *Penn GSE Perspective on Urban Education*, 5, 1, 1–21. www.urbanedjournal.org (retrieved February 21, 2008).

Pole, K. & Rogers, R. (2007). Educating for peace and justice: Using literacy as a tool for social change. *The Missouri Reader*, 32(1), 25–30.

Powell, R., Cantrell, S. C., & Adams, S. (2001). Saving Black Mountain: The promise of critical literacy in a multicultural democracy. *Reading Teacher*, 54(8), 772–781.

Power, B. & Chandler, K. (1998). *Well-chosen Words: Narrative assessments and report card comments.* York, ME: Stenhouse.

Powers, B. & Hubbard, R. (1999). *Living the Questions: A guide for teacher-researchers.* Portland, ME: Stenhouse.

Prendergast, C. (2003). *Literacy and Racial Justice: The politics of learning after Brown v. Board of Education.* Carbondale, IL: Southern Illinois University Press

Purcell-Gates, V. (1995). *Other People's Words: The cycle of low literacy.* Cambridge, MA: Harvard University Press.

Purcell-Gates, V. & Waterman, R. (2000). *Now we Read, we See, we Speak: Portrait of literacy development in an adult Freirean-based class.* Mahwah, NJ: Lawrence Erlbaum Associates.

Raphael, T. E., Florio-Ruane, S., & George, M. (2001). Book club plus: A conceptual framework to organize literacy instruction. *Language Arts*, 79(2), 159–168.

Reardon, B. (ed.) (1988). *Educating for Global Responsibility: Teacher-designed curricula for peace education, K-12.* New York: Teachers College Press.

Richardson, E. (2003). *African American Literacies.* New York: Routledge.

Rodgers, E. & Pinnell, G. S. (eds.) (2002). *Learning from Teaching in Literacy Education: New perspectives on professional development.* Portsmouth, NH: Heinemann.

Rogers, R. (2002). "That's what you're here for, you're supposed to tell us": Teaching and learning critical literacy. *Journal of Adolescent & Adult Literacy*, 45(8), 772–787.

Rogers, R. (2003). *A Critical Discourse Analysis of Family Literacy Practices: Power in and out of print.* Mahwah, NJ: Lawrence Erlbaum Associates.

Rogers, R. & Fuller, C. (2007). As if you heard it from your mother: Reconstructing histories of participation in an adult education classroom. In C. Lewis, P. Enciso, & E. Moje (eds.), *Identity, Agency, and Power: Reframing sociocultural research on literacy.* Mahwah, NJ: Lawrence Erlbaum Associates.

Rogers, R. & Kramer, M. (2008). *Adult Literacy Education Teachers Designing Critical Literacy Practices.* Mahwah, NJ: Lawrence Erlbaum Associates.

Rogers, R., & Mosley, M. (2004). Learning to be just: Peer learning in a working class classroom. In E. Gregory, S. Long, & D. Volk (eds.), *Many Pathways to Literacy: Learning with siblings, peers, grandparents, and in community settings* (pp. 142–154). New York: Routledge.

Rogers, R. & Mosley, M. (2006). Racial literacy in a second-grade classroom: Critical race theory, whiteness studies, and literacy research. *Reading Research Quarterly*, 41(4), 462–495.

Rogers, R. & Pole, K. (in press). A state take-over: The language of a school district crisis. In L. MacGillivray (ed.), *Literacy Practices in Times of Crisis*. New York: Routledge.

Rogers, R., Light, R., & Curtis, L. (2004). "Anyone can be an expert in something": Exploring the complexity of discourse conflict and alignment in a fifth grade classroom. *Journal of Literacy Research*, 36(2), 177–210.

Rogers, R., Mosley, M., & Kramer, M. (2005). Becoming socially just across the lifespan: A portrait of the Literacy for Social Justice Teacher Research Group. *The Missouri Reader*, 29(3), 76–87.

Rymes, B. (2001). *Conversational Borderlands: Language and identity in an alternative urban high school*. New York: Teachers College Press.

Schall, J. & Kauffmann, G. (2003). Exploring literature with gay and lesbian characters in the elementary school. *Journal of Children's Literature*, 29(1), 36–45.

Sheets, R. H. (1995). From remedial to gifted: Effects of culturally relevant pedagogy. *Theory into Practice*, 34(30), 186–193.

Sheets, R. H. & Fong, A. (2003). Linking teacher behaviors to cultural knowledge. *The Educational Forum*, 67, 372–379.

Shannon, P. (ed.) (1992). *Becoming Political: Readings and writings in the politics of literacy education*. Portsmouth, NH: Heinemann.

Shockley, B., Michalove, B., & Allen, J. (1995). *Engaging Families: Connecting home and school literacy communities*. Portsmouth, NH: Heinemann.

Shor, I. (1996). *When Students Have Power: Negotiating authority in a critical pedagogy*. Chicago, IL: The University of Chicago Press.

Shuart-Faris, N. & Bloome, D. (2004). *Uses of Intertextuality in Classroom and Educational Research*. Greenwich: Information Age.

Sims-Bishop, R. (1982). *Shadow and Substance: Afro-American experience in contemporary children's literature*. Urbana, IL: NCTE Press.

Sleeter, C. (2001). Preparing teachers for culturally diverse schools: Research and the overwhelming presence of whiteness. *Journal of Teacher Education*, 52(2), 94–106.

Smitherman, G. (1977). *Talkin' and Testifyin': The language of black America*. Boston, MA: Houghton Mifflin.

Souljah, S. (1996). *No Disrespect*. New York: Vintage Press.

Souljah, S. (2000). *The Coldest Winter Ever*. New York: Pocket Press.

Steinem, G. (1995). *Outrageous Acts & Everyday Rebellions*. New York: Owl Books (2nd edn).

Stevens, L. & Bean, T. (2007). *Critical Literacy: Context, research and practice in the K-12 classroom*. Thousand Oaks, CA: Sage.

Stewig, J. (1994). Self-censorship of picture books about gay and lesbian families. *The New Advocate*, 7(3), 184–192.

Stokes-Brown, C. (2002). *Refusing Racism: White allies and the struggle for civil rights*. New York: Teachers College Press.

Street, B. V. (2003). What's new in New Literacy Studies? Critical approaches to literacy in theory and practice. *Current Issues in Comparative Education*, 5(2), 1–14.

Street, B. V. (2005). *Literacy, 'Technology' and Multimodality: Implications for pedagogy and curriculum.* Paper presented at the 55th Annual Meeting of the National Reading Conference, Miami, FL.

Sumara, D. & Davis, B. (1999). Interrupting heteronormativity: Toward a queer curriculum theory. *Curriculum Inquiry,* 29(2), 191–208.

Swartz, P. (2003). It's elementary in Appalachia: Helping prospective teachers and their students understand sexuality and gender. *Journal of Gay and Lesbian Issues in Education,* 1(1), 51–71.

Sweeney, M. (1997). "No easy road to freedom": Critical literacy in a fourth-grade classroom. *Reading & Writing Quarterly: Overcoming Learning Difficulties,* 13, 279–290.

Tatum, B. (1992). Talking about race, learning about racism. *Harvard Educational Review,* 62(1), 1–24.

Tatum, B. (1997). *Why Are All the Black Kids Sitting Together in the Cafeteria? And other conversations about race.* New York: Basic Books.

Tatum, B. D. (1994). Teaching white students about racism: The search for white allies and the restoration of hope. *Teachers College Record,* 95(4), 462–476.

Taylor, D. (1997). *Many Families, Many Literacies.* Portsmouth, NH: Heinemann.

Thomas, J. C. (2003). *Linda Brown. You Are Not Alone. The Brown v. Board of Education decision: A collection.* New York: Jump at the Sun/Hyperion Books for Children.

Urrieta, L. & Mendez Benavidez, L. R. (2007). Community commitment and activist scholarship: Chicana/o professors and the practice of consciousness. *Journal of Hispanic Higher Education,* 6(3), 222–236.

Van Ausdale, D. & Feagin, J. (2001). *The First R: How children lead race and racism.* Boulder, CO: Rowman & Littlefield.

Van Sluys, K., Lewison, M., & Flint, A. (2006). Researching critical literacy: A critical analysis of classroom discourse. *Journal of Literacy Research,* 38(2), 197–233.

Vasquez, V. (2003). *Getting Beyond "I Like the Book": Creating space for critical literacy in K-6 classrooms.* Newark, DE: International Reading Association.

Vasquez, V. M. (2004). *Negotiating Critical Literacies with Young Children.* Mahwah, NJ: Lawrence Erlbaum Associates.

Waggoner, D. (1991). Report finds African-American and Hispanic students less likely to take advanced math courses. Numbers and needs: Ethnic and linguistic minorities in the United States (ERIC Document Reproduction Service No. EDJ45837).

Wiedeman-Ramirez, C. (2002). Teacher preparation, social justice, equity: A review of the literature. *Equity & Excellence in Education,* 35(3), 200–211.

Willis, A. I. (1997). Focus on research: Historical considerations. *Language Arts,* 74(5), 387–397.

Wilson, B. & Corbett, D. (1999). *Focus on Basics: Adult basic education and professional development; Strangers for too long.* New York: Focus on Basics.

Wink, J. (2000). *Critical Pedagogy: Notes from the real world.* New York. Longman.

Yagelski, R. P. (2000). *Literacy Matters Writing and Reading the Social Self.* New York: Teachers College Press.

Yolan, Y. (1998). *The Devil's Arithmetic.* New York: Penguin Press.

Zeichner, K. (1996). Educating teachers to close the achievement gap: Issues of pedagogy, knowledge, and teacher preparation. In B. Williams (ed.), *Closing the Achievement Gap* (pp. 56–76). Alexandria, VI: ASD.

Index

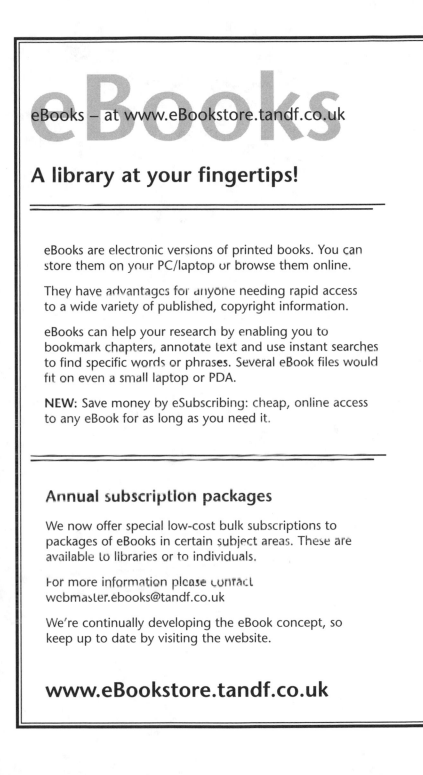